Tax Treaty Dispute Resolution: Lessons from the Law of the Sea

Series on International Taxation

VOLUME 85

Series Editors

Prof. Ruth Mason, University of Virginia School of Law
Prof. Dr Ekkehart Reimer, University of Heidelberg

Introduction & Contents

The Series on International Taxation deals with a wide variety of topics in the global tax arena. The authors include many of the field's leading experts as well as talented newcomers. Their expert views and incisive commentary have proven highly useful to practitioners and academics alike.

Objective

The volumes published in this series are aimed at offering high-quality analytical information and practical solutions to international tax practitioners.

Readership

Practitioners, academics and policy makers in international tax law.

Frequency of Publication

2-3 new volumes published each year.

The titles published in this series are listed at the end of this volume.

Tax Treaty Dispute Resolution: Lessons from the Law of the Sea

Rachna Matabudul

Wolters Kluwer

Published by:
Kluwer Law International B.V.
PO Box 316
2400 AH Alphen aan den Rijn
The Netherlands
E-mail: lrs-sales@wolterskluwer.com
Website: www.wolterskluwer.com/en/solutions/kluwerlawinternational

Sold and distributed by:
Wolters Kluwer Legal & Regulatory U.S.
920 Links Avenue
Landisville, PA 17538
United States of America
E-mail: customer.service@wolterskluwer.com

ISBN 978-94-035-3407-7

e-Book: ISBN 978-94-035-3417-6
web-PDF: ISBN 978-94-035-3427-5

For my parents, Hoop & Ritta

Table of Contents

List of Figures

List of Tables

List of Abbreviations

ALP	Arm's-Length Principle
BEPS	Base Erosion and Profit Shifting
BIAC	Business and Investment Advisory Committee
BIT	Bilateral Investment Treaty
CFA	Committee of Fiscal Affairs
CIA	Comparative Institutional Analysis
CPRs	Common Pool Resources
DST	Digital Services Tax
DSB	Dispute Settlement Body
DSU	Dispute Settlement Understanding
DTT	Double Tax Treaty
ECOSOC	Economic and Social Council
EEZ	Exclusive Economic Zone
FDI	Foreign Direct Investment
FTA	Forum on Tax Administration
IAD	Institutional Analysis and Development
ICJ	International Court of Justice
ICNT	Informal Composite Negotiating Text
IF	Inclusive Framework
ISA	International Seabed Authority
ISDS	Investor-State Dispute Settlement
ISNT	Informal Single Negotiating Text
ITLOS	International Tribunal for the Law of the Sea
ITR	International Tax Regime
ITT	International Tax Tribunal
JWG	Joint Working Group

LSA	Location-Specific Advantages
LOSC	Law of the Sea Convention
MAP	Mutual Agreement Procedure
MC	Multilateral Convention under Pillar One
MEMAP	Manual on Effective Mutual Agreement Procedures
MNE	Multinational Enterprise
ODI	Outbound Direct Investment
OECD	Organisation of Economic Co-operation and Development
PCA	Permanent Court of Arbitration
PE	Permanent Establishment
pIAD	Politicised Institutional Analysis and Development
PPT	Principle Purpose Test
SCS	South China Sea
SDC	Seabed Disputes Chamber
SRFC	Sub-Regional Fisheries Commission
STA	State Taxation Administration
TPDC	Transfer Pricing Disputes Chamber
UNCLOS	United Nations Convention on the Law of the Sea
UNCLOS III	Third United Nations Conference on the Law of the Sea
VCLT	Vienna Convention on the Law of Treaties
WHT	Withholding Tax
WTO	World Trade Organization

Preface

Since the launch of the OECD/G20 BEPS Project in 2015, the international tax regime has been in a state of ebullition, striving to level the international tax playing field between the developed and the developing worlds. Yet the debate on international tax dispute resolution has remained relatively timid and rather exclusive. This book is an attempt to not only widen the discussion on tax treaty dispute resolution but also cast a slightly different light on the topic by emphasising its potential catalytic effects for achieving international cooperation on current and future international tax negotiations.

To my knowledge, this book offers the first comparative analysis of international dispute resolution systems in the international tax and law of the sea regimes. Although somewhat unconventional, the choice of using the multilateral dispute resolution system under the United Nations Law of the Sea Convention (LOSC) as a benchmark for the purposes of improving tax treaty dispute resolution is the result of an in-depth analysis premised on geopolitical considerations underpinning both regimes in which developed and developing countries struggle to reconcile their often-conflicting interests and objectives. Just as the system of diplomatic and compulsory third-party settlement of disputes may have been the most significant justification for States to compromise towards a multilateral treaty under the law of the sea regime, my hope and humble contribution is that the new tax treaty dispute resolution system proposed in this book may also constitute a solid foundation for consensus-building towards a universal treaty in the international tax regime.

There are many people I wish to thank along the intellectual journey that led to the publication of this book, starting with my PhD supervisors at the London School of Economics, Eduardo Baistrocchi and Andy Summers, for making this book possible through their expert guidance, dedicated support, and cheerful outlook. I am also especially grateful to Ian Roxan and Veerle Heywaert for their careful and sharp feedback at the initial stages of this project. A special thank you goes to Jonathan Schwarz for introducing me to the world of international tax law at King's College London and for his continuing guidance and inspiration. A humble thank you also to Reuven Avi-Yonah and Malgosia Fitzmaurice for their insightful review of my work and their encouraging words that led to this publication. Last but not least, also a big thank you to the publishing team at Kluwer International for their prompt dealings and helpful expertise. As always, my family remains my biggest source of strength and solace through the ups and downs, and for that, I am forever grateful.

CHAPTER 1
Introduction

The mutual agreement procedure (MAP) needs improvement to address the tsunami of international tax disputes expected over the next decades in an increasingly multilateral international tax regime (ITR). Using the dispute resolution system under the law of the sea regime as a comparative benchmark, this book submits a proposal to restructure the MAP system for improving tax treaty dispute resolution in the ITR while taking into consideration the institutional contexts within which each system operates. Chapter 1 offers an overview of this comparative study that is premised on certain key geopolitical similarities that underpin both international regimes.

Existing international tax treaty dispute resolution mechanisms have often been criticised for their lack of effectiveness. Recourse to domestic remedies is a costly process, and courts are overburdened, leading to backlogs and delays.[1] The mutual agreement procedure (MAP), that constitutes the primary dispute resolution mechanism in bilateral tax treaties, has also led to a growing inventory of unresolved tax disputes,[2] and flaws have been pointed out by many authors.[3] To add to this, the global clamp down on aggressive tax planning through the launch of the base erosion and profit shifting (BEPS) project by the Organisation for Economic Co-operation and Development (OECD) and the G20 in 2015 has led tax administrations to take sterner

1. John C. Klotsche, *United States: Jousting with the Tax Man: An Extreme Makeover, IRS Edition* (3 July 2009) quoted in M. Markham, *Advance Pricing Agreements: Past, Present and Future* 19 (Kluwer Law International 2012); M. Markham, *Litigation, Arbitration and Mediation in International Tax Disputes: an Assessment of Whether This Results in Competitive or Collaborative Relationships* 11(2) Contemp. Asia Arbitr. J. 283 (2018).
2. *See* Table I.1: Map caseloads in Appendix I.
3. Michael Lang, *Introduction to the Law of Double Taxation Conventions* 148, 149 (Linde IBFD 2013); Roland Ismer, *Article 25: The Mutual Agreement Procedure,* in *Klaus Vogel on Double Taxation Conventions* 1801, 1810 (E. Reimer and A. Rust eds, Wolters Kluwer 2015); Jasmin Kollmann and Laura Turcan, *Overview of the Existing Mechanisms to Resolve Disputes and Their Challenges,* in *International Arbitration in Tax Matters* 25 (Michael Lang and Jeffrey Owens eds, IBFD 2015).

measures for protecting their domestic tax base.[4] Currently, the ITR is also in the midst of a revolutionary attempt to uphaul its century-old international tax rules through the planned implementation of the OECD's Two-Pillar Solution in 2024 (BEPS 2.0).[5] All these factors have led to the expectation that a tsunami of tax treaty disputes is to be expected in the next decade or so on all continents across the ITR.[6]

Accordingly, almost all stakeholders in the international taxation community agree that existing dispute resolution processes are in serious need of improvement, and a global consensus must be achieved so that global tax disputes can be resolved in a way that serves the interests of all stakeholders.[7] This is emphasised in the work of the G20 and the OECD on the topic of 'tax certainty', where improving international tax dispute resolution is noted as a major element.[8] In an attempt to contribute to the development of an improved dispute resolution system for the 21st-century ITR, this book offers a potential restructuring of the tax treaty dispute resolution system based on a comparative institutional analysis of the dispute resolution mechanisms under the ITR (prescribed through Article 25 of the OECD Model[9] or UN Model[10]) and the law of the sea regime (embedded under Part XV of the LOSC[11]). This comparative study is the first of its kind, and it is premised on the common geopolitical context that underpins both regimes, despite the differences from a substantive legal perspective.

The reform proposed in this book impacts tax treaty dispute resolution at all three levels of institutionalised decision-making.[12] At the operational level, I propose three new dispute resolution mechanisms based on the LOSC's system, which, along with

4. Sriram Govind, *The New Face of International Tax Dispute Resolution: Comparing the OECD Multilateral Instrument with the EU Dispute Resolution Directive* 27(6) EC Tax Review 309 (2018) DOI: 10.54648/ecta2018034.
5. Pillar One aims at relocating taxing rights to market jurisdictions irrespective of the existence of a physical presence, and Pillar Two introduces a global minimum corporate tax regime of 15%. *See* OECD, *Statement on a Two-Pillar Solution to Address the Tax Challenges Arising From the Digitalisation of the Economy* (8 Oct. 2021) (Statement on a Two-Pillar Solution) www.oecd.org/tax/beps/statement-on-a-two-pillar-solution-to-address-the-tax-challenges-arising-from-the-digitalisation-of-the-economy-july-2021.pdf accessed 4 Mar. 2022.
6. Kollmann and Turcan, *supra* n. 3, at para. 2.2.
7. McDermott Will & Emery, *Preparing for a Tsunami of International Tax Disputes* (14 Mar. 2016) www.taxcontroversy360.com/2016/03/preparing-for-a-tsunami-of-international-tax-disputes/ accessed 20 Mar. 2022; Howard Mann, *The Expanding Universe of International Tax Disputes: A Principled Analysis of the OECD International Tax Dispute Settlement Proposals*, 31(1) Asia-Pac. L. Rev. 268 (2023) DOI: 10.1080/10192557.2022.2102593.
8. IMF & OECD, *IMF/OECD Report for the G20 Finance Ministers* (March 2017) 22, 31-32 www.oecd.org/tax/tax-policy/tax-certainty-report-oecd-imf-report-g20-finance-ministers-march-2017.pdf accessed 21 Mar. 2021; *IMF & OECD, OECD/IMF Report on Tax Certainty: 2018 Update* www.oecd.org/tax/tax-policy/g20-report-on-tax-certainty.htm accessed 20 Mar. 2021. *See also* Mann, *supra* n. 7, at 8-9.
9. *OECD Model Tax Convention on Income and on Capital 2017 (Full Version)* (25 Apr. 2019) (OECD Model).
10. *United Nations Model Double Taxation Convention between Developed and Developing Countries 2017 Update* (August 2018) (UN Model).
11. *United Nations Convention on the Law of the Sea* (adopted 10 Dec. 1982, entered into force 16 Nov. 1994) 1833 UNTS 396 (LOSC).
12. Elinor Ostrom, *Understanding Institutional Diversity* (Princeton University Press 2005). According to Elinor Ostrom, there are three levels of institutionalised decision-making including the operational, policymaking and constitutional levels as discussed further in s. 3.2.5 below.

the MAP, form a comprehensive legal framework for resolving increasingly multilateral tax disputes. At the policymaking and constitutional levels, I recommend the use of specific consensus-building techniques to facilitate the implementation of the proposed mechanisms across the Inclusive Framework (IF).[13] These techniques were developed during the Third United Nations Conference on the Law of the Sea (UNCLOS III) that produced the LOSC through universal consensus among 157 participating countries.[14] Another salient lesson that emerges from this comparative analysis is the foundational role that an effective and robust dispute resolution system may hold for negotiating a universally agreed multilateral treaty in the ITR today, as evidenced through the negotiations of the LOSC. So far, the MAP system has remained largely unchanged since its inception in the 1920s, which presumably limits its impact for achieving the compromises needed to secure universal consensus across the ITR.

As with any comparative project, it is crucial to clearly identify and establish the institutional context within which the comparative analysis will take place prior to making any policy recommendations. This book aims to do just that by posing three research questions: (1) What are the institutional arrangements that underpin the current tax treaty dispute resolution system and the LOSC's dispute resolution system? (2) Which aspects of the LOSC's dispute resolution system may be relevant for improving tax treaty dispute resolution? and (3) How can the tax treaty dispute resolution system be restructured by adapting the relevant aspects identified in the LOSC's system? These three questions, as defined in Chapter 2, constitute the theoretical framework for the thesis, and each question is addressed in a separate chapter, as explained further below. Chapter 2 also analyses the appropriateness of the LOSC's dispute resolution system as a benchmark for developing an improved tax treaty dispute resolution system, compared to the dispute settlement systems under the World Trade Organization (WTO) and the bilateral investment treaty (BIT) regime.

Chapter 3 describes the research methodology used for conducting a comparative institutional analysis of the dispute resolution systems in the ITR and the LOSC. It is based on a three-step analytical approach (Steps A, B and C). Step A addresses the first research question posed and maps out the institutional arrangements[15] (i.e., rules, norms and strategies) that underpin the dispute resolution systems in the ITR and the LOSC. Step B addresses the second question and compares the patterns of interaction resulting from the institutional arrangements in the ITR and the LOSC and the inclusivity (participation) levels across the two systems to identify aspects of the LOSC's system that may be relevant for improving tax treaty dispute resolution. Step C

13. The BEPS Inclusive Framework (IF) was created in June 2016 as part of the original BEPS project that requires all members to work on equal footing to ensure a level the playing field in matters of international tax rules. As of November 2021, there were 141 IF members. *See* list of IF members at www.oecd.org/tax/beps/inclusive-framework-on-beps-composition.pdf accessed 2 Jun. 2022.
14. Richard J. Payne and Jamal R. Nassar, *The New International Economic Order at Sea* 17(1) J. Dev. Areas 31 (1982).
15. Institutional arrangements refer to the configurations of rules, norms and strategies within a specific policy setting that affect decision-making. *See* Elinor Ostrom, *Institutional Rational Choice: An Assessment of the Institutional Analysis and Development Framework*, in *Theories of the Policy Process* (Paul A. Sabatier ed., Westview Press 2007).

addresses the third and final research question and offers a potential restructuring of the tax treaty dispute resolution system that fits more appropriately in the 21st-century ITR. Chapter 3 also explains the comparative institutional tool used for analysing the two dispute resolution systems: the politicised Institutional Analysis and Development (pIAD) framework.[16]

Chapters 4 and 5 map out the institutional arrangements underpinning the tax treaty dispute resolution system and the LOSC's system, respectively, as outlined in Step A of the methodology. It applies the pIAD framework to gather necessary information (working rules, community attributes and physical conditions) in a systematic manner for each of the mechanisms being studied, taking into account the political and economic context and the relevant discourse that may influence the development of dispute resolution under each regime. Step A is crucial to ensure an accurate comparison of the two systems.

Chapter 6 addresses Step B of the methodology and integrates the analysis of the institutional arrangements mapped out in the two dispute resolution systems to compare the relevant patterns of interaction generated throughout the two systems. The aim is to identify aspects of the LOSC's system that may be relevant for improving tax treaty dispute resolution at the operational level. Step B also compares the inclusivity levels across the two dispute resolution systems at the policymaking and constitutional levels to identify consensus-based techniques that may be applied in the ITR to facilitate the implementation of the proposed reform across the IF.

Chapter 7 addresses the final Step C of the methodology. Based on the comparative analysis conducted in Chapter 6, Step C proposes a potential restructuring of the tax treaty dispute resolution system that aims to achieve an effective, predictable and equitable resolution of multilateral tax disputes across the ITR in the 21st century. The proposed structure includes three new mechanisms in addition to the MAP: an international tax tribunal (ITT), an IF arbitration mechanism and a special IF arbitration mechanism, each of which will address a different category of international tax disputes. The proposal also includes the implementation of consensus-building techniques for achieving universal consensus across the IF. Finally, Chapter 8 offers a conclusion on the lessons learnt from comparing the dispute resolution systems under the ITR and the LOSC.

16. The pIAD framework is based on Elinor Ostrom's Institutional Analysis and Development (IAD) framework developed originally in the 1980s. *See* Floriane Clement, *Analysing Decentralised Natural Resource Governance: Proposition for a 'Politicised' Institutional Analysis and Development Framework* 43 Pol'y Sci. 129 (2010) DOI: 10.1007/s11077-009-9100-8.

CHAPTER 2

Defining the Research Questions

Chapter 2 explores predominantly the international tax and law of the sea literature to define the three underlying research questions of this thesis. It demonstrates the urgent need for an overhaul of the tax treaty dispute resolution system by addressing the actual and expected challenges facing the current system in the post-BEPS ITR. It also reviews the work done so far with respect to reforming the MAP system, including the proposed dispute resolution mechanism under Pillar One and emphasises the need for a more holistic review of the system from an institutional perspective. This chapter also elaborates on key geopolitical similarities in both regimes that may justify using the LOSC's system as a comparative benchmark for the purpose of improving tax treaty dispute resolution in the ITR despite the substantive legal and institutional differences between the two systems. The LOSC's system is also compared to the dispute resolution systems under the WTO and the BIT regimes to further highlight its eligibility for the purposes of this comparative analysis.

2.1 INTRODUCTION

In the ITR, international tax dispute resolution (referred to as tax treaty dispute resolution for the purposes of this book) involves the MAP as prescribed under Article 25 of the OECD Model or the UN Model. If a taxpayer considers that it suffered from taxation that is not in accordance with the applicable tax treaty, it may file a request with the competent authority of the relevant contracting state to initiate a MAP. If the request is admissible, then the competent authority will attempt to resolve the issue on its own, and if not possible, then it will liaise with the competent authority of the other contracting state to endeavour to resolve the tax dispute through mutual agreement. The MAP is a diplomatic mechanism, although it may also include a supplementary arbitration process if agreed by the contracting states on a bilateral basis.

In contrast, the international dispute resolution system embedded under Part XV of the LOSC not only represents one of the longest and most intricate dispute settlement provisions ever drafted through universal consensus,[17] but it was also developed in the 1970s with the aim of maintaining peace and equitable economic order amid growing international tensions in relation to the governance of the oceans.[18] Arguably, the ITR now seems to be following in a similar direction as the risks of international tax conflict[19] soar among countries across an increasingly connected and multilateral tax regime. From this perspective, I argue that the LOSC's dispute resolution system constitutes a more appropriate benchmark for developing an improved tax treaty dispute resolution system compared to dispute settlement systems under other regimes like the WTO or the BIT regime.

This present chapter explores predominantly the international tax and law of the sea literature to define the three underlying research questions of this thesis. It attempts to demonstrate, first and foremost in section 2.2, the urgency of specific changes needed in the tax treaty dispute resolution system by addressing the actual and expected challenges facing the current system in the ITR. Section 2.3 then reviews the existing proposals for reforming the tax treaty dispute resolution system, emphasising the need for a more in-depth institutional analysis of the tax treaty dispute resolution system in the post-BEPS era (i.e., after the launch of the BEPS project in 2015). Section 2.4 explores the various reasons that contribute to the LOSC being held as a benchmark in the context of this research for improving international tax dispute resolution in the

17. Cesare P.R. Romano, *The Settlement of Disputes under the 1982 Law of the Sea Convention: How Entangled Can We Get?* 103(1) J. Int'l. L. & Dipl. 84, 87 (2004). For various perspectives on the dispute settlement provisions of the Convention, *see also* Willem Riphagen, *Dispute Settlement in the 1982 United Nations Convention on the Law of the Sea*, in *The New Law of the Sea* 281 (Christos L. Rozakis and Constantine A. Stephanou eds, North-Holland Publishing Company 1983); Elliot L. Richardson, *Dispute Settlement under the Convention on the Law of the Sea: A Flexible and Comprehensive Extension of the Rule of the Law to Ocean Space,* in *Contemporary Issues in International Law: Essays in Honor of Louis B Sohn* 149 (Thomas Buergenthal ed., N P Engel 1984); Yogesh K. Tyagi, *The System of Settlement of Disputes under the Law of the Sea Convention: An Overview* 25(2) Indian J. Intl. L. 191 (1985); Gerhard Erasmus, *Dispute Settlement in the Law of the Sea* Acta Juridica 15 (1986); Mahdi El-Baghdadi, *The Binding Nature of the Disputes Settlement Procedure in the Third U.N. Convention on the Law of the Sea: The International Seabed Authority* 6 J. Min L. & Pol'y 173 (1990/1991); John E. Noyes, *The Third-Party Dispute Settlement Provisions of the 1982 United Nations Convention on the Law of the Sea: Implications for States Parties and for Non-parties,* in *Entry into Force of the Law of the Sea Convention* 213 (M. H. Nordquist and J. N. Moore eds, Martinus Nijhoff Publishers 1995); Robin R. Churchill and Alan V. Lowe, *The Law of the Sea* 447 (Manchester University Press 1999); Jon M. Van Dyke, *Louis B Sohn and the Settlement of Ocean Disputes* 33 Geo. Wash. Intl. L. Rev. 31 (2000); Igor V. Karaman, *Dispute Resolution in the Law of the Sea* 1 (Brill Publications 2012).
18. Tommy Koh, *A Constitution for the Oceans*, Remarks of the President of the Third United Nations Conference on the Law of the sea at the Conference at Montego Bay (10 Dec. 1982), www.un.org/depts/los/convention_agreements/texts/koh_english.pdf accessed 2 Feb. 2022.
19. For the sake of simplicity, the terms 'dispute' and 'conflict' and related expressions are used synonymously, though it is recognised that there exists a body of literature that distinguishes between the two. *See* John Collier and Vaughan Lowe, *The Settlement of Disputes in International Law: Institutions and Procedures* 1 (Oxford University Press 1999); Douglas H. Yarn, *Conflict* in *Dictionary of Conflict Resolution* 115 (Douglas H. Yarn ed., Jossey-Bass 1999); Louis Kriesberg, *The Development of the Conflict Resolution Field* in *Peacemaking in International Conflict* 64-65 (William Zartman and Lewis Rasmussen eds, United States Institute of Peace Press 1997).

ITR, compared to the dispute resolution systems under the WTO and the BIT regimes. The three research questions are formulated in section 2.5, further below, following a critical review of the literature.

2.2 WHY DOES THE CURRENT TAX TREATY DISPUTE RESOLUTION SYSTEM NEED REFORM?

This section explores the current and expected challenges within the MAP and arbitration system in an attempt to highlight the urgency of reforming the current system despite the implementation of the BEPS Action 14 minimum standard that aims to make the MAP more effective among the IF jurisdictions.[20]

2.2.1 Capacity Issues Within MAP

Based on the OECD MAP Statistics from 2016 to 2020[21] (*see* Table I.1 in Appendix I), the total number of MAP cases being opened and cases being closed in the year has increased steadily (with a slight decrease in 2020, which may be due to COVID-19-related disruptions). This means that not only are there more disputes being referred to the MAP by taxpayers, but also that competent authorities are able to resolve MAP cases more rapidly. Such results would suggest that the implementation of the BEPS Action 14 minimum standard across IF members may be having a positive impact on the effectiveness of the MAP.

However, despite the improvements made to the MAP in terms of access and resolution, there is also a marked increase in the inventory of MAP caseload over the years, as the ending inventory levels in 2020 have almost quadrupled since 2016 (*see* Table I.1 in Appendix I). This may be explained by the fact that the rate at which new MAP cases are being opened every year consistently exceeds the rate of resolution of cases. The resulting build-up of MAP cases undoubtedly puts pressure on the tax administrations in terms of allocating (already scarce) resources across their various functions, resulting in potential capacity constraint issues.[22] In the long run, such administrative pressures may also compromise the independence and efficiency of the competent authority units whose work is based on the concept of good faith.

---

20. BEPS Action 14 is one of the four minimum standards under the OECD/G20 BEPS Project. It sets out mandatory rules and best practices that aim to strengthen the effectiveness and efficiency of the MAP process in four areas: (1) preventing disputes, (2) making MAP more accessible, (3) resolving MAP cases, and (4) implementing MAP agreements. *See* OECD, *Making Dispute Resolution Mechanisms More Effective, Action 14-2015 Final Report* (OECD Publishing 2015).
21. The MAP cases listed include those received on or after 1 January 2016 or 1 January of the year of joining the BEPS IF as these cases have been reported under the OECD's agreed reporting framework, thus ensuring greater reliability in the statistics. The cases received prior to 1 January 2016 were based on each reporting jurisdictions' own methodology, without a jurisdiction by jurisdiction breakdown, making it impossible to reconcile the cases reported across jurisdictions. This is because aggregate reporting for old cases included double counting of cases reported by two reporting jurisdictions in their respective inventory and was therefore less reliable.
22. OECD, *Manual on Effective Mutual Agreement Procedures* 39-40 (OECD Publishing 2007) (MEMAP).

A closer examination of the outstanding MAP cases also shows that transfer pricing cases make up the majority of the outstanding MAP caseload (*see* Table I.1 in Appendix I). This trend is especially alarming for transfer pricing cases, which shows an increase in ending inventory levels of 133% since 2017 compared with a 79% increase for non-transfer pricing cases. This may be explained by the fact that transfer pricing cases require much more case-specific information from the taxpayer due to their more complex nature, as reflected in the longer length of time for resolution, as shown in Table I.2 in Appendix I. In fact, the average time for resolving transfer pricing cases consistently exceeds the recommended timeline of 24 months under BEPS Action 14 minimum standard to last approximately over 30 months.

The MAP statistics discussed above demonstrate that although the MAP may be effective in resolving the majority of the increasing non-transfer pricing disputes since 2016 (resolved under the 24-month period), the results are less impressive with regard to the resolution of transfer pricing cases (average resolution period of 30-35 months). Given the increased risks of tax treaty disputes resulting from the interpretation of ambiguous BEPS provisions in transfer pricing cases and permanent establishment (PE) cases (discussed in section 2.2.2.2 below), it is expected that the effectiveness of the MAP, especially with regard to transfer pricing cases, will continue to be limited, resulting in growing capacity constraints on the existing MAP mechanism. As one commentator noted, the length and inefficiency of a MAP 'seems to be a function of the bureaucratic exigencies of the states involved rather than anything intrinsic in the MAP process'.[23] This suggests the need for an overall institutional approach to ensure a targeted response to the increasing resource and capacity issues within the dispute resolution system.

2.2.2 Failure to Provide Tax Certainty

2.2.2.1 Absence of Obligation to Resolve MAP Cases in a Timely Manner

The structure of the MAP provision under Article 25(2) of the OECD or UN Model requires the competent authorities to only 'endeavour' to reach an agreement for resolving the tax issue. This means they are not legally obligated to find a solution, in which case, sometimes, the taxpayer may not find any relief to the double tax issue despite incurring potential legal and/or accounting costs for preparing a MAP submission.[24] Although the majority of MAP cases are resolved – MAP Statistics show that, on average, 80% of MAP cases are resolved through unilateral relief or bilateral agreement (*see* Table I.3 in Appendix I) – any risks of unresolved cases may exacerbate the taxpayer's lack of trust in the MAP system for obtaining a guaranteed resolution of the tax issue. Non-resolution, especially after the competent authorities have worked on

23. Chloe Burnett, *International Tax Arbitration* 36(3) Aust. Tax Rev. 173, 174 (2007).
24. Jeff Owens, *Mandatory Tax Arbitration: The Next Frontier Issue*, 46(8/9) Intertax 610 (2018); Robert A. Green, *Antilegalistic Approaches to Resolving Disputes Between Governments: A Comparison of the International Tax and Trade Regimes*, 23 Yale J. Int'l L. 79 (1998); Gustaf Lindecrona and Nils Mattsson, *Arbitration in Taxation* 25 (Kluwer Law and Taxation Publishers 1981).

the case for a few years, may also constitute a wastage of resources for both the taxpayer and the competent authorities.

To address the lack of a guaranteed resolution in the MAP process, the OECD Model prescribes an optional provision to refer a MAP case to mandatory arbitration if no MAP agreement is reached within 24 months.[25] A similar clause is also introduced in the UN Model. However, the UN Model arbitration is a voluntary mechanism, which could only be triggered through mutual agreement of the competent authorities if they were unable to reach a solution within a period of three years.[26] Despite such efforts, it is difficult to analyse the effectiveness of such provisions at this point as mandatory arbitration has not been widely implemented (only 31 countries out of the 141 IF members as of June 2022, and most signatories opted for mandatory binding arbitration with reservations);[27] even in those jurisdictions where it would be applicable, the arbitration mechanism has not been used often; and even when it is triggered, arbitration decisions are not generally made public.[28] For example, as of 2014, the US had four double tax treaties (DTTs) in force that contained voluntary arbitration provisions, although there is no known arbitration case pursuant to these arbitration provisions.[29]

Although the lack of obligation to reach a MAP agreement persists, the implementation of the BEPS Action 14 minimum standard brought some relief for taxpayers by introducing mandatory timelines for the resolution of the MAP cases and the implementation of MAP agreements. Before BEPS, the MAP provision did not specify any timeline for resolving MAP cases, giving competent authorities unlimited periods to endeavour to resolve the case.[30] Arguably, such practice could leave the taxpayer in a conundrum when considering whether to withdraw from the MAP and file a case with the domestic courts instead to ensure that the applicable limitation of a statute is

25. Article 25(5) OECD Model.
26. Article 25 Alternative B UN Model.
27. Countries include Andorra, Australia, Austria, Barbados, Belgium, Canada, Curacao, Fiji, Finland, France, Germany, Greece, Hungary, Ireland, Italy, Japan, Lesotho, Liechtenstein, Luxembourg, Malta, Mauritius, The Netherlands, New Zealand, Papua New Guinea, Portugal, Singapore, Slovenia, Spain, Sweden, Switzerland and the United Kingdom. *See* OECD, *List of signatories and parties to the Multilateral Convention to Implement Tax Treaty Related Measures to Prevent Base Erosion and Profit Shifting* (28 Jun. 2022) www.oecd.org/tax/treaties/beps-mli-signatories-and-parties.pdf accessed 20 Jul. 2022.
28. The IBFD database as on April 2017 suggests a total of 217 tax treaties in force in the English language that contain a mandatory arbitration clause out of the existing 3,000 or so tax treaties. *See* Sriram Govind and Shreya Rao, *Designing an Inclusive and Equitable Framework for Tax Treaty Dispute Resolution: An Indian Perspective,* 46(4) Intertax 313, 321 (2018) DOI: 10.54648/taxi2018032.
29. *See* David Rosenbloom, *Mandatory Arbitration of Disputes Pursuant to Tax Treaties: The Experience of the United States,* in *International Arbitration in Tax Matters* 160 (Michael Lang and Jeffrey Owens eds, IBFD 2016).
30. An extreme example is of a dispute between Luxemburg with another OECD country that was closed in 2009 that took 16 years and 4 months to be decided: *See* OECD, *MAP Program Statistics for the 2015 reporting period, Country: Luxembourg* (2015) www.oecd.org/ctp/dispute/MAP%20PROGRAM%20STATISTICS%20FOR%202015%20LUX.pdf accessed 10 Nov. 2021 DOI: 10.1787/rev_fish_stat_en-2014-20-en; *see also* Qiang Cai, *A Package Deal Is Not a Bad Deal: Reassessing the Method of Package Negotiation Under the Mutual Agreement Procedure,* 46(10) Intertax 746 (2018) DOI: 10.54648/taxi2018081.

not exceeded. BEPS Action 14 introduced certain mandatory rules to address these issues by requiring MAP cases to be resolved in 24 months[31] and MAP agreements to be implemented irrespective of the time limits under domestic law.[32] Although it is noted that in practice, currently, the average resolution time period for transfer pricing cases remains well above the prescribed timeline (an average of 30-35 months, as summarised in Table I.2 in Appendix I). Such outcomes undoubtedly put pressure on the proper functioning of the MAP system and may even impact the taxpayers' reliability on the MAP, suggesting the need for alternative dispute resolution mechanisms.

2.2.2.2 Indeterminacy in Interpreting International Tax Regulations

One of the top factors identified as creating uncertainty in the ITR is related to inconsistency or conflicts between two or more tax administrations in the interpretation of international tax standards.[33] International tax regulations and treaty rules, in particular, are not precise and can be interpreted to apply very differently in any specific case, giving rise to various forms of indeterminacy.[34] The first is the general level of language that sets the linguistic context and hence the meaning of certain words or phrases or how to express a particular concept. In certain social and linguistic contexts, meanings are assigned in a very strict fashion and in others, meanings are more fluid with various levels of interpretation, which unavoidably creates complexities when interpreting terms under international standards. An example would include the conflicted interpretation of certain generally accepted terms such as 'value creation' or 'source income' among the various multilingual jurisdictions of the ITR.[35]

The second form of indeterminacy flows from conflicts in interpreting abstract principles under the rule of law when applying them to specific cases. In fact, Herzfeld argues that in order to be accepted by most countries, the BEPS Action Plan had to be diluted to an almost meaningless point with vague outcomes that can be interpreted liberally by tax administrations, thus leading to conflicting interpretative issues and increased risk of disputes.[36] These risks are particularly relevant in the new PE rules under Action 7 and the revised transfer pricing guidelines under Actions 8-10.[37]

31. OECD, *BEPS Action 14 on More Effective Dispute Resolution Mechanisms: Peer Review Documents*, para. 16C2 (OECD Publishing 2016) (Action 14 Peer Review Documents).
32. Action 14 Peer Review Documents, *supra* n. 31, at paras 17.D2 and D3.
33. IMF and OECD, 'Tax Certainty: IMF/OECD Report for the G20 Finance Ministers' 32 (March 2017) www.oecd.org/tax/tax-policy/tax-certainty-report-oecd-imf-report-g20-finance-ministers-march-2017.pdf accessed 21 Mar. 2021.
34. Sol Picciotto, *Constructing Compliance: Game Playing, Tax Law, and the Regulatory State* 29(1) L. & Pol'y 11 (2007) DOI: 10.1111/j.1467-9930.2007.00243.x.
35. *See* Michael Lennard, *Act of Creation: The OECD/G20 Test of 'Value Creation' as a Basis for Taxing Rights and Its Relevance to Developing Countries* 25(3) Transnat'l Corp 55 (2018) DOI: 10.18356/3db18835-en; Michael Devereux and John Vella, *Are We Heading Towards a Corporate Tax System Fit for the 21st Century?* 35 Fisc. Stud. 449 (2014) DOI: 10.1111/j.1475-5890.2014.12038.x.
36. Mindy Herzfeld, *The Case Against BEPS: Lessons for Tax Coordination* 21 Florida Tax Review 52 (2017); *see also* Michelle Markham, *Seeking New Directions in Dispute Resolution Mechanisms: Do We Need a Revised Mutual Agreement Procedure?* 70 (1-2) Bull. Int'l Tax'n 82 (2016).
37. Herzfeld, *supra* n. 36, at 52.

Additionally, with respect to BEPS Action 6, that tackles the issue of treaty shopping by introducing a principle purpose test (PPT) in the treaty provision,[38] some tax scholars and practitioners have argued that the subjective reading of the PPT provision places an undue burden on the taxpayer to disprove the tax authority's interpretation of a tax benefit being the primary motive for a transaction, emphasising the need for more precise treaty language to avoid treaty disputes.[39]

The third type of indeterminacy is attributed to the fact that the interpretation of the law is an exercise in normative judgment, implying that even the core meaning of a legal norm might depend on a shared view of the values or purposes that underlie it. The differing views about those values in various social and political contexts may therefore result in different interpretations of the meaning of the norm, which may be equally potentially acceptable.[40] More importantly, such fragmented interpretation may give more weight to the views of the more politically influential parties.[41] For instance, the texts of the new PE provisions under BEPS Action 7 were scaled back as a result of pressure from business groups, including the Business and Investment Advisory Committee (BIAC) to the OECD, that argued that tighter PE rules would negatively impact cross-border transactions.[42] The details were instead included in the Commentaries of the Action 7 report, which do not strictly constitute 'context' for purposes of treaty interpretation under the Vienna Convention on the Law of Treaties (VCLT),[43] thus making it harder to defend in court. It is noted, however, that in practice, OECD commentaries are followed by many courts in both developed and developing countries, which may counter such interpretative conflicts.[44]

Overall, as discussed above, international tax interpretation is prone to various sources of indeterminacy, which may create a conflicting and fragmented understanding among the competent authorities as well as taxpayers, which increases the risks of double-taxation, tax avoidance and evasion. Given that the MAP is based on a non-binding, bilateral mechanism, it has limited potential to build a collective interpretation of the international tax rules on a multilateral level and, therefore, may need to be supplemented with alternative legalistic mechanisms that apply at a more multilateral level.

38. OECD, *Preventing the Granting of Treaty Benefits in Inappropriate Circumstances, Action 6: 2015 Final Report* (OECD Publishing 2015).
39. Michael Lang, *BEPS Action 6: Introducing an Anti-abuse Rule in Tax Treaties* 74 Tax Notes Int'l 655 (2014) DOI: 10.2139/ssrn.2500827.
40. Sol Picciotto, *Indeterminacy, Complexity, Technocracy and the Reform of International Corporate Taxation* 24 *Soc. Legal Stud.* 165 (2015) DOI: 10.1177/0964663915572942.
41. *See* Herzfeld, *supra* n. 36, at 29. *For e.g.*, Herzfeld argues that the changes in the revised transfer pricing rules simply ignored some countries' (e.g., China and France) requests for a complete re-examination of the existing arm's-length standard.
42. Herzfeld, *supra* n. 36, at 56.
43. *Vienna Convention on the Law of Treaties* (adopted 23 May 1969, entered into force 27 Jan. 1980) 1155 UNTS 331 Art. 33 (VCLT).
44. Eduardo Baistrocchi, *Patterns of Tax Treaty Disputes: A Global Taxonomy*, in *A Global Analysis of Tax Treaty Disputes* (Eduardo Baistrocchi ed., Cambridge University Press 2017).

2.2.2.3 *Lack of Transparency and Accountability*

One of the main criticisms associated with the current dispute resolution system refers to the lack of transparency associated with certain operational aspects of the MAP, including the limited publication of government reports of their practices through digests, diplomatic notes and agreements.[45] The MAP involves a private and confidential negotiation process between the competent authorities of the two contracting states for resolving the taxpayer's cross-border tax issue. The taxpayer whose case is being discussed is not allowed to participate in any way in this process, arguably to preserve the confidentiality of government-to-government communications. This is clearly demonstrated through the recent UK First-Tier Tribunal decision in *McCabe v. Revenue & Customs*.[46]

Such opacity within the MAP has inevitably raised taxpayers' doubts regarding the accountability of the competent authorities to objectively apply the rules of the treaty in good faith, fuelling concerns of 'package deals' being struck between the officials to maximise tax revenue collections without any scrutiny.[47] Such fears may be amplified for some taxpayers given the large amounts of financial information that they are required to submit to the tax administrations from their end in the course of the MAP, thus increasing the risks of being audited in the future if no MAP agreement is reached.[48] In fact, the Canadian Revenue Agency (CRA) reported in 2018 that one of the reasons for MAP failures was the refusal by taxpayers to provide requested information.[49]

While the arbitration mechanism recommended under the OECD and the UN Models may mitigate to some extent the issue of accountability, as the MAP case is submitted to an independent panel of arbitrators for resolution, the problem of lack of transparency would likely persist. This is because the tax arbitration process and the arbitration award are usually kept private and confidential unless both competent authorities and the concerned taxpayer agree to publish the decision. However, this is not common practice in the ITR, as evidenced by the lack of case law generated through MAP because of the limited publication of the MAP and arbitration decisions (except in redacted form in very rare cases).[50] This failure to develop an evolving body of published MAP and arbitration decisions that can serve as guidance for future interpretation of important issues makes it difficult to establish 'certainty' in the interpretation of international tax standards,[51] and it also hinders the development of international tax law.[52]

---

45. Allison Christians, *How Nations Share* 87 Ind. L. J 1407 (2012).
46. Jonathan Schwarz, *Mutual Agreement Procedure: Taxpayer Access to Information* (Kluwer International Tax Blog, 12 Jun. 2019) http://kluwertaxblog.com/2019/06/12/mutual-agreement-procedure-taxpayer-access-to-information/ accessed 4 Mar. 2022.
47. Christians, *supra* n. 45, at 1451.
48. MEMAP, *supra* n. 22, at 35.
49. Canada Revenue Agency, *Mutual Agreement Procedure: Program Report – 2018 (Annex A)* (CRA MAP Report 2018) www.canada.ca/en/revenue-agency/services/tax/international-non-residents/competent-authority-services/2018map.html#toc17 accessed 20 Mar. 2021.
50. Christians, *supra* n. 45, at 1410.
51. Markham, *Litigation, Arbitration and Mediation in International Tax Disputes, supra* n. 1, at 297.
52. Christians, *supra* n. 45.

2.2.3 Inequitable Dispute Resolution Processes and Outcomes Across the ITR

2.2.3.1 Limitations of a Bilateral MAP

The MAP is inherently a bilateral mechanism based on the applicable tax treaty, and it is, therefore, up to the competent authorities of the contracting states to determine the extent and outcome of the negotiations. The process may thus be subject to power dynamics resulting from economic, technical or political inequities between the competent authorities if the dispute involves, for example, a developed and a developing country. The competent authority of the developing country may feel pressured to accept the views of the more skilled and powerful developed country counterpart, leading to inequitable solutions through MAP. For the purpose of this thesis, inequitable solutions refer to outcomes that do not allocate taxes to the jurisdiction where the activity takes place through a balanced consideration of relevant circumstances of all parties involved. This is based on the definition of 'tax fairness' under the BEPS Project, which involves allocating profits and taxes where value is created by taking into consideration the economic substance of the transactions (e.g., adequate amount of operating expenditure and labour).[53] In the case of transfer pricing disputes, relevant circumstances to consider may involve the comparability factors present in the transaction, as defined in the OECD's Transfer Pricing Guidelines (e.g., contractual terms, functions performed by the parties, characteristics of the good or service transferred, economic circumstances of the parties and the business strategies pursued by the parties).[54]

In today's increasingly multilateral ITR, tax treaty disputes, especially those related to transfer pricing issues, often involve third or fourth jurisdictions, which makes it particularly difficult to administer through an inherently bilateral MAP process. In addition, multilateral negotiations also increase the difficulties for competent authorities to find a commonly accepted solution to the distributive conflicts arising from the transfer pricing cases in question. When dealing with disputes involving several countries (e.g., profit allocation disputes under Pillar One), it would appear to be onerous and inefficient for one competent authority to establish which of the other tax authorities might be affected by the dispute in question and to invite them to participate in the multilateral process.[55] This situation is particularly true in a scenario in which the issue is whether the multinational enterprise (MNE) in question falls within the scope of the OECD's Pillar One, i.e., whether residual profits (Amount A) should be allocated to the market jurisdiction (discussed further in section 2.3.1.3

53. OECD, *Resumption of Application of Substantial Activities for No or Nominal Tax Jurisdictions – BEPS Action 5* (OECD Publishing 2018).
54. OECD, *Transfer Pricing Guidelines for Multinational Enterprises and Tax Administrations 2022* para. 1.36 (OECD Publishing 2022) (OECD Transfer Pricing Guidelines 2022).
55. Spyridon E. Malamis and Qiang Cai, *International Tax Dispute Resolution in Light of Pillar One: New Challenges and Opportunities* 75(2) Bull. Int'l Tax'n 94, 100 (2021).

below).[56] Thus, reliance on the MAP solely may aggravate potential bargaining problems and exacerbate the risks of inequitable solutions in a multilateral ITR.

2.2.3.2 Uneven Application of MAP Across the DTT Network

The MAP addresses most issues arising within a bilateral tax treaty. Under Article 25(1), the MAP covers disputes in relation to double taxation that is not in accordance with the treaty, arising from transfer pricing transactions, the creation of PE, dual residence, withholding tax payments and employment income tax levies. Under Article 25(3), the MAP provision also covers tax disputes related to the treaty that require clarification or interpretation and double tax issues in cases that are not otherwise provided for in the treaty. However, there are certain disputes which may be excluded from MAP and the treaty, including, for example, the case involving a third-country resident that has a PE in both contracting states under the treaty.[57] In addition, certain countries may also disallow the resolution of tax disputes arising under transfer pricing cases in the absence of Article 9(2) of the OECD or UN Model that provides for corresponding adjustments of income among associated enterprises,[58] despite the recommendations to that effect in the Commentaries to Article 25 in both the OECD and the UN Models.[59] It is worth noting that BEPS Action 14 addressed this issue by recommending that all IF jurisdictions should provide access to MAP in transfer pricing cases.[60]

In other aspects, Action 14 was less effective in tackling certain scope limitations of the MAP. For instance, MAP applies only to taxes specified in the particular treaty (*see* OECD Model Article 2), which would not capture disputes arising from certain types of digital services tax (DST) schemes like the Indian Equalisation Levy on digital services, designed to operate outside the scope of tax treaties.[61] Currently, it is also unclear how the MAP will deal with potential disputes under Pillar Two regarding the application of the minimum tax regime. The limited scope of the current MAP thus leads to uneven coverage of potential disputes across the ITR as each jurisdiction may decide unilaterally to apply MAP to certain types of disputes (e.g., the UK issued legislation in 2021 to make Diverted Profits Tax one of the taxes in respect of which a

56. Malamis and Cai, *supra* n. 55, at 100.
57. If there is no treaty between the state of residence of the taxpayer and either of the states where PE is located, the taxpayer may not be eligible for MAP which is usually a bilateral process. It is noted however that there have been multilateral MAPs in the derivative financial industry between the US, the UK and Japan in the 1990s.
58. Under Art. 9(2), relief may be provided if profits are reallocated among associated companies of a group and tax had already been charged on the profit prior to being reallocated to another jurisdiction where it will be taxed again.
59. *See* OECD Model: Commentary on Article 25, para. 10 and UN Model: Commentary on Article 25, para. 9.
60. Action 14 Peer Review Documents, *supra* n. 31, at paras 14.B3 and 17.D1.
61. All parties joining Pillar One have agreed in principle to remove existing DSTs and other relevant similar measures to implement instead the new nexus rules. *See* Statement on a Two-Pillar solution, *supra* n. 5, at 3. *See also* USTR, *Termination of Action in the Digital Services Tax Investigation of India and Further Monitoring* (Federal Register, 2 Dec. 2021) www.federalregister.gov/documents/2021/12/02/2021-26198/termination-of-action-in-the-digital-services-tax-investigation-of-india-and-further-monitoring accessed 5 Mar. 2022.

MAP outcome could potentially be implemented).[62] Such uneven application of rules leads to unequal treatment across jurisdictions, which may exacerbate the risks of inequitable solutions to cross-border tax disputes.

2.2.4 Implications in This Study

The analysis in section 2.2 clearly demonstrates that the incremental improvements brought to the MAP and arbitration system through BEPS Action 14 fall short of addressing some of the most pertinent issues identified within the current tax treaty dispute resolution system. These issues include capacity constraints, lack of certainty and inequitable solutions across jurisdictions. Arguably, the planned implementation of the Two-Pillar Solution in 2024 to reform the allocation of taxing rights and set out a global minimum tax regime is also expected to result in an increase in cross-border tax disputes along with rising uncertainty levels across the ITR. These risks are further emphasised through the competing tax revenue needs of countries in the wake of the COVID-19 pandemic,[63] which call for an urgent and more radical restructuring of the dispute resolution system that addresses the issues mentioned above.

2.3 IDENTIFYING THE RIGHT TYPE OF REFORM WITHIN TAX TREATY DISPUTE RESOLUTION

In order to devise an appropriate research design that can provide a targeted policy reform of the current tax treaty dispute resolution system, it is important to understand what has been proposed in the past and what impact such proposals have had. This section scans the international tax literature and relevant tax policy material to analyse existing reform proposals. The analysis identifies a lack of appropriate institutional analysis regarding international dispute resolution in the post-BEPS ITR and recommends a strategic use of comparative institutional analysis to ensure a targeted reform of the current system.

2.3.1 Review of Existing Proposals for Reforming Tax Treaty Dispute Resolution

2.3.1.1 Proposals to Improve Existing Mechanisms

A review of several studies within the international tax law and policy literature reveals various analyses of the deficiencies of the current dispute resolution mechanisms in the ITR, as discussed in section 2.2, and suggestions for reform. These analyses focus

62. HMRC, *Policy Paper: Mutual Agreement Procedure Decisions Relating to the Diverted Profits Tax* (HMRC, 27 Oct. 2021) www.gov.uk/government/publications/mutual-agreement-procedure-map-decisions-relating-to-the-diverted-profits-tax/mutual-agreement-procedure-map-decisions-relating-to-the-diverted-profits-tax accessed 20 Mar. 2022.
63. *See* Baker Mckenzie (Newsroom, 17 Feb. 2022) www.bakermckenzie.com/en/newsroom/2022/02/tax-disputes-in-2021 accessed 2 Apr. 2022.

mostly on analysing the existing arbitration processes and seem to endorse, at least from a theoretical standpoint, the OECD's proposed mandatory binding arbitration approach, in spite of the potential sovereignty-related costs cited by several developing countries.[64] In fact, although the OECD had stated that the adoption of a binding arbitration system would represent an 'unacceptable surrender of fiscal sovereignty' in 1984, it endorsed the opposite view in the post-BEPS period.[65] Even developed countries like Japan and the US strongly opposed binding arbitration until the mid-2000s.[66] One potential explanation for this change, offered by Hearson and Tucker, refers to the instrumental business power driving a process of incremental change through layering to overcome states' preference to retain sovereignty.[67] This strategy started with the publication of the mandatory arbitration provision in the 2008 OECD Model (discussed in section 4.3.5.4.3 further below).

Certain studies also discuss the potential use of mediation to facilitate collaborative exchanges among competent authorities,[68] even though there is no record of any formal mediation being applied to resolve MAP cases.[69] Litigation through domestic courts has been revealed as the least favoured mechanism in the ITR for both taxpayers and competent authorities due to the costly and time-consuming procedures and differential outcomes across jurisdictions (discussed further in section 3.5.2 below).[70]

2.3.1.2 In-Depth Institutional Studies Advocating New Tax Dispute Resolution Structures

To the best of my knowledge, Daniel Altman's 2005 ground-breaking study on dispute resolution under tax treaties constitutes the most comprehensive institutional analysis of the tax treaty dispute resolution system as it existed in the pre-BEPS era.[71] The study compares dispute resolution systems under the MAP, the WTO dispute settlement understanding (DSU) and the European Arbitration mechanism. It takes an in-depth look at the mechanisms used to resolve such disputes and how they interact with the interests of the various parties involved in the process, including international organisations, governments and taxpayers, based on international relations theory.

64. Markham, *Litigation, Arbitration and Mediation in International Tax Disputes, supra* n. 1, at 298; Owens, *supra* n. 24; Hans Mooij, *Tax Treaty Arbitration* 35(2) Arb. Int'l 195 (2018); Benjami Angles Juanpere, *The Resolution of Tax Disputes and International Tax Arbitration* 5(1) Eur. J. Bus. & Manag. Res. 1, 6 (2020) DOI: 10.24018/ejbmr.2020.5.1.174.
65. *See* Martin Hearson and Todd N. Tucker, *An Unacceptable Surrender of Fiscal Sovereignty: The Neoliberal Turn to International Tax Arbitration* 1 (2021) www.cambridge.org/core/journals/perspectives-on-politics/article/an-unacceptable-surrender-of-fiscal-sovereignty-the-neoliberal-turn-to-international-tax-arbitration/C3E4CDD17A00C985AEFC782CB3ADC2D0 accessed 20 May 2022 DOI: 10.1017/s1537592721000967.
66. Hearson and Tucker, *supra* n. 65, at 2.
67. *Ibid.*, at 8-12.
68. Markham, *Litigation, Arbitration and Mediation in International Tax Disputes, supra* n. 1.
69. Mooij, *supra* n. 64, at 197.
70. Markham, *Litigation, Arbitration and Mediation in International Tax Disputes, supra* n. 1, at 297.
71. Zvi Daniel Altman, *Dispute Resolution under Tax Treaties* 1 (Doctoral Series Volume 11, 1-5, IBFD 2005).

When relevant data is available, the study also conducts a quantitative analysis of tax and trade disputes and their resolution through the MAP and the WTO.[72] The study uses a common framework of analysis (checklist) developed specifically to measure the impact of the proposals made in the study. It concludes by recommending the establishment of a new international organisation with links to domestic judicial networks in order to address some of the challenges faced within tax treaty dispute resolution at the time (i.e., pre-BEPS era).

Another study conducted earlier in 1998 by Professor Robert Green also draws upon international relations theory to compare the dispute resolution systems under MAP and the WTO that replaced the General Agreement on Tariffs and Trade (GATT) in 1995.[73] According to Green, the legalistic model of the WTO system was not an ideal model for the resolution of income tax disputes that would benefit more from negotiations and diplomatic means. Green's conclusions are based on three main arguments. First, legalistic dispute resolution procedures are more useful for managing unilateral strategies and in international trade, states tend to resort regularly to retaliatory strategies to enforce international compliance with WTO obligations, which is not the case in the ITR. Second, legalistic procedures are needed in non-transparent institutions to ensure that information is being disseminated to all users. According to Green, the ITR was much more transparent than the WTO regime and, therefore, did not need a legalistic dispute resolution system as in the WTO. Third, the costs of setting up a legalistic system in the ITR, including administration and other costs related to the potential breakdown of diplomatic and political relations through adversarial processes, would largely outweigh its benefits.

2.3.1.3 The OECD's Dispute Resolution Mechanism Proposed under Pillar One

In addition to the academic literature review, the OECD's new mandatory and binding dispute resolution mechanism proposed under Pillar One also merits attention, although it is still being developed. The proposed mechanism is expected to come into force in 2024 through the adoption of a Multilateral Convention (MC) to ensure a consistent and synergised implementation across the IF.[74] It may be applied to resolve disputes relating to the allocation of the residual profits (amount A) to market jurisdictions and also to issues related to Amount A (e.g., transfer pricing and business profits disputes).[75] A closer examination of the mechanism proposed reveals, however, that with respect to amount A, more emphasis is laid on dispute prevention measures by advocating for early tax certainty processes, including self-assessment returns and review panels with the tax authorities concerned to settle any disputes amicably (Panel

72. Altman, *supra* n. 71, at 184.
73. Green, *supra* n. 24, at 138.
74. Statement on Two-Pillar Solution, *supra* n. 5, at 6. *See also* OECD, *Tax Challenges Arising from Digitalisation – Report on Pillar One Blueprint: Inclusive Framework on BEPS* para. 824 (OECD Publishing 2020) (Report on Pillar One Blueprint).
75. Statement on a Two-Pillar Solution, *supra* n. 5, at 2.

Review Process) followed by binding panel arbitration decisions (Determination Panel Process) if no amicable settlement is reached.[76] Certain exceptions may apply for developing countries that have no or low levels of MAP cases.[77]

A review of the Pillar One proposals by Malamis and Cai highlights an apparent paradox in that the profit allocation mechanisms intended to provide greater certainty to taxpayers are themselves associated with dispute prevention and/or resolution on a case-by-case-basis,[78] which may perpetuate opportunistic behaviours among tax authorities, especially in a multilateral setting involving tax authorities across several countries. For instance, the mechanism requires a 'leading tax authority' of the MNE to initiate and take charge of the dispute prevention and or resolution process (e.g., formulate questions, consider the scenario of the filtering out of 'lower-risk groups' during an initial review or concluding that a panel's review is not required based on specific criteria).[79] This would affect the Panel Review Process and also filter the disputes that proceed to binding resolution under the Determination Panel Process, arguably exacerbating power disparities among competent authorities that could compromise the independence of the legal process through blocking and abusive tactics.[80] Similar views are also reflected in Howard Mann's analysis of the Pillar One mechanism, emphasising, in addition, the absence of a focus on tax certainty for governments compared to MNEs of developed countries that will benefit the most from the proposed mechanism.[81]

Additionally, just as in the current OECD mandatory arbitration process, the Pillar One mechanism favours a baseball arbitration approach (where the arbitrators settle on one of the solutions proposed by each of the competent authorities) as the default rule instead of the independent opinion method (where the arbitrators reach a decision based on their own independent legal analysis of the facts). This means that the Determination Panel has to settle on one of the alternative outcomes submitted by the jurisdictions involved in the MAP unless the competent authorities agree otherwise.[82] However, such practice may be particularly problematic when there are several parties involved, as any single offer cannot settle the positions for the remaining parties, potentially resulting in more dissatisfaction among the competent authorities.[83] The lack of transparency associated with this process also keeps the competent authorities in the dark regarding the reasoning behind the decisions, which may perpetuate tax uncertainty across the ITR. These approaches are further explored in section 4.3.2.1.5.2 below.

The double-edged relevance of the dispute resolution mechanism proposed under Pillar One cannot be understated in the context of this book. On the one hand, it certainly brought about the first radical step in the reform of tax treaty dispute resolution by rallying developing countries to implement a mandatory and binding mechanism for resolving multilateral disputes across the IF. Traditionally, developing

76. Report on Pillar One Blueprint, *supra* n. 74, at para. 706.
77. Statement on Two-Pillar Solution, *supra* n. 5, at 2.
78. Malamis and Cai, *supra* n. 55, at 97.
79. *Ibid.*, at 100.
80. *Ibid.*
81. Mann, *supra* n. 7, at 5-6, 9-10, 15.
82. Report on Pillar One Blueprint, *supra* n. 74, at paras 774, 803.
83. Malamis and Cai, *supra* n. 55, at 103; Mann, *supra* n. 7, at 13, 15.

countries have been reluctant to establish binding arbitration, which may explain why only 31 of the 141 IF members had implemented the OECD mandatory arbitration by June 2022.[84] On the other hand, the Pillar One mechanism in its current form (it is still being developed) seems to apply to certain types of disputes of in-scope groups under Pillar One only, potentially excluding disputes under Pillar Two (although it is expected that the proposed mechanism will expand both in scope of issues and number of companies covered after the initial seven years).[85] It is also uncertain at this point how it will relate to the existing MAP system to achieve an effective resolution of the new generation of disputes expected from the proposed implementation of BEPS 2.0 across the ITR.

2.3.2 Need for More Relevant Institutional Analysis of Dispute Resolution in the ITR

With the noted exception of Green's 1998 study, followed by Altman's 2005 study, most studies on international tax dispute resolution tend to focus on critical analyses of existing mechanisms like MAP and arbitration without exploring the possibilities for newer and more appropriate mechanisms. This is particularly puzzling given the various issues that have been identified with the existing mechanisms as the ITR has developed. In fact, the institutional dynamics within the ITR have evolved considerably since Altman's 2005 study. As discussed in section 2.2, the ITR is rapidly evolving into a multilateral regime through the rise of global business models spanning multiple countries, the implementation of increasingly standardised international tax rules across IF jurisdictions since 2015 (e.g., BEPS minimum standards) and more recently with the implementation of new nexus rules for allocating global taxing rights and a minimum corporate tax regime (under the OECD's Two-Pillar Solution). It follows that tax treaty disputes would also be increasingly multilateral in nature, emphasising the need for more multilateral dispute resolution solutions.

Altman's analysis was conducted before BEPS was introduced, and therefore it may not be relevant for designing a dispute resolution system fit for the post-BEPS era. In fact, Altman's analysis suggested that the MAP was underused by taxpayers, with an average of only 25 new transfer pricing cases a year among European countries, 160 new cases in the United States and much smaller or non-existent MAP cases in other countries.[86] In comparison, the latest MAP Statistics show that in 2020, approximately 2,500 MAP cases were filed, with the highest number of cases being filed in Germany, followed by the US, France and India.[87] Such differences call for an updated institutional analysis of dispute resolution in the ITR for designing a comprehensive tax treaty dispute resolution system that can cater for the rising number and new types of international tax disputes (e.g., disputes regarding DSTs).

84. OECD, *supra* n. 27.
85. Mann, *supra* n. 7, at 7.
86. Altman, *supra* n. 71, at 194.
87. OECD, *2020 MAP Statistics* www.oecd.org/tax/dispute/mutual-agreement-procedure-statistics-2020-per-jurisdiction-inventory.htm accessed 26 Jan. 2022.

The recent trend towards more multilateral, consensus-based agreements across the IF in the post-BEPS era also suggests increasing cooperation levels among the IF jurisdictions in developing new international tax rules, where multilateral institutions, such as the IF, play a major role in shaping states' decision-making processes. Accordingly, any proposed dispute resolution reform needs to consider not only the procedural aspects but also the consensus-building structures that affect the decision-making process within a multilateral framework. In this regard, it may be useful to examine and compare the international dispute resolution systems established in other multilateral regimes, as in the separate studies conducted by Altman and Green discussed in section 2.3.1. It is noted, however, that the analysis in the latter studies used the WTO DSU as a comparator and was based primarily on theories of international relations. In contrast, the comparative exercise in this thesis will apply an institutionalist theory based on cooperative and strategic interactions rather than the international relations theory based mainly on realist assumptions that interactions are mostly the result of power struggles for domination (as in, for example, the studies of Altman, Green and Hearson and Tucker discussed previously) For this purpose, the universally agreed international dispute resolution system under the LOSC developed to ensure a peaceful resolution of maritime disputes may constitute an appropriate benchmark for comparative analysis as discussed in section 2.4 below.

2.4 COMPARING DISPUTE RESOLUTION IN THE ITR AND THE LAW OF THE SEA REGIME

This section examines the geopolitical elements that underpin the ITR and the law of the sea regime to justify using the LOSC as a comparative benchmark in the context of this thesis. Some analysis is also included on the unsuitability of dispute resolution systems under the WTO and the BIT regimes as comparators for the purpose of reforming dispute resolution in the ITR.

2.4.1 Similarities in the Geopolitical Context

2.4.1.1 Consensus-Based Decision-Making

International tax rules, especially in the post-BEPS ITR, just as the rules governing the oceans under the modern law of the sea regime, are developed through consensus-based negotiations among the members of the IF and the LOSC, respectively. Since its creation in June 2016, the number of participants engaged in developing international tax rules on a consensus-basis across the IF has increased from an original OECD/G20 group of 89 members to 141 IF members as of November 2021.[88] The LOSC, for its part, was finalised through the participation of 157 countries at the UNCLOS III that spanned over 11 sessions of international negotiations lasting nine years from 1973 to 1982.[89]

88. *See* list of IF members, *supra* n. 13.
89. Koh, *supra* n. 18.

Under both regimes, the members constitute developed and developing countries that arguably have different interests and objectives, which makes the process of reaching an agreement by consensus very difficult. In fact, in addition to the sheer size of the UNCLOS III, comprising over 150 jurisdictions, each having various and often conflicting interests regarding the governance of the seas, the challenges involved in sustaining the momentum and productivity of the negotiations over such long periods also added to the complexities of achieving consensus.[90] Although certain key compromises had to be made, the resulting LOSC was developed through universal consensus based on the desire of states to 'establish true universality in the effort to achieve a just and equitable international economic order governing ocean space'.[91] It is noted that the term 'equitable' is not explicitly defined in the LOSC, although it may refer to the balancing of rights of the relevant parties against their obligations, as evidenced throughout the length of the Convention.[92]

Similar dynamics prevail in the ITR, as the developed, developing, and emerging countries across the IF aim to establish a level playing field in the ITR to ensure that jurisdictions are allocated their 'fair share of taxes' based on where value is created.[93] Although the concept of international distributive justice when it comes to the allocation of global taxing rights is not new in international tax, based on arguments of inter-nation equity developed in the 1980s,[94] the launch of the BEPS initiatives has arguably given new momentum to the debate on distributive justice in the ITR. In addition to collectively addressing tax avoidance, the 141 IF members are currently in the midst of redefining the allocation of global taxing rights through Pillar One and Pillar Two to achieve a more equitable distribution of the international tax base.

For the purposes of this book, it is assumed that the IF and the LOSC, comprising 141 and 157 parties at the time of the UNCLOS III negotiations, respectively, have comparable memberships.[95] As a result, I also assume that although substantive laws differ between the two regimes, the challenges for achieving cooperation/consensus across the diverse members of the IF (each with their own interests and objectives) may be similar to the challenges faced during UNCLOS III. The LOSC thus provides a

---

90. *Ibid.*
91. *Ibid.*
92. For an express reference to the term 'equity' throughout the LOSC, *see* Ruth Lapidoth, *Equity in International Law* 81 Am. Soc. Int'l L. 138, 140 (1987) DOI: 10.1017/s0021223700016575.
93. *See* OECD, *Addressing the Tax Challenges of the Digital Economy, Action 1 – 2015 Final Report* (OECD Publishing 2015). *See also* Irene Burgers and Irma Mosquera, *Corporation Taxation and BEPS: A Fair Slice for Developing Countries* 10(1) Erasmus L. Rev. 29, 41 (2017) DOI: 10.5553/elr.000077.
94. *See* Peggy B. Musgrave, *Taxation of Foreign Investment Income: an Economic Analysis* (John Hopkins Press 1963). *See also* Richard A. Musgrave and Peggy B. Musgrave, *Inter-Nation Equity*, in *Modern Fiscal Issues: Essays in Honor of Carl S Shoup* 63, 85 (Richard Bird and John G. Heads eds, University of Toronto Press 1972). Inter-nation equity makes a compelling argument for allocating the international tax base in a way that acknowledges the entitlement of countries to tax income arising in their territories while making allowance for some degree of international redistribution.
95. *See* list of IF members, *supra* n. 14. For the list of participating countries to the Third United Nations Conference on the Law of the Sea (UNCLOS III), *see* https://treaties.un.org/doc/Publication/MTDSG/Volume%20II/Chapter%20XXI/XXI-6.en.pdf accessed 20 Mar. 2022.

useful benchmark in terms of consensus-building techniques developed to encourage states to reach a compromise. Given that the IF and the LOSC both comprise largely similar state members, diplomatic negotiations may inevitably involve political deal-making across both institutions to maximise the mutual benefits of the common members under both regimes, reinforcing the connection between the two regimes. Another important consideration is that in October 2021, the Group of 77 – a coalition of over 130 developing countries which negotiate together in the United Nations – tabled a proposal for an intergovernmental tax negotiation at the United Nations to discuss the reallocation of taxing rights to ensure a more balanced process.[96] This new development shows the increasing urge of developing countries to participate more fully in the decision-making processes of the ITR, just as in the 1970s when they set into motion the UNCLOS III negotiations to develop the LOSC.[97]

2.4.1.2 Distributive Rules over Scarce Resources to Manage Conflict

The global tax base in the ITR and the oceans under the law of the sea regime both constitute scarce/common pool resources (CPR) that need to be allocated among jurisdictions across the ITR and the LOSC, respectively. Under economic theory, such scarce/CPRs[98] may be defined as goods that generate a finite flow of benefits where it is costly to exclude beneficiaries (non-excludable) and where one member's consumption subtracts from the amount of benefits available to others (subtractable).[99] For example, an MNE's global tax base is a scarce resource because it constitutes a finite good that is divided among various jurisdictions where the MNE has operations; even if the size of the tax base was increased, for example, by applying higher tax rates, the tax base being distributed across relevant jurisdictions would still be limited through distributive rules. The ocean also constitutes a finite good that is divided among various neighbouring countries for use and control. As such, both the ITR and the law of the sea regime constitute multilateral ecosystems characterised by dynamics of creeping jurisdictions as countries compete for increased control over scarce resources (i.e., global tax base and oceans) based on self-interest.

In fact, the term 'creeping jurisdictions' was first defined in the law of the sea regime as groups of states claimed wider areas of the oceans under national jurisdiction, resulting in increasingly conflictual relations with regard to the exploitation of the oceans, especially in the latter half of the 20th century.[100] The oceans not only

---

96. Alex Cobham, Tax Justice Network Blog (25 Nov. 2021) https://taxjustice.net/2021/11/25/power-concedes-nothing-without-a-demand-the-oecd-the-g77-and-a-un-framework-convention-on-tax-proposal/ accessed 20 May 2022.
97. UNCLOS III, Division for Ocean Affairs and the Law of the Sea www.un.org/depts/los/convention_agreements/convention_historical_perspective.htm#Third%20Conference accessed 20 May 2022.
98. Common pool resources (CPR) constitute one of the four types of goods under standard economic theory as discussed further in s. 3.2.2.3.
99. Ostrom, *supra* n. 15, at 40.
100. For an informative account on the nature of maritime disputes and brief description of the main disputes, *see* Ted L. McDorman and Aldo Chircop, *The Resolution of Maritime Disputes*, in *Maritime Affairs: A World Handbook* 344-386 (Edgar Gold ed., Longman Group UK 1991).

represent one of the most conflict-prone sectors of the planet, with conflicts taking place at all levels, from the 'local to the super-power',[101] but also constitute an arena of conflicting uses and interests that are expected to increase in magnitude and extent with the passage of time.[102] These dynamics prompted, in part, the establishment of the international legal framework under the LOSC to manage such international conflicts in a more peaceful manner. For example, Articles 74 and 83 of the LOSC provide clearly for the delimitation of the exclusive economic zone (EEZ) and of the continental shelf, respectively, to be agreed 'on the basis of international law in order to achieve an equitable solution'.

In the ITR as well, similar dynamics of creeping jurisdiction have manifested as states started to compete for more significant shares of cross-border tax revenue from MNEs through the proliferation of intangibles in the 1960s,[103] resulting in increasingly complex transfer pricing rules to manage the rising international tax disputes over the past decades.[104] This is evidenced not only through the increase in MAP cases (*see* Table I.1 in Appendix I) but also through the enactment of largely uncoordinated DSTs and other unilateral digital tax measures in various jurisdictions (e.g., DSTs in France, Italy and the UK) for securing tax revenue across the digital economy. In addition, the interpretation and application of increasingly complex international rules under the BEPS project and BEPS 2.0 may also lead to a new generation of interpretive tax conflicts as IF jurisdictions, especially as developing and emerging countries become more assertive in establishing their rights and interests, which may often conflict with the interests of developed countries when allocating global tax bases. In this respect, it is worth noting that one of the conditions for implementing the new nexus rules under OECD's Pillar One for allocating global tax bases includes the elimination of DSTs at the domestic level.[105]

Based on the analysis above, it is clear that both the ITR and the law of the sea regime have developed distributive mechanisms to manage the risks of international conflict over the allocation of the global tax base and the oceans, respectively. In addition, the rapid pace of changes within both regimes also requires a dynamic implementation of rules to address issues effectively, such as rules to regulate the jurisdiction of artificial islands under the LOSC or the jurisdictional rights regarding the taxation of digital transactions in the ITR. The fact that one of the aims of the LOSC was to manage the risks of conflict through overlapping jurisdictions makes the LOSC a useful benchmark to examine potential mechanisms that the ITR may adopt to address similar jurisdictional conflicts.

101. Donald C. Watt, *The Future Governance of the Seas: An Inaugural Lecture for the Inauguration of the M Sc Course in Sea Use: Law, Economics and Policy – Making* 10 (The London School of Economics and Political Science, London, 10 Oct. 1979).
102. Independent World Commission on the Oceans, *The Ocean Our Future: The Report of the Independent World Commission on the Oceans* 140 (Cambridge University Press 1998).
103. *See, e.g., Nestle Company Inc v. Commissioner*, 22 TCM 46, 62 (1963) in which the Tax Court analysed the royalty rate for a valuable intangible for which no comparable could be found.
104. Dani Rodrik and Tanguy Van Ypersele, *Capital Mobility, Distributive Conflict and International Tax Coordination* 54(1) J. Int'l Econ. 57 (2001) DOI: 10.3386/w7150.
105. Statement on Two-Pillar Solution, *supra* n. 5, at 6.

2.4.1.3 *Addressing Collective Action Issues*

As explained in section 2.4.1.2 above, the global tax base and the oceans both constitute CPRs (or scarce resources). Since CPRs are available to all users, overuse or uncoordinated exploitation of CPRs may result in collective action problems where certain users may reap benefits in their own interests while avoiding related costs or pushing costs to others. Tax avoidance by MNEs is an example of such dynamics in the ITR, where an MNE may benefit from the infrastructure of a state to grow its business but also exploit the loopholes across the overlapping domestic and treaty rules to avoid paying any taxes to that state or even other states where it is doing business. This leads to lost revenue for the affected jurisdictions, affecting their ability to adequately service their public infrastructure and higher costs to jurisdictions for implementing stricter legislation to counter such avoidance actions.[106] The BEPS project, launched in 2015, was developed specifically to address such loopholes by the IF members through stricter domestic and treaty rules and compliance-monitoring based on peer review. These include the implementation of certain minimum standard provisions (i.e., mandatory rules) under BEPS Action points 5, 6, 13 and 14 for all IF members.[107]

Collective action problems also arise in the law of the sea regime in regard to the pollution of marine environments. For example, plastic waste thrown in seas and oceans from one state contributes to filling ocean bottoms, endangering the livelihood of marine life or littering coastal areas of other neighbouring states, negatively impacting their quality of life and also resulting in higher clean-up costs for other states that did not cause pollution. The LOSC addresses such issues through the use of regional cooperation to protect marine environments, enforcement mechanisms, and anti-pollution measures. Examples include general obligations to protect and preserve the marine environment,[108] control pollution of the marine environment from any source[109] and ensure that pollution from one state does not spread beyond the areas where they exercise sovereign rights.[110] By considering the unique economic and environmental capacity of each area, the LOSC also encourages states to harmonise and create regional frameworks to serve the larger goal of reducing marine pollution.[111]

Based on the above discussion, both the ITR and the law of the sea regime face collective action issues. In fact, for the comparative purpose of this book, unacceptable

106. The 2015 OECD/G20 BEPS Report estimated that the global corporate income tax revenue losses could be between USD 100 and 240 billion annually. *See* OECD, *Explanatory Statement, OECD/G20 Base Erosion and Profit Shifting Project* (OECD Publishing 2015).
107. BEPS Action 5 counters harmful tax practices more effectively; Action 6 counters treaty shopping and treaty abuse; Action 13 requires the exchange of Country-by-Country Reporting (CbCR); and Action 14 introduces measures to make dispute resolution under MAP more effective.
108. Article 192 LOSC.
109. Article 194.1 LOSC.
110. Article 194.2 LOSC.
111. *See* Law Explorer, *United Nations Convention on the Law of the Sea and the Regional Seas Agreements* (5 Oct. 2015) https://lawexplores.com/united-nations-convention-on-the-law-of-the-sea-and-the-regional-seas-agreements/ accessed 2 May 2022.

international tax avoidance in the ITR is assumed to be functionally equivalent to pollution under the law of the sea. Since the modern law of the sea regime has dealt with such issues since its conception in the 1970s with the aim of establishing a peaceful and equitable economic order, the development of the LOSC may arguably provide some useful insights for developing a more cooperative, multilateral framework within the ITR to ensure peaceful and equitable relationships among countries in the area of tax treaty dispute resolution.

2.4.1.4 The Role of Customary International Law

Customary international law is recognised as one of the sources of international law by Article 38(1) of the ICJ Statute,[112] and it refers to international obligations among states arising from established international practices, as opposed to obligations arising from formal written conventions or treaties.[113] Based on a review of the academic literature, I argue that despite some distinctly polarised views in the ITR,[114] customary international law plays a significant role in the development of the legal systems within both the ITR and the LOSC.

In fact, in the law of the sea regime, the notion of customary international law is almost universally accepted as being one of the main pillars on which the LOSC was developed.[115] According to Lee, this is reflected mainly in the LOSC's ability to meet all three criteria of the ICJ for qualifying as customary international law.[116] These criteria were developed in the *North Sea Continental Shelf* case and include the ability to: (1) codify or modify pre-existing customary international norms, (2) crystallise emerging customary international norms, and (3) initiate a progressive process of developing customary international norms.[117] In addition, Lee also suggests that the 'package deal theory' used during UNCLOS III for negotiating and adopting the LOSC as a single, indivisible package may also constitute an additional source of customary international law.[118] There are also several provisions of the LOSC and the earlier 1958 Geneva

112. Statute of the International Court of Justice (adopted 26 Jun. 1945, entered into force 24 Oct. 1945) 33 USTS 993 (ICJ Statute).
113. ILC, *Report of the International Law Commission on the Work of its 70th Session* (30 Apr.-1 Jun. and 2 Jul.-10 Aug. 2018) UN Doc. A/73/10, at para. 65.
114. Dirk Broekhuijsen and Irma Mosquera Valderrama, *Revisiting the Case of Customary International Tax Law* 23 Int'l Cmty. L. Rev. 79, 88, n. 44 (2021) DOI: 10.1163/18719732-12341459. Claims of customary international tax law are refuted on rational arguments that such practices were borne predominantly out of self-interest rather than a sense of legal obligation.
115. Bernard H. Oxman, *The Rule of Law and the United Nations Convention on the Law of the Sea* 7 Eur. J. Int'l L. 353 (1996) DOI: 10.1093/oxfordjournals.ejil.a015517; Martin Lishexian Lee, *The Interrelation Between the Law of the Sea Convention and Customary International Law* 7 San Diego Int'l L. J. 405 (2006); Ashley J. Roach, *Today's Customary International Law of the Sea* 45(3) Ocean Dev. & Int'l L. J. 239 (2014) DOI: 10.1080/00908320.2014.929460.
116. Lee, *supra* n. 115, at 409.
117. *Ibid.*
118. *Ibid.*, at 418.

Conventions[119] that have been identified as customary international law by international courts and tribunals.[120]

In the ITR, Avi-Yonah argues that the existence of customary international tax law is evident through the widely followed international tax practices such as the arm's-length principle (ALP) for allocating global income and the extensive use of more than 2,000 bilateral tax treaties based on the UN or OECD Model.[121] Such claims were reinforced even further recently, based on the use of other traditional elements of international tax law, such as the PE threshold and the residence-source principle in tax treaties for allocating taxing rights.[122] Another argument in favour of customary law in the ITR focuses on the application of the nexus principle, which refers to the qualifying connection between a state's territory and income.[123] Although it could be argued that such examples may be less applicable in the future under the new nexus rules of Pillar One that eliminate the traditional residence-source principle, there is new evidence in light of the recent multilateral developments that also support the use of customary international law in the ITR. These include the policy challenges for tackling aggressive tax planning and tax avoidance through the implementation of mechanisms such as the BEPS project, the Multilateral Instrument (MLI) and the IF[124] that present characteristics of the prisoner's dilemma.[125] To give a more specific example, Broekhuijsen and Valderrama argue that the adoption of the PPT among all IF members to curb treaty shopping and treaty abuse under BEPS Action 6 minimum standard could qualify as customary international law under the third criterion of initiating the progressive development of customary international law through norm-making.[126]

To sum up, it is clear that while customary international law constitutes a pillar in the interpretation and application of the LOSC's provisions, it also plays an increasingly important role in the development of legal rules in the ITR to ensure equitable solutions, especially for developing countries. What makes the use of customary international law even more relevant in both regimes is that although the US

119. The Geneva Conventions adopted in 1958, are the product of the First United Nations Conference on the Law of the sea (UNCLOS I) and comprise four different treaties governing different aspects of the oceans. All four treaties were amalgamated within the LOSC adopted in 1982, following UNCLOS III.
120. Roach, *supra* n. 115.
121. Reuven Avi-Yonah, *International Tax as International Law* 57 Tax L. Rev. (2004); Reuven Avi-Yonah, *International Tax as International Law: An Analysis of the International Tax Regime* 5 (Cambridge Tax Law Series 2007).
122. Reuven Avi-Yonah, *Does Customary International Tax Law Exist?* U. Mich. Law & Econ. Working Papers 161 (2019).
123. Stjepan Gadžo, *The Principle of 'Nexus' or 'Genuine Link' as a Keystone of International Income Tax Law: A Reappraisal* 46(3) Intertax (2008).
124. Broekhuijsen and Valderrama, *supra* n. 114.
125. The prisoner's dilemma describes a decision-making situation where two rational individuals fail to reach an optimal outcome by acting in their own self-interests rather than cooperating towards a more strategic outcome for their mutual benefit. Prisoner's dilemmas are involved in many cooperative structures in international relations (including international taxation). *See* Robert O. Keohane, *After Hegemony: Cooperation and Discord in the World Political Economy* 85-110 (Princeton University Press 1984).
126. Broekhuijsen and Valderrama, *supra* n. 114, at 92-103. *See also* Mosquera Valderrama, *BEPS Principal Purpose Test and Customary International Law* 33(3) Leiden J. Int'l L. 745 (2020).

is not a member of the LOSC, it applies the rules of the LOSC as customary international law. Similarly, in the ITR, although the US may not sign the MC proposed under Pillar One, it may apply the rules of Pillar One as customary international law. This aspect also makes the LOSC an appropriate benchmark for the purposes of this study.

2.4.1.5 *Dispute Resolution: Emphasis on Diplomacy*

The dispute resolution systems in both the ITR and the LOSC give primacy to diplomatic means for resolving disputes, following which adjudication procedures may be applied if no amicable settlement is reached, as shown in the overall structure of the two dispute resolution systems in Figure 1. Both structures emphasise the need to maintain peaceful diplomatic relations within the regime.

Figure 1 Dispute Resolution Systems under ITR and LOSC

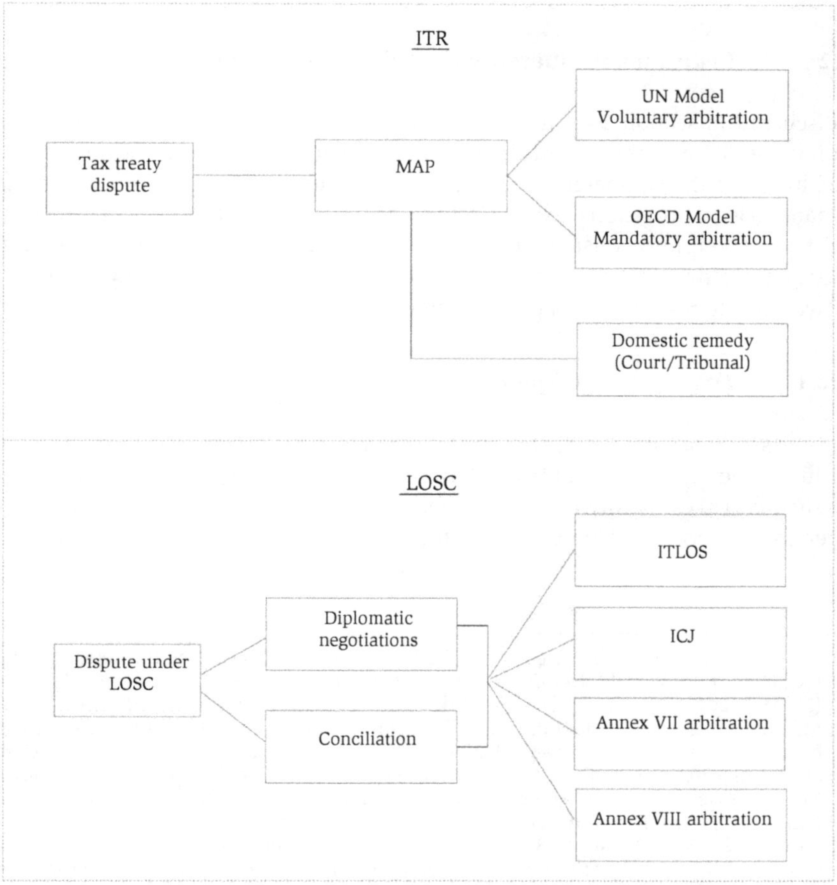

As shown in Figure 1, the LOSC's dispute resolution system includes at least four adjudicative mechanisms: the International Tribunal for the Law of the Sea (ITLOS or the Tribunal), the International Court of Justice (ICJ or the Court) and arbitral tribunals under Annexes VII and VIII of the LOSC. However, the ITR includes only two types of treaty-based arbitration mechanisms (excluding domestic remedy): voluntary arbitration under the UN Model and mandatory arbitration under the OECD Model.

Based on Green's 1998 study (discussed in section 2.3.1.2), although it was not considered relevant at the time, a more legalistic system may now be needed in the ITR to ensure compliance with the increasingly multilateral international tax standards. To this end, the LOSC's system, with its multiple adjudicative procedures, may indeed provide appropriate guidance to this effect. However, it is important to take into consideration the fact that only a few maritime disputes are started every year under the LOSC mechanisms (e.g., in 2019, only five cases were lodged under the LOSC's dispute settlement system)[127] while over 2,600 MAP cases were started in 2019.[128] This would invariably impact the design of the dispute resolution procedures in the ITR compared to the LOSC.

2.4.2 Institutional Differences to Take into Account

As discussed in section 2.4.1 above, there are several geopolitical similarities underpinning the ITR and the law of the sea regime that justify the use of the LOSC as a benchmark for the comparative purposes of this study, despite the differences in the substantive legal provisions. However, there are two main institutional differences that need to be taken into consideration when comparing the dispute resolution systems under ITR and the LOSC. These include the frequency of disputes being lodged under the two dispute resolution systems and the actors involved in the disputes.

2.4.2.1 Frequency of Disputes

As discussed in section 2.2.1, capacity constraints constitute a significant issue in the ITR due to the increasing number of MAP cases being opened every year and the fact that such cases, especially the increasingly complex transfer pricing cases, may take longer to be resolved. This creates bottlenecks within the MAP at the level of the

127. In 2019, four cases were started under the ITLOS: (1) case concerning the detention of three Ukrainian naval vessels (*Ukraine v. Russian Federation*), Provisional Measures, Case No. 26 (25 May 2019); (2) the M/T 'San Padre Pio' Case *(Switzerland v. Nigeria)*, Provisional Measures, Case No. 27 (6 Jul. 2019); (3) dispute concerning delimitation of the maritime boundary between Mauritius and Maldives in the Indian Ocean *(Mauritius/Maldives)* Case No. 28 (18 Aug. 2022); and (4) the M/T 'San Padre Pio' (No. 2) Case *(Switzerland v. Nigeria)*, Case No. 29 (29 Dec. 2021). One Annex VII case was initiated under the PCA: *Dispute Concerning the Detention of Ukrainian Naval Vessels and Servicemen (Ukraine v. the Russian Federation)*, PCA Case No. 2019-28 (2 Mar. 2023). No LOSC related cases were started under the ICJ in 2019.
128. OECD, *2019 MAP Statistics* www.oecd.org/tax/dispute/mutual-agreement-procedure-statistics-2019.htm accessed 3 Jan. 2022.

competent authorities. As shown in Table I.1 in Appendix I, in 2019, 2,600 MAP cases were opened.

In contrast, there does not seem to be a capacity issue in the LOSC's dispute resolution system based on the limited number of dispute cases being opened under the LOSC. Unlike the MAP, no information is available on the number of negotiations being started every year under the LOSC (due to the private and confidential nature of the process); however, information on the number of cases being lodged under other LOSC dispute resolution mechanisms including the ITLOS, the ICJ and even the arbitral tribunals under Annex VII is publicly available. In fact, in 2019, only four cases were lodged under the ITLOS, and one case was initiated under Annex VII arbitration, as discussed in section 2.4.1.5 above. Such differences in the frequency of disputes would inevitably need to be considered when adapting LOSC mechanisms into the ITR.

2.4.2.2 Institutional Actors

Both dispute resolution systems involve predominantly state-to-state mechanisms; however, in the ITR, a tax treaty dispute is always initiated by the taxpayer and negotiated on behalf of the taxpayer by the competent authorities through the MAP (three-way transactions). The potential resolution of the dispute through a competent authority agreement not only affects the tax revenue in the contracting states but also directly affects the tax paid by the taxpayer as reflected in its tax returns, both of which are private and confidential between the disputant parties and the taxpayer. In some cases, the competent authority agreements may also be drafted into formal government memos (e.g., the US-Mexico Mutual Agreement of 22 December 2005 on the criteria and procedures to be applied for purposes of granting treaty benefits to fiscally transparent entities).[129] The taxpayer also has the final say in whether to accept the MAP decision or not. The taxpayer is, therefore, a key actor in tax treaty dispute resolution, although the taxpayer has no decision-making powers in the MAP process. In certain circumstances, the taxpayer may, however, be able to participate in the arbitration process if no MAP agreement is reached between the two competent authorities. Accordingly, the taxpayer's rights and obligations need to be considered in the tax treaty dispute resolution process.

In contrast, interpretative disputes under the LOSC are usually initiated at the governmental level (e.g., the delimitation of maritime borders or the prompt release of vessels detained by another country). The resolution of such disputes is usually in the form of a treaty, a bilateral or multilateral agreement that is publicly known and may impact the operations of users other than the disputant parties. The resolution process is restricted to government officials of the disputant states unless the states agree to resort to third-party settlement (under conciliation or adjudication, as shown in Figure 1). It is noted, however, that in disputes relating to activities in the seabed Area (Area),[130] private contractors involved in such activities, such as mining, would be

129. MEMAP, *supra* n. 22, at 10.
130. *See* Part XI of the LOSC. The Area and its resources are the common heritage of mankind.

allowed to participate directly in the dispute resolution process through the Seabed Disputes Chamber (SDC) of the ITLOS.[131] To some degree, this process may be similar to the participation of taxpayers in the arbitration process. It may therefore be interesting to examine the rights and responsibilities allotted to such private contractors under the LOSC (discussed in section 5.3.3.1.1.1.1 below).

As discussed above, although both resolution systems constitute mainly intergovernmental transactions, the dispute resolution process is initiated and terminated by the private taxpayer, and therefore the mechanisms in the ITR need to reflect this fact. There is no similar entity under the LOSC as the diplomatic mechanism is started and terminated by the governmental parties involved.

2.4.3 Other International Dispute Settlement Systems under Consideration

This research thesis also considered other dispute resolution systems under the WTO and the bilateral investment regime as potential benchmarks for comparison, as trade and tax treaties generally share the same original intent of reducing barriers to trade. However, they were found to be less appropriate than the LOSC for the purposes of reforming the current tax treaty dispute resolution system, as explained in this section.

2.4.3.1 The WTO DSU

The WTO DSU provides two mechanisms for resolving disputes: bilateral consultations between parties to find a mutually agreed solution followed by adjudication (including the implementation of the panel and Appellate Body Reports) if necessary, which is binding upon the parties once adopted by the dispute settlement body (DSB).[132] The DSB is composed of representatives of all WTO Members who belong to either the trade or the foreign affairs ministry of the WTO Member they represent, and it oversees the entire dispute settlement process from beginning to end.[133]

Both Green's and Altman's studies that compared the international tax and trade regimes (discussed in section 2.3.1.2) concluded that the WTO's dispute resolution system was not appropriate for resolving tax treaty disputes in the ITR. According to Green, although the WTO's legalistic dispute resolution was effective for mitigating retaliatory strategies[134] and disseminating information[135] in a cooperative regime like the trade regime, it was unnecessary in the ITR based on the political and financial costs involved. He recommended instead a softer approach that involved diplomatic negotiations and interpretation of treaties, including compliance monitoring, to be led

131. Articles 187(c) and 188 LOSC.
132. *See* Understanding on the Rules and Procedures Governing the Settlement of Disputes, Annex 2 to the Marrakesh Agreement Establishing the World Trade Organization, 1869 UNTS 401, 33 ILM 1226 Arts 4, 6, 17. (1994) (DSU).
133. Article 2 DSU.
134. Green, *supra* n. 24, at 110.
135. *Ibid.*, at 127.

by the OECD.[136] Altman, however, found that the DSU, especially at the consultation stage, was used primarily by states as a political pressure-inflicting and deflecting instrument rather than for resolving disputes and, as such, did not constitute an appropriate comparator for the MAP,[137] although some elements at the WTO's adjudication stage were considered relevant for improving the resolution rates of the MAP.[138]

Although these earlier comparative studies found the DSU to have limited relevance in relation to the MAP, it was reassessed as a potential comparator for the purposes of this thesis because the institutional dynamics among the IF jurisdictions in today's post-BEPS ITR have evolved since. The unprecedented emphasis on cooperative and collaborative strategies in the ITR (through the IF, the BEPS project and the OECD's work on Pillar One and Two) may, in fact, benefit from a more legalistic system that mitigates retaliatory measures like unilateral DSTs (following Green's analysis). However, in line with Altman's arguments, the present analysis found that the political aspects associated with the DSU's adjudication mechanism impacted, at least in perception, its judicial independence.[139] The perceived lack of judicial independence is based on the fact that the DSB that administers the dispute settlement comprises delegates who receive instructions from their capitals on the positions to take and the statements to make in the DSB.[140] This is in spite of the fact that decision-making at the level of the DSB is based on consensus, and there are procedures in place to insulate the panel and the Appellate Body from government interference. For example, when government officials serve as panellists, they do so in their individual capacity, and WTO Members are directed not to give them instructions.[141]

The concept of independence is primordial in tax treaty dispute resolution in relation to the process or the outcome. The MAP system prioritises the need for competent authorities to maintain an independent character during the negotiation process to interpret the terms of the treaty in 'good faith'.[142] The recommended

136. *Ibid.*, at 139.
137. Altman, *supra* n. 71, at 178.
138. *Ibid.*, at 190.
139. The concept of judicial independence under the WTO is quite polarised with some commentators praising the high level of judicial independence set by the WTO as a 'true court of the world trade'. *See* Steve Charnovitz, *Judicial Independence in the World Trade Organization*, in *The Path of World Trade Law in the 21st Century* (Steve Charnovitz ed., World Scientific Publishing 2015); Robert Howse, *The World Trade Organization 20 Years On: Global Governance by Judiciary* 27(1) Eur. J. Int'l L. 9 (2016) DOI: 10.1093/ejil/chw011.
    Others have denounced the WTO's lack of independence at various levels. *See* Joost Pauwelyn, *The WTO 20 Years On: 'Global Governance by Judiciary' or, Rather, Member-Driven Settlement of (Some) Trade Disputes Between (Some) WTO Members?* 27(4) Eur. J. Int'l L. (2016) DOI: 10.1093/ejil/chw062; Rishi Gulati, *'Judicial Independence at International Courts and Tribunals: Lessons Drawn from the Experiences of the International Court of Justice and the Appellate Body of the World Trade Organisation* KFG Working Paper Series, No. 41 https://papers.ssrn.com/sol3/papers.cfm?abstract_id=3519891 accessed 23 Mar. 2021.
140. WTO, *A Handbook on the WTO Dispute Settlement System* 24 (2nd edn, Cambridge University Press 2017).
141. Article 8.2 DSU.
142. *See* Action 14 Peer Review Documents, *supra* n. 31, at paras 16.C4 and C5. These provisions require jurisdictions to implement measures to ensure that competent authorities conduct dispute resolution processes without interference from other tax administration personnel.

mandatory binding arbitration procedure under the OECD Model also prioritises judicial independence by requiring the competent authorities to implement the decision reached by the independent panel of arbitrators,[143] although the taxpayer has a final right to veto the decision. Accordingly, the DSU, with its politically charged adjudication mechanism and the potential independence issues that it may raise, falls short of the requirements of a benchmark for the ITR. The fact also that the WTO is undertaking a structural reform of its Appellate body system following a breakdown in consensus[144] makes it even less apt to be held as a benchmark institution. In this respect, the LOSC offers four types of adjudication mechanisms, including international courts (ICJ and ITLOS) and independent arbitral tribunals (under Annexes VII and VIII), all of which prioritise the process of judicial independence, thus making the LOSC system a more appropriate benchmark.

2.4.3.2 The Investor-State Dispute Settlement

The Investor-State Dispute Settlement (ISDS) constitutes a stand-alone dispute resolution system in the BIT regime that provides investors with the right to sue a foreign state before an independent arbitration tribunal for breaching a provision of the relevant BIT. In fact, the ISDS mechanism in BITs has also been used to resolve tax disputes under the investment treaty.[145] The BIT and DTT networks are not only among the most extensive treaty networks in existence, with roughly 2,200 BITs[146] and 3,000 DTTs[147] currently in force but also the most influential from the perspective of the protection and treatment that they provide to individuals. In both cases, the bilateral treaties between states are concluded to protect a private party (investors or taxpayers), and they also share the goal of promoting cross-border investment.[148] Hence, a taxpayer-state arbitration system, based on the investor-state practice, could potentially be a successful system for addressing tax treaty disputes. A more critical analysis of the policy rationale that underpins the BIT and DTT regimes, however, indicates that such a format would not be appropriate in the ITR.

The main policy rationale for concluding a BIT is to provide a legal framework that protects non-nationals and encourages them to invest their capital in a given

143. *See OECD Model: Sample Mutual Agreement on Arbitration, Annex to Commentary on Article 25* Art. 12 (OECD Model: Sample Arbitration Agreement).
144. Marianne Schneider-Petsinger, *Reforming the World Trade Organisation* (Chatham House, 11 Sep. 2020) www.chathamhouse.org/2020/09/reforming-world-trade-organization accessed 20 Feb. 2021.
145. Since 1999 at least 32 tax related cases have been brought to international investment arbitration. *See* Julien Chaisse, *The Treatment of (National) Taxes in Tax and Non-Tax (International) Agreements* (6th meeting of the Asia – Pacific FDI network) www.unescap.org/sites/default/files/5.%20Julien%20Chaisse_Tax.pdf accessed 21 Mar. 2021.
146. UNCTAD Investment Policy Hub https://investmentpolicy.unctad.org/international-investment-agreements accessed 4 Mar. 2022.
147. *See* Govind and Rao, *supra* n. 28, at 321.
148. Rudolf Dolzer and Christoph Schreuer, *Principles of International Investment Law* 229-233 (OUP 2012); *see also* Jerome Monsenego, *Does the Achmea Case Prevent the Resolution of Tax Treaty Disputes Through Arbitration?* 47(8) Intertax 728, 729 (2019) DOI: 10.54648/taxi2019071.

country, often a developing country or an economy in transition.[149] The focus is on strengthening the rights of foreign investors and preventing any expropriation of their investment for reasons that may be connected with policy changes in the government of the investee country.[150] From this perspective, the BIT may be considered an instrument of private international law by which states bind themselves to recognise the protection of the rights of investors. In contrast, the main objective of the DTT is to allocate taxing rights across two contracting states in order to eliminate double taxation and reduce tax avoidance and evasion. It is predominantly a state-to-state instrument for allocating taxing rights across jurisdictions with less focus on the individual rights of the taxpayers. The DTT thus constitutes an instrument of public international law for regulating conflicts between states.

This fundamental difference in rationale between the BIT and the DTT limits the relevance that the ISDS mechanism may bring to tax treaty dispute resolution. Although it could be argued that the enhanced and more transparent ISDS procedures[151] may be useful to address the transparency issues in the current MAP system as well as the limited taxpayer participation rights in the process, the inherent state-to-state nature of the MAP mitigates the relevance of such elements in the ITR. This view is emphasised through the arguments of several international tax scholars and arbitrators that the participation of taxpayers should be limited when it comes to government transactions.[152]

Another fundamental policy difference between the BIT and the DTT regimes that makes the ISDS a less appropriate benchmark for the purposes of the ITR involves the level of sovereign control that states are willing to exercise in the two regimes. Historically, the aim of the ISDS, as formulated in the BIT, was to allow investors to submit their grievances and disputes directly to an independent arbitration panel for resolution and thus avoid the involvement of the contracting governments in disputes that may damage the diplomatic relations between the two countries.[153] In contrast, in the ITR, governments, especially competent authorities, are reluctant to surrender control of the dispute resolution process and the related outcome. In fact, competent

149. Michael Lang et al., *The Impact of Bilateral Investment Treaties on Taxation* 3 (IBFD 2017).

150. *Ibid.*, at 7. *See e.g.*, the French policy throughout the 1960s that promoted BITs with unilateral effects in favour of French investors abroad and the German policy that prioritised developing countries when it concluded its first BITs, possibly due to fear that legal instability in such countries could pose immediate threats to German outbound investment. For an introductory note on the topic, *see* Stefano Castagna, *ICSID Arbitration: BITs, Buts and Taxation – An Introductory Guide* 70(7) Bull. Int'l Tax'n 370-378 (2016).

151. The arbitration procedure under ISDS is held privately, raising issues of transparency and legitimacy as in the MAP and arbitration system in the ITR. However, the ISDS implemented enhanced rules on transparency by adopting the United Nations Commission on International Trade Law (UNCITRAL) Rules on Transparency in Treaty-based Investor-State Arbitration in 2013 followed by the UN Convention on Transparency in Treaty-based Investor-State Arbitration in 2015.

152. *See e.g.*, Hugh Ault and Jacques Sasseville, *2008 OECD Model: The New Arbitration Provision* 63(5) Bull. Int'l Tax'n 210 (2009); Rosenbloom, *supra* n. 29, at 160-162; John F. Avery Jones, *Types of Arbitration Procedure* 49(8/7) Intertax (2019).

153. Spyridon E. Malamis, *The future of OECD Tax Arbitration: The Relevance of Investment Treaty and WTO Dispute Settlement Practice in Promoting a Gradual Evolution of the International Tax Dispute Resolution System* 48(11) Intertax 966, 969 (2020) DOI: 10.54648/taxi2020099.

authorities tend to use the MAP primarily as a negotiating tool not only to resolve the taxpayer's issue but also to leverage good diplomatic relations between contracting states through mutual compromise rather than through adversarial means.[154] Thus, even though the ISDS may have some useful insight in terms of enhancing transparency and taxpayer's rights, the significant differences in the underlying policy rationale between the BIT and the DTT regimes mitigate the use of the ISDS as a benchmark for tax treaty dispute resolution. The LOSC's system is more relevant in this respect as it also prioritises diplomatic relations in state-to-state dynamics, as discussed in section 2.4.1.5.

2.5 DEFINING THE RESEARCH QUESTIONS

As explained in section 2.3.2, the tax treaty dispute resolution system is in urgent need of reform to address the existing and new generation of international tax disputes more appropriately. A review of the proposals made to date shows a clear need for an updated institutional analysis of the post-BEPS ITR in order to recommend targeted policy reforms to the current tax treaty dispute resolution system. Although the OECD's proposed dispute resolution mechanism under Pillar One certainly brings some improvement in terms of implementing a mandatory and binding mechanism at a multilateral level, several potential issues were identified which may mitigate the effectiveness of the mechanism. More importantly, the Pillar One mechanisms fall short of addressing the issues identified with the current MAP and arbitration procedures, including potential capacity constraints at the MAP level, rising uncertainty among taxpayers with respect to the processes and outcomes and inequitable processes and outcomes across the IF jurisdictions for both taxpayers and competent authorities.

The aim of this study is to develop a new tax treaty dispute resolution system that takes into consideration the issues identified above to achieve an effective and predictable dispute resolution process that yields equitable solutions across the ITR. For this purpose, this thesis uses the dispute resolution system under the law of the sea regime as a benchmark to explore relevant aspects of the LOSC's system that can be adapted into the ITR. As discussed in section 2.4.1, the ITR and the law of the sea regime both reflect similar geopolitical dynamics that make such comparison relevant.

Given the different institutional contexts of the ITR and the law of the sea regime, a comparative analysis of the dispute resolution systems would need to consider the various institutional aspects that underpin both systems. Accordingly, the analysis in this research thesis is based on the following three research questions:

(1) What are the institutional arrangements that underpin the current tax treaty dispute resolution system and the LOSC's dispute resolution system?
(2) Which aspects of the LOSC's dispute resolution system may be relevant for improving tax treaty dispute resolution?

154. Stephen B. Golberg et al., *Dispute Resolution: Negotiation, Mediation and Other Processes* 64-66 (Wolters Kluwer Law & Business/Aspen Publishers 2003); *see also* Altman, *supra* n. 71, at 253-255.

(3) How can the tax treaty dispute resolution system be restructured by adapting the relevant aspects identified in the LOSC's system?

2.6 CONCLUSIONS

The current tax treaty dispute resolution system has remained largely unchanged since it was first conceived in the 1920s, despite the rapidly evolving ITR in which it operates, rendering it less and less appropriate for addressing the increasingly complex and multilateral tax disputes within the ITR. As discussed in section 2.2, the MAP and arbitration mechanisms present significant limitations, including growing capacity constraint issues, increased uncertainty and inequitable processes and outcomes across the ITR. The dispute resolution mechanism proposed under the OECD's Pillar One, set to launch in 2024 among IF members, also falls short of addressing these issues and may even further emphasise the power imbalances across the IF jurisdictions, as discussed in section 2.3.1.3.

Taking into consideration the failure of past reform proposals to tackle existing issues, this study applies an innovative approach to propose a new tax treaty dispute resolution system by using the dispute resolution system under the LOSC as a benchmark. The analysis will compare the institutional arrangements that underpin international dispute resolution in the ITR and the law of the sea regime to identify relevant aspects of the LOSC's system that can be adapted into the ITR. As discussed in section 2.4, the LOSC's system constitutes an appropriate benchmark based on the common geopolitical logic that underpins both regimes.

In order to develop a new tax treaty dispute resolution system, this book is divided into three parts, each part addressing a specific research question. The first question maps out the institutional arrangements underpinning the dispute resolution systems in the ITR and the LOSC within their respective institutional context; the second question compares the institutional arrangements and patterns of interaction across the two systems to identify relevant aspects of the LOSC's system for improving tax treaty dispute resolution in the ITR; and the final third question proposes a potential restructuring of the tax treaty dispute resolution system by adapting the relevant aspects identified in the LOSC's system.

CHAPTER 3
Methodology

Chapter 3 sets out the research design that underpins this comparative study through a three-step analytical approach, each step addressing a separate research question. Step A maps out the institutional arrangements that underpin the dispute resolution systems in the ITR and the LOSC. Step B integrates the analysis of the institutional arrangements mapped out in Step A and compares the patterns of interaction and outcomes generated within both systems to identify relevant aspects of the LOSC's system that can be adapted into the ITR. Step B also compares the inclusivity (participation) levels across both systems to enhance consensus-building within the ITR. The final Step C proposes a restructured tax treaty dispute resolution system based on the relevant aspects identified in the LOSC's system. Chapter 3 also elaborates on the 'politicised' Institutional and Development (pIAD) Framework that constitutes the central analytical tool used in Steps A and B. The pIAD Framework applies a comparative institutional analysis (CIA) approach to ensure an accurate comparison of the two systems, despite the differences in the institutional context of the two regimes.

3.1 INTRODUCTION

This study compares the dispute resolution systems under the ITR and the LOSC in search of normative lessons that can be applied in the ITR to develop a more appropriate tax treaty dispute resolution system that is fit for the 21st century. Given the institutional differences between the ITR and the law of the sea regime, the methodology employed in this research thesis aims to clearly identify and establish the institutional context within which the comparative analysis will take place. It applies an analytical tool developed by Elinor Ostrom and refined subsequently by Floriane Clement, the pIAD framework,[155]

155. Clement, *supra* n. 16.

separately to the dispute settlement systems under the ITR and the LOSC to map out and analyse the relevant institutional arrangements that underpin both dispute resolution systems.

Section 3.2 provides an overview of the pIAD framework that constitutes the central analytical element of the research method for analysing the relevant institutional arrangements underpinning the dispute resolution system under the ITR and the LOSC. It also includes a schematic diagram of the pIAD framework showing its main components (Figure 2). Section 3.3 then sets out the detailed analytical steps to be followed for applying the pIAD framework in the context of this research design, which constitutes a three-step analytical approach (Steps A, B and C). Section 3.4 explains why the pIAD analysis is the method of choice for this research, and any limitations associated with the methodology are explored in section 3.5 before concluding in section 3.6.

3.2 OVERVIEW OF THE pIAD FRAMEWORK

The pIAD framework provides a systematic method for breaking up often complex policy activities into identifiable and more manageable components, as shown in Figure 2. As the name suggests, the pIAD framework is based on the original Institutional Analysis and Development (IAD) framework developed by Elinor Ostrom in the 1980s for studying the highly contested notion of 'institutions'[156] from a public choice perspective.[157] Clement's pIAD framework builds on the original IAD version by locating the analysis within a power-centric context.[158] This is particularly relevant in this research thesis as the dispute resolution systems in the ITR and the LOSC are both subject to power dynamics under international law (discussed further in section 3.4), and the pIAD framework will ensure an accurate analysis of the two systems by taking into consideration the power structures in which they operate. Other than that, the analysis is based on Ostrom's IAD framework. Figure 2 shows the main components of the pIAD framework. A more detailed explanation of the various components follows.

---

156. Elinor Ostrom adopted slightly different definitions of the term 'institutions' depending on the time of writing and the intended function of the term within a specific analysis. Since the analysis in this research thesis covers two different institutional contexts, this thesis will adopt a broad definition of institutions as 'shared concepts used by humans in repetitive situations organised by rules, norms, and strategies'. *See* Ostrom, *supra* n. 15, at 37. *See also* Daniel H. Cole, *The Varieties of Comparative Institutional Analysis,* Articles by Maurer Faculty (2012) www.repository.law.indiana.edu/facpub/834 accessed 19 Dec. 2018 DOI: 10.2139/ssrn.2162 691. Cole explores the multiple (functional) definitions of institutions used across multi-disciplinary literature i.e., economics, political science, law and sociology.
157. Elinor Ostrom, *An Agenda for the Study of Institutions* 48(1) Pub. Choice 3 (1986) DOI: 10.1007/bf00239556. The foundations of the public choice perspective were developed by James Buchannan who posits that government actions are the result of individuals making decisions in their roles as elected officials, appointed officials, or bureaucrats who are implicitly self-interested and motivated through an economic system of incentives and constraints.
158. *See* Clement, *supra* n. 16. The original IAD framework included the analysis of three contextual variables: working rules, community attributes and physical conditions. The pIAD framework includes two additional variables: the politico-economic context and discourses that influence the policy activity under study, as shown in Figure 2. Other than that, for the purposes of this thesis, the mechanics of the pIAD framework and the IAD framework are functionally similar and use the same core terminology.

Figure 2 Overall Structure of the pIAD Framework (Adapted from Revised IAD Framework, Clement 2010)

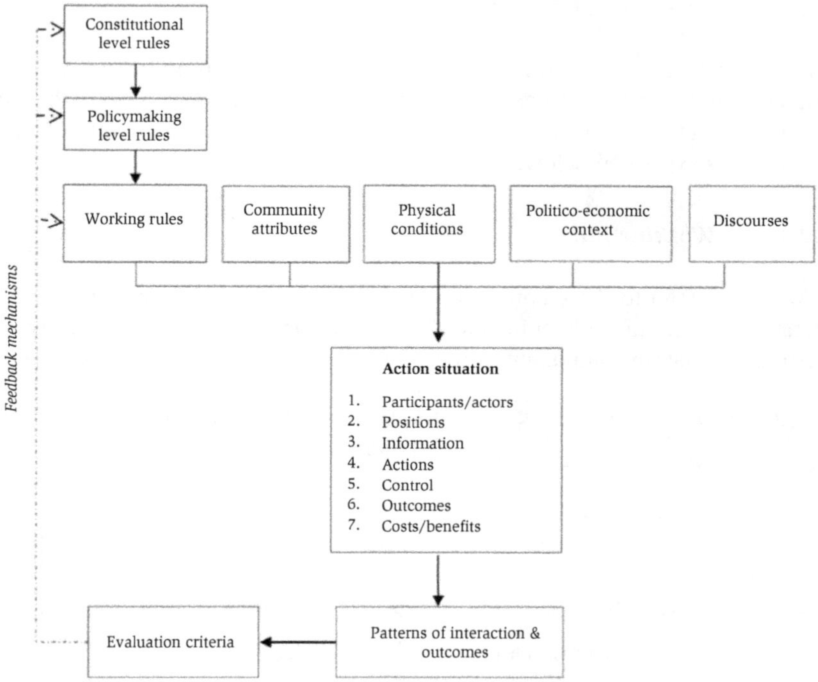

3.2.1 The Action Situation

The focal point of the pIAD framework is the action situation. It represents the specific policy activity under study, and it comprises the conceptual space where relevant actors/participants engage with each other in decision-making processes. In fact, most policy situations are composed of multiple distinct but overlapping action situations that are linked sequentially or simultaneously across several levels of procedural rules (e.g., the tax treaty dispute resolution system comprises three separately linked action situations: MAP and arbitration mechanisms under the UN and the OECD Models). Depending on the policy question, several action situations may need to be analysed, and it is, therefore, important to narrow the policy question as much as possible.

As shown in Figure 2, the action situation itself can be broken down further into seven components for analysis: (1) the set of actors in (2) positions (playing specific roles) who must decide among diverse actions based on the (3) information that they possess about (4) how actions are linked to potential outcomes, (5) the control they have over their action in this situation, (6) the potential outcomes that are linked to an individual sequence of actions and (7) the costs and benefits assigned to actions and outcomes that serve as incentives or deterrents. Each of these seven components of an identified action situation is governed by a specific working rule as defined in section 3.2.2.1 below.

3.2.2 Five Sets of Contextual Variables

As shown in Figure 2, the seven components that make up an action situation are influenced by five sets of contextual variables.[159] These variables include the working rules, community attributes, physical conditions, the politico-economic context and discourses, as explained below.

3.2.2.1 Working Rules

Working rules refer to shared prescriptions (must, must not or may) that are mutually understood and predictably enforced.[160] There are seven types of working rules, each governing a separate component of the action situation, as shown in Figure 3.

Figure 3 Relationship Between Working Rules and Components of the Action Situation

	Working rules		Action situation
1.	Boundary rules	→	Participants/actors
2.	Position rules	→	Positions
3.	Information rules	→	Information
4.	Authority rules	→	Actions
5.	Aggregation rules	→	Control
6.	Scope rules	→	Outcomes
7.	Payoff rules	→	Costs/benefits

159. Ostrom's IAD framework uses the term 'exogenous variables' to refer to the physical conditions, community attributes and working rules. Arguably, these variables are endogenised to the framework as the patterns of interaction and related outcomes can and do affect the variables through feedback mechanisms. Therefore, the term 'contextual variables' will be used to refer to the five sets of variables in the pIAD framework.

160. Ostrom, *supra* n. 15, at 36. 'Working rules' are also referred to as 'rules-in-use' in Ostrom's IAD framework. For simplification, the term 'working rules' only will be used in this thesis.

(1) Boundary rules specify the entry and exit criteria for participants in an action situation. For example, to be an eligible MAP applicant, a taxpayer needs to be a resident of either one of the contracting jurisdictions under the applicable bilateral tax treaty.
(2) Position rules specify the set of positions or roles that participants assume in an action situation, each of which has a unique combination of resources, opportunities, preferences and responsibilities. For example, in MAP, there are two main positions that participants may assume: MAP applicant and MAP administrator. Taxpayers may assume the position of a MAP applicant to request MAP assistance, and competent authorities assume the role of MAP administrator to resolve the MAP case initiated by the MAP applicant.
(3) Information rules affect the type and amount of information made available to participants in an action situation. For example, in MAP, information rules specify the conditions under which MAP decisions or other guidance materials are made public.
(4) Authority rules specify a range of permitted actions that participants in particular positions in an action situation may, must or must not take. For example, when a competent authority receives a MAP request from a taxpayer, it may, as the MAP administrator, either accept or reject the MAP request.
(5) Aggregation rules affect the level of control that a participant in a position exercises in choosing a specific course of action among the range of permitted actions. To illustrate with the same MAP example as above, the action of the competent authority to accept or reject the MAP request submitted by the taxpayer is controlled through the applicable time limits for submission of MAP requests or the scope of the tax issues that qualify for MAP under the treaty.
(6) Scope rules delimit the effect of potential outcomes within the action situation and specify whether these outcomes are final or not. With respect to the analysis of international dispute resolution systems, the scope rules specify the jurisdiction of the decisions issued and the finality of such decisions. For instance, under the OECD Model, arbitration decisions in the ITR are final and legally binding on the competent authorities if certain conditions are met.
(7) Payoff rules determine how costs and benefits are distributed in the action situation, thus establishing the incentives or deterrents for action among the various participants. For example, the arbitration mechanism in the ITR is less attractive for competent authorities compared to taxpayers. This is because the financial costs for setting up the arbitration panel are borne entirely by the competent authorities, while decision-making power is also shifted away from them to an independent panel of arbitrators. Whereas for the taxpayer, arbitration guarantees a decision for resolving the taxpayer's issue, subject to the taxpayer's acceptance.

These seven types of working rules that govern day-to-day activities are nested within multi-layered rules structures, including policymaking level rules and constitutional level rules, as shown in Figure 2. These will be further elaborated in section 3.2.5 when discussing the multiple levels of institutionalisation on which the pIAD framework is based.

3.2.2.2 Community Attributes

Community attributes constitute the second set of contextual variables influencing decision-making in the action situation. They refer to the generally accepted norms about policy activities, the degree of common understanding potential participants share about activities in the policy area, and the extent to which potential participants' values, beliefs, and preferences about policy-oriented strategies and outcomes are homogeneous.[161] For example, in the ITR, there is a distinct difference between developed and developing countries in relation to the implementation of mandatory arbitration based on the lack of technical expertise and resources that most developing countries suffer from compared to their more developed counterparts.

3.2.2.3 Physical Conditions

Physical conditions include the physical and human capabilities that support the production and provision of goods and services within an action situation. These conditions include production inputs like capital, labour and technology, as well as sources of finance, storage, and distribution channels.[162] They may restrict or direct the possibilities for action of participants in specific ways (strategies) and thus have significant implications for policy design, politics, and collective action, which are all critical aspects of the policymaking process. In the pIAD (and IAD) frameworks, the analysis of such physical conditions is based on the economic nature of goods and services using standard economic theory.[163]

The economic nature of a good or service can be determined by two attributes: (1) the extent to which access to consumption can be controlled (excludability) and (2) the extent to which one person's consumption reduces the supply available to others (subtractibility). High subtractibility implies individual consumption; low subtractibility implies that more than one person may consume the good or service at the same time. High excludability implies that consumers will have difficulty consuming the good or service without contributing to its cost; low excludability implies that consumers may be able to 'free-ride', consuming the good or service without contributing to the cost of provision or production.[164] This classification scheme is summarised in Table 1, which shows four broad categories of goods and services: private,

161. *Ibid.*, at 43.
162. *Ibid.*, at 40-42. The IAD framework differentiates between production and provision: production refers to those activities that involve transforming inputs into outputs and provision refers to activities associated with financing and distribution activities.
163. *Ibid.*, at 40-41.
164. Mancur Olson, *The Logic of Collective Action: Public Goods and the Theory of Groups* (Harvard University Press 1965).

toll, CPR, and public. As explained in section 2.4.1.2, the global tax base and the oceans both constitute CPRs.

Table 1 Determining the Economic Nature of Good or Service

	High excludability	*Low excludability*
High subtractibility	**Private good** (e.g., clothes, electronics)	**Common pool resource (CPR)** (e.g., fisheries, forests)
Low subtractibility	**Toll good** (e.g., telephone, private club)	**Public good** (e.g., air, knowledge)

The matrix in Table 1 also shows that except for private goods, most goods have benefits that are not purely private or public and exist as impure public goods.[165] In fact, it has been argued that the public or private characteristics of any good are typically constructed through legal and political processes rather than arising from inherent properties of the underlying problem.[166] Therefore, analysing the economic nature of the different aspects of a policy activity may reveal important information on which resources, capabilities and coordination mechanisms may be required to implement a policy and address relevant collective action issues. The analysis of the public-private good characteristics for the purposes of this thesis is discussed further in section 3.3.1.3 below.

3.2.2.4 Politico-economic Context

The analysis of the politico-economic context (and discourses) proposed under the pIAD framework is meant to bring the analyst to explicitly consider power and values within the action arena. More specifically, it should explain how power has been distributed among the actors who make decisions and how political and economic interests have driven actors' decisions within a particular set of working rules.[167] Given the complex geopolitical implications that underpin the ITR and the law of the sea regime, it is particularly important to analyse and compare the power dynamics across the two regimes to ensure an accurate comparison of the international dispute resolution mechanisms from a political perspective. For example, in relation to MAP, the politico-economic context may refer to the impact that developing/emerging

165. Inge Kaul, Isabelle Grunberg and Marc A. Stern, *Defining Global Public Goods*, in *Global Public Goods: International Cooperation in the 21st Century* 4 (Inge Kaul, Isabelle Grunberg and Marc A. Stern eds, Oxford University Press 1999).
166. *See* Inge Kaul and Ronald U. Mendoza, *Advancing the Concept of Public Goods*, in *Providing Global Public Goods: Managing Globalization* 78, 86-87 (Inge Kaul ed., Oxford University Press 2003); Samuel Cogolati, Linda Hamid and Nils Vanstappen, *Global Public Goods and Democracy in International Legal Scholarship* 5(1) Cambridge J. Int'l & Compar. L. 4, 13-14 (2016) DOI: 10.4337/cilj.2016.01.02; Daniel Augenstein, *To Whom It May Concern: International Human Rights Law and Global Public Goods* 23(1) Ind. J. Glob. Legal Stud. 225, 229-232 (2016) DOI: 10.2979/indjglolegstu.23.1.225.
167. Clement, *supra* n. 16, at 140.

countries may have on the development of the MAP process compared to the developed countries.

3.2.2.5 Discourses

Discourses constitute the fifth and final contextual variable in the pIAD framework. Discourses confer power to institutions by reinforcing or undermining their credibility and are themselves dependent on the politico-economic context in which they are embedded.[168] Just as the analysis of the politico-economic context, discourse analysis is also intended to highlight certain aspects of the underlying power dynamics within a specific policy activity by asking not whether a representation is true or false but what the political implications of adopting a particular representation are. This will ensure that the policy recommendations being proposed in this thesis are viable from an international political perspective.

It is important to note that there are multiple variations in defining the concept of discourses and discourse analysis depending on the epistemological framework of a project, and summarising these is beyond the scope of this book.[169] However, for the purposes of analysing the circulation of power that influences the development of international dispute resolution mechanisms in the ITR and the LOSC, this study will adopt a historical discourse analysis approach developed by Asgeir Johannesson.[170] Historical discourse analysis is based on the work of Michel Foucault and Pierre Bourdieu and constitutes a process-oriented approach that takes into consideration the notion of social strategies and includes the analysis of social practices and institutional structures.[171] For example, in the ITR, discourse analysis may be applied to study how the geographical composition of the treaty negotiating groups has influenced the design of the MAP system. A step-by-step description of this approach is provided in section 3.3.1.5 below.

3.2.3 Patterns of Interaction and Related Outcomes

Once the constraints of contextual variables are taken into consideration, patterns of interaction flow logically from the behaviour of actors in the action situation, as shown in Figure 2. Patterns of interaction refer to the structural characteristics of an action situation and the conduct of actors in the resulting structure based on the influence of

168. *Ibid.*
169. Discourse analysis has been taken up in a variety of disciplines in the humanities and social sciences, including linguistics, education, sociology, anthropology, social work, cognitive psychology, social psychology, area studies, cultural studies, international relations, human geography, environmental science, communication studies, biblical studies, public relations and translation studies, each of which is subject to its own assumptions, dimensions of analysis and methodologies.
170. Asgeir Johannesson, *The Politics of Historical Discourse Analysis: A Qualitative Research Method?* 31(2) Discourse: Studies in the Cultural Politics of Education 251 (2010) DOI: 10.1080/01596301003679768.
171. *Ibid.*, at 253-254.

contextual variables.[172] In tightly constrained policy action situations where participants have a limited (or regulated) range of strategies in an action situation, a policy analyst can make strong inferences and specific predictions about likely patterns of behaviour and the resulting outcomes. Conversely, in such situations, the analyst may also work backwards through the framework to identify the sources of risks and specific problem areas within the institutional arrangements that give rise to certain outcomes. For example, in the ITR, since the MAP is the only mechanism for resolving tax treaty disputes at the international level, if the number of MAP users increases and there is no other alternative mechanism to relieve the pressure off competent authorities, it would be expected to find an increase in the number of unresolved tax disputes, as evidenced through the MAP statistics since 2016.

3.2.4 Evaluation Criteria

The final key component of the pIAD framework involves an evaluation criterion being applied to the patterns of interaction and the outcomes to assess the performance of the policy activity under study. The evaluation criteria may consist of any objective standard or principle as required to make appropriate policy recommendations.[173]

For the purposes of this comparative analysis of the dispute resolution systems under the ITR and the LOSC, this study will use 'inclusivity' as an evaluation criterion. The assessment of inclusivity will be based on the participation of relevant actors and the rules that govern the decision-making processes. As Bird argues, the process for reaching an agreement in the ITR is as relevant as the agreement in itself because if some of the contracting parties do not accept that the process was sufficiently fair and inclusive, then it may be difficult for them to be bound by the outcome.[174] Accordingly, inclusivity plays a critical role in the implementation of potential policy reforms across the ITR.

Interestingly, the LOSC constitutes an ideal benchmark for examining inclusivity as it is not only one of the most widely ratified treaties globally, but it is also known for applying a wide range of consensus-building techniques to achieve universal consensus among almost 160 parties present at the UNCLOS III.[175] In this study, inclusivity will be assessed at the policymaking and constitutional levels of decision-making (discussed in section 3.2.5 below).

---

172. Margaret M. Polski and Elinor Ostrom, *An Institutional Framework for Policy Analysis and Design* in *Elinor Ostrom and the Bloomington School of Political Economy*: *Volume 3, A Framework for Policy Analysis* 31 (Daniel H. Cole and Michael D. McGinnis eds, Rowman and Littlefield Publishers Inc. 2010).
173. Ostrom, *supra* n. 15, at 34. The evaluation criteria may involve baselines set through the relevant programs or policies or they may include more common political-economic standards, such as economic efficiency, fiscal equivalence, re-distributional equity, accountability and adaptability.
174. Richard M. Bird, *Reforming International Taxation: Is the Process the Real Product?* Int'l Ctr. Pub. Pol'y Working Paper Series paper 1503 (2016) DOI: 10.7866/hpe-rpe.16.2.5.
175. *See* Koh, *supra* n. 18.

3.2.5 The Multi-level Rules Structure

According to Ostrom's logic of institutions, social choice processes operate at three levels of institutionalisation: operational level, policymaking level and constitutional level.[176] Accordingly, we must distinguish between three levels of rules that cumulatively affect the actions taken and outcomes generated in any policy situation. The linkage among the different levels of rules within the pIAD framework is illustrated in Figure 2, and they are defined as follows:

(1) Operational level rules directly govern the day-to-day activities among the participants in any policy setting (e.g., rules specifying how and where to file a MAP request).
(2) Policymaking rules determine the design of the operational level rules (e.g., rules of treaty negotiation that determine the MAP process).
(3) Constitutional level rules determine the participants and the rules governing decisions at the policymaking level (e.g., rules governing the treaty negotiation process).

Such multi-level rules analysis is especially relevant in this study for examining international dispute resolution mechanisms that are developed across multiple governance levels and across different countries. For example, in tax treaty dispute resolution, a taxpayer may usually submit a request for MAP assistance within a period of three years of being notified of the tax issue by the tax authority – this represents an operational level rule. This operational level rule specifying the timeframe for submission of MAP requests is based on the MAP treaty provision that was negotiated by treaty negotiators into the bilateral tax treaty. This is the policymaking level, and an example of a policymaking level rule could be a rule specifying the level of expertise of a potential treaty negotiator. The rules governing the negotiation processes at the policymaking level are, in turn, dictated by the international treaty-making rules that are usually specified in the VCLT.[177] The rules of the VCLT identify who can take part in the decision-making processes at the policymaking level and thus represent constitutional level rules. In relation to the ITR, the rules that govern the multilateral processes for developing the OECD and the UN Models represent the constitutional level rules.

3.3 THE RESEARCH DESIGN: A THREE-STEP ANALYTICAL APPROACH

The present research design applies a three-step approach (Steps A, B and C) to address each of the three research questions posed. This section sets out these three steps and

176. Ostrom, *supra* n. 12. Ostrom's IAD framework and Clement's pIAD framework both use the term 'collective-choice level' but this thesis uses the term 'policymaking level' instead as it is more specific for the purposes of this book.
177. *See supra* n. 43.

explains how the pIAD framework is applied in the context of this study for mapping out the institutional arrangements that underpin dispute resolution across the ITR and the LOSC (Step A) and comparing the resulting patterns of interaction and inclusivity levels (Step B). Based on this comparative analysis, a potential restructuring of the tax treaty dispute resolution system is offered (Step C).

3.3.1 Step A: Mapping out Institutional Arrangements

Step A addresses the first research question and applies the pIAD framework to the ITR and the LOSC to map out the institutional arrangements (i.e., rules, norms and strategies) that underpin each dispute resolution system within their respective institutional context. The pIAD framework breaks up the dispute resolution activities into smaller components, including relevant action situations and five sets of contextual variables that influence behaviour within and across the identified action situations. This step is applied separately to the ITR and the LOSC for comparative purposes. As shown in Figure 4, the pIAD analysis in Step A includes two parts.

Figure 4 Applying Step A of pIAD Analysis in Two Parts

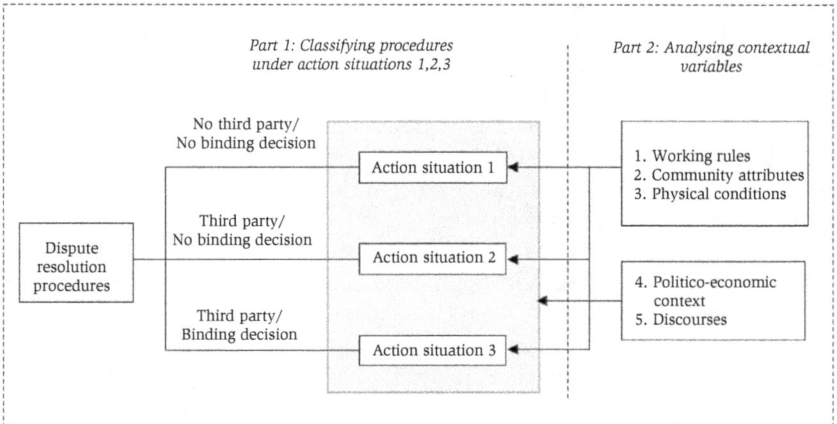

Part 1 of the analysis classifies the dispute resolution procedures into one of three separately linked action situations based on the extent to which third parties can legitimately participate in determining the settlement and, conversely, the extent to which the parties can reject a settlement proposed by the third party (i.e., whether the decision is legally binding). For example, the current tax treaty dispute resolution system comprises the MAP and a supplementary arbitration mechanism under the OECD or the UN Models.[178] The MAP involves negotiation between the competent

178. Article 25(5) OECD Model; Art. 25(5) Alternative B UN Model.

authorities of the disputing states with no third party. Arbitration involves an arbitration panel as an independent third party that may issue a legally binding decision on the MAP case under the OECD Model and a non-binding decision under the UN Model, resulting in three separately linked action situations for analysis in the ITR. Such classification of dispute resolution mechanisms across three separately linked action situations allows for a common basis of comparison across the two regimes.

Part 2 of Step A then analyses the five sets of contextual variables (working rules, community attributes, physical conditions, politico-economic context and discourses) that influence decision-making within and across the identified action situations. As shown in Figure 4, the analysis of the (1) working rules, (2) community attributes, and (3) physical conditions will be conducted for each of the three separately linked action situations identified. The analysis of the (4) politico-economic context and (5) discourse will apply to the dispute resolution system as a whole (not at the level of each separately linked action situation) to examine the more pervasive power dynamics that may impact decision-making in the system.

3.3.1.1 Working Rules

To examine relevant working rules governing dispute resolution in the ITR, information was collected from the BEPS Action 14 Peer Review Documents that sets out mandatory rules that IF jurisdictions must apply in relation to the MAP.[179] The BEPS Action 14 report also includes best practices for improving the effectiveness of the MAP. Additionally, relevant information on the MAP rules was also collected from the Commentaries of Article 25 of the 2017 OECD and UN Models that implements the BEPS Action 14 minimum standard. In order to supplement any missing information, the recommendations made in the 2007 OECD Manual on Effective Mutual Agreement Procedures (MEMAP) were also consulted, where applicable.[180] Information regarding the arbitration mechanisms was obtained from the 2017 OECD and UN Models and related Commentaries on Article 25 and, more specifically, from the 'Sample Mutual Agreement' proposed in the OECD and UN Model that countries may use as a guide to implement arbitration within their jurisdictions.

To examine the working rules under the dispute settlement system under the LOSC, relevant information on the working rules was obtained from the Convention, more specifically in Part XV on the dispute settlement procedures and the related Annexes,[181] as well as relevant UN Handbooks.[182] The analysis of the formal rules in

179. *See* Action 14 Peer Review Documents, *supra* n. 31.
180. *See* MEMAP, *supra* n. 22.
181. *See* Arts 279-299 LOSC in Part XV and Annexes V-VIII, dealing respectively with conciliation, ITLOS, arbitration and special arbitration.
182. *See e.g.*, United Nations, *Handbook on the Delimitation of Maritime Boundaries* (Division for Ocean Affairs and the Law of the sea Office for Legal Affairs, United Nations 2000) (UN Handbook on delimitation on maritime boundaries).

the Convention was also supplemented with the practical application of the procedures as obtained from key case studies within the law of the sea, where applicable.[183]

3.3.1.2 Community Attributes

Based on the definition of community attributes in section 3.2.2.2, the analysis of the community attributes in the context of this comparative thesis focuses on the objectives and interests of the relevant actors in relation to the dispute resolution mechanisms in both the ITR and the LOSC. The aim is to identify potential trends that may affect the distribution of participants across jurisdictions.

3.3.1.3 Physical Conditions

As explained in section 3.2.2.3, the analysis of physical conditions is rooted in the economic nature of goods and services. For the purposes of this study, the analysis focuses more specifically on the economic rationale of global public goods in international law,[184] which examines the public-private good characteristics associated with the specific functions linked with the various dispute resolution mechanisms under the ITR and the LOSC. These characteristics affect the distribution of costs and benefits across the system. For example, since the benefits of a public good are usually available to all users, they should all contribute to its cost.

The aim is to compare the degree to which the various mechanisms contribute to global public goods (e.g., as an intermediate or ultimate public good).[185] Both international tribunals as institutions and the specific outputs they produce, such as judgments or decisions, most likely constitute intermediate public goods. This is because they are not created for their own sake but, rather, as part of attempts to provide ultimate public goods such as the protection of the marine environment or a trustworthy international tax system.[186] For example, in the case of the LOSC, if we accept the protection of whales as a global public good, then Australia's winning claim before the ICJ against Japan's continued pursuit of a large-scale program of whaling in the Antarctic may help to produce that good and may therefore constitute an intermediate public good.[187] Such analysis may be useful for examining how the dispute resolution mechanisms under the ITR and the LOSC address collective action issues

183. For list of ICJ Reports and ITLOS cases, *see infra* n. 527. For list of LOSC Annex VII cases administered under the Permanent Court of Arbitration (PCA), *see infra* n. 529.
184. *See* Fabrizio Cafaggi, *Global Public Goods Amidst a Plurality of Legal Orders: A Symposium* 23 Eur. J. Int'l L. 643 (2012) DOI: 10.1093/ejil/chs049; Ernst-Ulrich Petersmann, *Mini-Symposium on Multilevel Governance of Interdependent Public Goods* 15 J. Int'l Econ. L. 709 (2012); Nico Krisch, *The Decay of Consent: International Law in an Age of Global Public Goods* 108 Am. J. Int'l L. 1 (2014) DOI: 10.5305/amerjintelaw.108.1.0001; Joshua Paine, *International Adjudication as a Global Public Good?* 29(4) Eur. J. Int'l L. 1223 (2019).
185. Andre Nollkaemper, *International Adjudication of Global Public Goods: The Intersection of Substance and Procedure* 23 Eur. J. Int'l L. 769,783 (2012) DOI: 10.1093/ejil/chs041.
186. *Ibid.*, at 783.
187. *See* Whaling in the Antarctic *(Australia v. Japan: New Zealand intervening)* Judgment (31 Mar. 2014), I.C.J Rep. 2014, 226.

that affect the wider field of international tax governance and oceans governance,[188] respectively.

3.3.1.4 Politico-economic Context

As discussed in section 2.4.1, the ITR and the LOSC both share common geopolitical elements that give rise to evolving power dynamics among countries, influencing not only the development of general international law but also the dispute resolution systems under the two regimes. In this context, it is clear that China's economic superpowers have caused a gradual shift in the political economy's centre of gravity from the US to China. This is evidenced by the fact for the first time since the 19th century, emerging and developing countries have contributed over 50% of the global gross domestic product,[189] and China's economy even surpassed that of the US in 2014.[190] If soft power mirrors but lags behind economic power, this may signal a gradual corresponding shift in political influence towards the east, which could alter the power dynamics between developed, developing and emerging countries in distinct ways.

The impact of China is notable also in its swift transformation on the international legal platforms from a rule-taker to rule-maker status, as seen through the increasingly assertive influences of China on the development of the OECD and UN Models (e.g., the incorporation of China's transfer pricing concept of location-specific advantages (LSA) in the 2017 OECD Model, despite heavy criticism by the US, as discussed in section 4.3.4.3). Within the law of the sea regime, the political and economic dominance of China in maritime affairs, especially in the South China Sea (SCS) relations, is also undeniable (discussed in section 5.3.4). Given the increasingly dominant role of China within the ITR and the law of the sea regime, the analysis of the politico-economic context in this study will compare the role of China within the power shifts under the two regimes. The aim is to compare the potential cooperation dynamics among developed, developing and emerging countries in relation to international dispute resolution in the two regimes.

188. Oceans governance is a term that is increasingly used in academic literature, involving multiple dimensions. For the purposes of this analysis, 'oceans governance' will be described as a chosen course of collective action that follows a given set of goals and identifies tools and mechanisms to steer it towards those goals. This definition is taken from Anshuman Chakraborty, *Dispute Settlement under the United Nations Convention on the Law of* the *Sea and Its Role in Oceans Governance* (LLM thesis, Victoria University of Wellington 2006) DOI: 10.26686/wgtn.16945630.v1. *See also* James N. Rosenau, *Governance in the Twenty-First Century* 1 Global Governance 13, 14 (1995).

189. Eduardo Baistrocchi, The *International Tax Regime and Global Power Shifts* 20(2) Va. Tax Rev. 219 (2021).

190. *Ibid.* In 2014, the IMF estimates the size of the US economy was USD 17.4 trillion and the size of China's economy was USD 17.6 trillion.

3.3.1.5 *Discourses*

The discourse analysis in this study will examine the development of the dispute resolution provisions under the ITR and the LOSC in an attempt to understand the motivations underpinning the two systems. This analysis may be useful for assessing the applicability of certain aspects of the LOSC's system in the ITR in light of any contextual differences.

As mentioned in section 3.2.2.5, a historical discourse analysis approach will be applied, which involves the study of discourses within a historical context, i.e., over a certain time period. To this end, this study applies a four-step approach:

(1) The first step identifies the relevant discursive event/situation to be studied. For example, to analyse the underlying motivations in the ITR, the first step would specify the relevant negotiations/conferences to be studied (e.g., the conferences held by the League of Nations and the OECD).
(2) The second step selects the texts and material that would throw light on the issue or event that is being studied. In the ITR, for example, these would include the negotiation texts that deal with dispute resolution provisions (e.g., the MAP provisions of the OECD or the UN Models).
(3) Since the analysis is based on historical conjunctures, the third step chooses specific events or points in time for studying the evolution of the identified texts. Specific points in time at which the MAP provisions are studied may include its original formulation in 1927 by the League of Nations, the 1963 draft OECD Model provision, the 2008 Model provision and the 2015 post-BEPS format.
(4) The final step four analyses the content of the selected texts at different points in time to identify potential patterns and tensions in the discourse. The use of guiding questions will be relevant in this step, such as: What are the treaty provisions regarding dispute resolution? What is the geographical composition of the decision-making group and their views? How are the views of the decision-makers reflected in the treaty?

The aim is to capture 'the interplay between the historical and political conditions and the arguments for ideas and practices'[191] that could explain the motivations in the two regimes with respect to dispute resolution.

3.3.2 Step B: Comparing Patterns of Interaction and Inclusivity Levels

As shown in Figure 2, the institutional arrangements mapped out in the action situation lead to patterns of interaction and outcomes. While Step A of the pIAD analysis analyses the contextual variables to map out the institutional arrangements that underpin dispute resolution in the ITR and the LOSC, Step B integrates the analysis of

191. Johannesson, *supra* n. 170, at 253.

the institutional arrangements in each system and compares the resulting patterns of interaction. More specifically, Step B analyses the patterns of interaction relating to the issues in the current tax treaty dispute resolution system, as identified in section 2.2. These issues include capacity issues, failure to provide certainty and inequitable dispute resolution processes and outcomes across the ITR. A similar analysis will then be applied to the LOSC, held as a benchmark, to compare aspects of the LOSC's dispute resolution system that could be relevant for addressing the identified issues in the ITR.

Step B also assesses the inclusivity (participation) levels at the policymaking and constitutional levels of decision-making in both dispute resolution systems (as explained in section 3.2.4) by analysing the actors and the rules that govern the decision-making processes at the policymaking and constitutional levels. The aim is to identify consensus-building techniques used in the universally accepted LOSC that may be adapted at the policymaking and constitutional levels of tax treaty dispute resolution to facilitate the implementation of policy reforms across the IF through consensus. Step B thus addresses the second research question of identifying aspects of the LOSC's system that may be relevant for improving tax treaty dispute resolution.

3.3.3 Step C: Restructuring the Tax Treaty Dispute Resolution System

The final Step C of the research methodology addresses the final research question of this study and proposes a restructuring of the tax treaty dispute resolution system based on the comparative analysis in Step B. The aim is to develop a comprehensive legal framework that may achieve an effective, predictable and equitable resolution of multilateral tax disputes in the ITR in the 21st century. The reform proposal also includes recommendations to facilitate the implementation of the newly proposed mechanisms across the IF through consensus.

3.4 WHY IS THE pIAD ANALYSIS RELEVANT TO THIS RESEARCH?

This section explains the underlying motivations for using the pIAD framework as the method of choice for the comparative purposes of this research thesis.

3.4.1 Applying a Comparative Institutional Approach

First and foremost, the pIAD framework constitutes an ideal tool for applying a comparative institutional analysis (CIA) method in the context of this research instead of relying on a single institutional analysis. Single institutional analysis tends to focus on one chosen characteristic, giving rise to potential cycling problems, i.e., situations where the solution to a perceived institutional problem turns into a problem and the new solution involves reverting back to the original situation.[192] An example of an

192. Cole, *supra* n. 156, at 104.

institutional cycling problem is where market failures lead to government solutions, which in turn lead to government failures that again raise calls for market solutions.

In contrast, the CIA method examines institutional data through the lens of all four dominant categories of institutionalism: rational choice, historical, normative/sociological and constructivist to produce a complete analysis of the institutional context.[193] Rational choice focuses on the actor's preferences within a structure of incentives; historical institutionalism explains evolution from the perspective of structural choices made at the inception of the institution; normative institutionalism understands political behaviour through values that individuals acquire from membership in the institution, while the constructivist approach grapples with the strategic complexities of institutional change.[194] It is thus expected that by adopting a CIA approach, this thesis will conduct a complete analysis of the institutional arrangements that underpin the regimes under study to avoid the pitfalls of single institutional analysis.

3.4.2 Breaking up Complex Policy Situations into Components

There are many methods advocated under the CIA approach that take into consideration various aspects of the particular institution under study.[195] However, the mechanics of the pIAD framework are found to provide the most relevant analysis in the context of this research as it provides a common framework for comparing the dispute resolution system under the ITR and the LOSC despite their different institutional contexts. As shown in Figure 2, the pIAD framework breaks up a complex policy situation into smaller and more manageable components (e.g., action situation, contextual variables, patterns of interaction, outcomes) to allow for a systematic study of the various institutional factors that impact decision-making within the system.

By mapping out the information into specific components, it becomes possible to compare the institutional elements that underpin the dispute resolution mechanisms across the ITR and the LOSC from the perspective of a common baseline for a more accurate comparison. For example, operational rules are categorised into seven types

193. *See* Colin Hay, *Constructivist Institutionalism* (Oxford University Press 2008).
194. *Ibid.*
195. *See e.g.*, Oliver E. Williamson, *The Economic Institutions of Capitalism: Firms, Markets, Relational Contracting* (The Free Press 1985) for CIA approach based on transaction costs across alternative governance structures; Douglass C. North, *Institutions, Institutional Change and Economic Performance* (Cambridge University Press 1991) for a more macroeconomic application of CIA to explain institutional change in state-economy interactions; Masahiko Aoki, *Towards a Comparative Institutional Analysis: Motivations and Some Tentative Theorization* 47(1) Japanese Econ. Rev. (1996) DOI: 10.1111/j.1468-5876.1996.tb00031.x for a game theoretic model of CIA based on a multiple equilibrium of the economic organisation; Neil K. Komesar, *Imperfect Alternatives: Choosing Institutions in Law Economics, and Public Policy* (University *of* Chicago Press 1994) on the participation-centred approach that links the competence of an institution to the participation of the institutional actors within it; Ostrom, *supra* n. 176 on the development of the IAD Framework used extensively in common-pool resources governance.

of working rules that produce specific components in any action situation (*see* Figure 3). Thus, in spite of any substantive differences, an analyst may compare the rules across the two systems by asking what rules produced each of the seven components in the identified action situations. In regard to the positions available, for instance, the analyst would be led to ask: which positions exist? What are the responsibilities and roles associated with each position? In regard to the actions that can be taken, the analyst would ask: why these actions rather than others? Are sets of actions time or path-dependent? Similar questions can be asked about each component of the action situation, and answers to these sets of questions can then be formalised as a set of relations that, combined with the other four sets of contextual variables, produce particular patterns of interactions and outcomes that can be compared in a more accurate manner.

In addition, the pIAD analysis also explicitly locates the analysis of institutional arrangements within a power-centric context by considering the politico-economic context and the prevailing discourse. Although power distribution is an important consideration in the design of any social institution, it is especially relevant in the development of international law mechanisms that operate within the context of international cooperation, such as the ITR and the LOSC.[196]

3.4.3 Analysing Multi-level Governance Structures

The pIAD framework also includes a multi-level decision structure whereby working rules are nested within policymaking level rules, which are in turn nested within overarching constitutional level rules (as shown in Figure 2). Such multi-level design prompts the analysis of the relationships among the different levels of decision-making and a deeper contextualisation of the applicable rules within the system. This is particularly important when analysing whether any dispute resolution mechanisms under the LOSC can be transposed into the ITR and under which circumstances that would be possible while taking into consideration the overarching governance structure. For example, in the ITR, MAP rules are based on the MAP provision in the treaty that was decided bilaterally between two governments. In contrast, the rules of the mechanisms within the LOSC were decided on a multilateral basis, requiring consensus among all 157 UN member countries present at UNCLOS III. There are vastly different considerations to take into account when the number and type of decision-makers differ, and comparing the development of the operational rules through the various governance levels (policymaking and constitutional levels) helps to bring these considerations to light.

196. *See* Sol Picciotto, *International Law: The Legitimation of Power in World Affairs*, in *The Critical Lawyer's Handbook 2* (P Ireland and Per Laleng eds, Pluto Press 1997); Nico Krisch, *International Law in Times of Hegemony: Unequal Power and the Shaping of the International Legal Order* 16(3) Eur. J. Int'l L. (2005) DOI: 10.1093/ejil/chi123 on the role of power in international law; *see also* Baistrocchi, *supra* n. 189 that explores the effect of hegemons on international tax regulations.

3.5 SCOPE AND LIMITATIONS OF THE RESEARCH METHOD

This research study aims to address the shortcomings identified within the current tax treaty dispute resolution system, including MAP and arbitration. The analysis focuses on the post-BEPS MAP and arbitration rules adopted among the IF countries, excluding the dispute resolution mechanisms under the EU framework and the domestic legal framework. This section highlights the reasons for such scope restrictions. The potential limitations of the pIAD analysis are also highlighted.

3.5.1 Excluding Analysis of EU Mechanisms

In 2017, the European Council adopted the EU Arbitration Directive (2017/1852) (EU Directive) to strengthen further the dispute resolution mechanisms in the EU Arbitration Convention (90/463) and in the bilateral tax treaties between Member States.[197] Although the EU Directive constitutes a well-established multilateral arbitration mechanism,[198] the processes under the EU Directive will be excluded from the scope of this analysis mainly because of the restricted group of actors affected by the EU Directive. The BEPS IF and the LOSC are both consensus-based institutions that have similar global memberships consisting of developed, developing and emerging countries around the world with often conflicting interests and objectives. In contrast, the decision-making processes under the EU Directive only affect 27 EU Member States, all of which share similar policy objectives within the EU. This renders the examination of the EU Directive arrangements less relevant, given the aim of designing an international tax dispute resolution system that can be used throughout the ITR by taking into consideration existing global geopolitical conflicts.

3.5.2 Excluding Analysis of Domestic Legal Dispute Resolution Mechanisms

This study also excludes any analysis related to the resolution of cross-border tax disputes within domestic legal structures (e.g., national court systems or other administrative arbitration courts). It is an important consideration because there are close interactions between these two systems that would invariably impact the potential sharing of resources among the various processes at the tax administration level, hence influencing the cost-benefit analyses of the MAP and arbitration procedures. For example, although the MAP process is conducted independently at the competent authority level, the implementation of the MAP decision may be constrained by the domestic legal and administrative context in terms of implementation timelines

197. *See Preamble, Council Directive (EU) on Tax Dispute Resolution Mechanisms in the European Union* 2017/1852 (10 Oct. 2017).

198. *See* European Commission, *Resolution of Double Taxation Disputes in the European Union* (Taxation and Customs Union) (19 Oct. 2016) https://ec.europa.eu/taxation_customs/business/company-tax/resolution-double-taxation-disputes_en_en accessed 20 Nov. 2021.

and any decision issued by the domestic court (if a case had been lodged at the court as well).

Historically, however, few taxpayers encountering cross-border tax disputes (transfer pricing being the main area of controversy in international tax) have elected to litigate their controversies in domestic courts, with a disproportionate number of such cases occurring in Canada, Germany and India.[199] According to one tax expert, this may be explained by the fact that litigation in court is generally too costly and time-consuming, sometimes taking up to 15 years (including a five-year audit, three years in appeals, and then another five years in court and two more on appeal).[200] Even in 2017, litigation through domestic court remained an unpopular, last-option resort, as about one in six companies (17%) reported having resorted to courts to resolve severe controversies, out of which 57% expressed dissatisfaction with the extended length of the process and variability of the outcomes.[201]

Thus, while there may be domestic policy concerns and national legislation that affect the resolution of international tax disputes within the MAP process, the study of domestic dispute resolution structures is not considered relevant for the purposes of this study. This is due to the reluctance of taxpayers to engage in litigation at the domestic level and also the potentially inherent competitive relations that may result from transfer pricing litigation (e.g., taxpayers may have an incentive not to cooperate by hiding information that is not in their interests).[202] In addition, each government has its own policy and political concerns to look after and may have concerns over setting a precedent that overrides neutral consideration of the facts of any individual case. It is only by contracting out of the national court that both parties can truly be heard before a neutral tribunal.[203] Therefore, this research will focus instead on studying the potential institutional challenges that need to be overcome to develop a more multilateral and comprehensive framework to resolve cross-border tax disputes.

3.6 CONCLUSIONS

The research methodology comprises a three-step analytical approach, and each step addresses a specific research question. Clement's pIAD framework constitutes the central element of the research methodology, and it is applied in Steps A and B,

199. Eduardo Baistrocchi and Martin Hearson, *Tax Treaty Disputes: A Global Quantitative Analysis*, in *A Global Analysis of Tax Treaty Disputes* 1518 (Eduardo Baistrocchi ed., Cambridge University Press 2017). *See also* Markham, *Litigation, Arbitration and Mediation in International Tax Disputes*, *supra* n. 1, at 283. According to a 2007-2008 Global Transfer pricing survey by Ernst & Young involving 850 multinational taxpayers across 24 countries, between 2003 and 2007 only 28 litigation cases were reported among these taxpayers and less than half (43%) of the taxpayers were satisfied with the process.
200. *See* Klotsche, *supra* n. 1.
201. Ernst and Young, *2016-2017 Transfer Pricing Survey Series: Controversy, Avoidance and Resolution* 11 (2017).
202. Eduardo Baistrocchi, *The Transfer Pricing Problem: A Global Proposal for Simplification* 59(4) The Tax Lawyer 941, 959 (2006).
203. Maya Ganguly, *Tribunal and Taxation: An Investigation of Arbitration in Recent US Tax Conventions* 29 Wis. Int'l L. J. 735, 746 (2012).

respectively. The pIAD analysis constitutes an ideal method for comparing the dispute resolution systems under the ITR and the LOSC because it breaks up the complex policy information into components and also analyses decision-making processes through multiple levels of governance (operational, policymaking and constitutional levels). The pIAD framework thus allows for a more complete and accurate comparative analysis across the different regimes.

Step A of the methodology addresses the first research question that involves mapping out the institutional arrangements (i.e., rules, norms and strategies) that underpin the dispute resolution systems in the ITR and the LOSC. This step is done in two parts. Part one identifies the relevant action situations by grouping the dispute resolution procedures in each regime based on the twin criteria of whether a third party is involved and whether the decision is legally binding on the disputant parties. Part two maps out the components of the relevant action situations by analysing the five sets of contextual variables that influence processes in the identified action situations. Step A is applied separately to the ITR and the LOSC, and the results will be mapped out in Chapters 4 and 5, respectively.

Step B addresses the second research question by integrating the analysis of institutional arrangements mapped out in Step A and then comparing the resulting patterns of interaction and outcomes generated across the dispute resolution systems in the LOSC and ITR. It also assesses the inclusivity (participation) levels among actors at the policymaking and constitutional levels of decision-making in both dispute resolution systems. The aim is to determine aspects of the LOSC's dispute resolution system that could be relevant for addressing the identified operational issues within tax treaty dispute resolution and also improve consensus-building across the ITR at the policymaking and constitutional levels. Step B analysis will be included in Chapter 6.

The final Step C addresses the final question and proposes a restructuring of the tax treaty dispute resolution system based on the pIAD analysis in Steps A and B. Based on the relevant aspects identified in the LOSC's system, held as benchmark, a targeted policy reform is offered that addresses the operational level issues identified and also facilitates the implementation of the new proposed system across the IF at the policymaking and constitutional levels. The proposed restructuring of the tax treaty dispute resolution system in Step C will be included in Chapter 7.

CHAPTER 4

Mapping out Institutional Arrangements in the ITR

Chapter 4 applies Step A of the research methodology to the ITR to map out the institutional arrangements (i.e., the rules, norms and strategies) that underpin each of the three mechanisms that make up the tax treaty dispute resolution system, including the MAP and arbitration under the UN and OECD Models along with the relevant political-economic context and discourse that influence the power dynamics across the system as a whole. The mapping process reveals growing capacity issues across the MAP, tax uncertainty through lack of predictability and excessive control by competent authorities, especially under the UN Model and inequitable solutions resulting from the uneven application of rules across developed and developing countries. With respect to the political-economic context, China's emerging economic superpower is gradually increasing its influence on international tax regulations. The discourse analysis shows that the MAP system developed in the early 20th century was focused mostly on facilitating a swift dispute resolution process for the benefit of a few developed countries that constituted the main cross-border trading partners at the time.

4.1 INTRODUCTION

As explained through the methodology in Chapter 3, this research thesis is based on a three-step analytical approach (Steps A, B and C). This chapter addresses Step A of the methodology to map out the institutional arrangements that underpin dispute resolution in the ITR by analysing the five contextual variables that influence decision-making across the current tax treaty dispute resolution system. This first step of the pIAD analysis is crucial not only to understand how the system works in detail but also to provide a common framework to ensure an accurate comparison with the LOSC's system that will be analysed in the following chapter.

As explained in section 3.3.1, this analysis will be done in two parts. Part 1 breaks up the dispute resolution system into three separately linked action situations based on the extent to which third parties can legitimately participate in determining the settlement of the dispute and, conversely, the extent to which the parties can reject a settlement proposed by the third party (i.e., whether the decision is legally binding). The analysis is set out in section 4.2, and the action situations identified in the ITR are illustrated in Figure 5. Part 2 of Step A is set out in section 4.3, and it analyses the five sets of contextual variables (working rules, community attributes, physical conditions, politico-economic context and discourses) that influence processes within and across each of the identified action situations.

4.2 IDENTIFYING ACTION SITUATIONS

The MAP involves a negotiation between the competent authorities of the disputant countries, resulting in a non-legally binding MAP decision. Depending on the applicable bilateral treaty between the contracting parties, if no MAP agreement is reached within a reasonable time limit, the MAP case may be submitted to a mandatory and binding arbitration procedure (under the OECD Model),[204] or it may also be submitted to voluntary arbitration involving a non-legally binding decision (under UN Model).[205] Therefore, the MAP and the arbitration mechanisms under the UN and OECD Models will each represent a separately linked action situation in relation to the tax treaty dispute resolution system in the ITR. The MAP will constitute action situation 1, and the arbitration mechanisms under the UN and OECD Models will constitute action situations 2 and 3, respectively, as shown in Figure 5.

In the second part of Step A, the analysis of the working rules, community attributes and physical conditions is conducted for each action situation, whereas the impact of the politico-economic context and discourse are analysed on the dispute resolution system as a whole and not on the individual action situations as explained in section 3.3.1. Figure 5 shows the pIAD analysis applied in Steps A and B of the methodology.

204. Article 25(5) OECD Model.
205. Article 25(5) Alternative B UN Model.

Figure 5 pIAD Analysis of Tax Treaty Dispute Resolution System

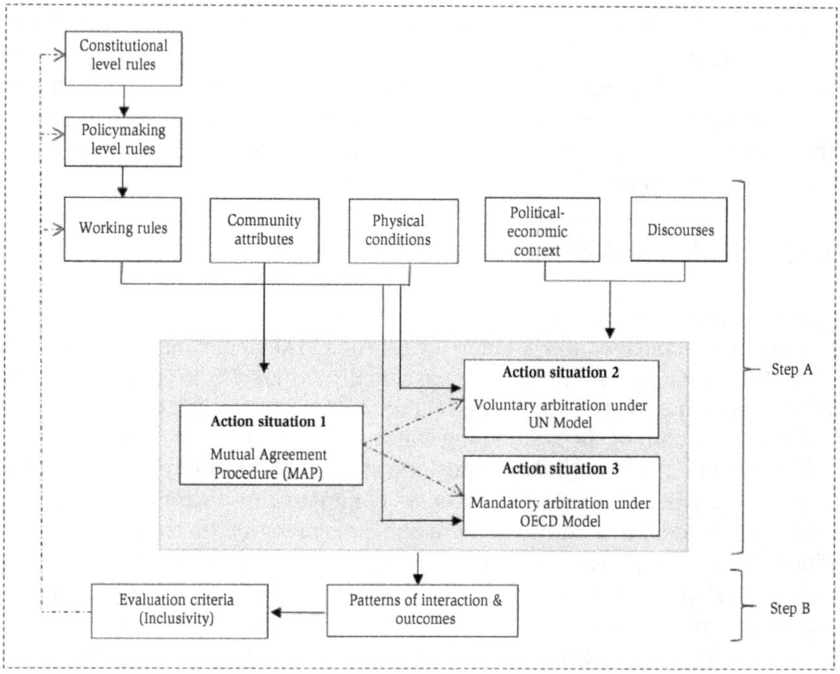

4.3 ANALYSING CONTEXTUAL VARIABLES

This section constitutes Part 2 of Step A, and it analyses the five sets of contextual variables that influence the processes in and across action situations 1, 2 and 3 identified in section 4.2.

4.3.1 Action Situation 1: MAP

4.3.1.1 Working Rules

4.3.1.1.1 Boundary Rules

The boundary rules specify the criteria of the actors participating in the MAP. There are two actors involved in the MAP: taxpayers and competent authorities. Taxpayers eligible to make a MAP request include individuals, companies or other bodies of persons that are a resident of either one of the contracting states.[206]

206. Article 3(1)(a) OECD Model.

Competent authorities administer the MAP on behalf of the taxpayer. The competent authority for each country is typically defined as the representative (position, person, or body) to whom issues can be addressed within the contracting state that is one of the two parties to a tax agreement.[207] It is recognised in the OECD and UN Models that the execution of the DDTs does not exclusively fall within the remit of the tax authorities, and therefore, each contracting state is allowed, under the Model treaty, to designate one or more authorities as competent. A typical designation would be 'the Minister of Finance or his authorised representative' or 'the Secretary of the Treasury or his delegate'.[208]

4.3.1.1.2 Position Rules

The position rules specify the roles and responsibilities of the various actors. With respect to MAP, a taxpayer may assume the role of a MAP applicant to initiate the MAP process. The MAP applicant need not have actually suffered from the tax that is not in accordance with the treaty – they may set the MAP in motion if it is probable that the actions of one or both of the contracting states will result in such taxation.[209]

Competent authorities hold the position of MAP administrators and negotiate in good faith[210] on behalf of the taxpayer to eliminate the taxation suffered by the taxpayer that is not in accordance with the provisions of the treaty (e.g., double taxation).[211] The competent authority function may be split between an area responsible for resolving taxpayer-specific cases (i.e., taxpayer requests about taxation that are not in accordance with the DTT) and a policy area for issues involving general interpretation as well as general issues concerning the application of the tax treaty where specific taxpayers are not involved.[212] The competent authority constitutes a separate function from the general tax audit functions of the tax authority in order to maintain the independence of the MAP process.[213]

4.3.1.1.3 Information Rules

Information rules govern the distribution of information at various stages of the MAP process. All information obtained or generated during a MAP process is fully protected by the confidentiality provisions of the applicable tax treaty, specifically the Exchange of Information article (Article 26 of the OECD and UN Models). MAP procedures

207. Article 3(1)(a) OECD Model; Art. 3(1) UN Model.
208. The OECD publishes country profiles that indicate who the competent authority is for a certain country, *see* OECD, *MAP Profiles* www.oecd.org/tax/dispute/country-map-profiles.htm accessed 12 Mar. 2022.
209. Article 25(1) OECD Model; Art. 25(1) UN Model.
210. This means that competent authorities are obliged to seek to resolve the case in a fair and objective manner, on its merits, and in accordance with the terms of treaty and applicable principles of international law on the interpretation of treaties as embodied in Articles 31 and 32 of the VCLT.
211. Paragraph 5.1 OECD Model, Commentary to Article 25.
212. MEMAP, *supra* n. 22, at 40-42.
213. *Ibid.*, at 41.

and decisions are therefore kept private and confidential between the concerned competent authorities. In addition, a competent authority should recognise that the disclosure of sensitive or confidential information, such as a trade secret, could harm a taxpayer's competitive position and should ensure that all measures are taken to protect such information.[214]

Although such practice may be necessary to protect the confidentiality of high-level government transactions, the lack of scrutiny associated with such transactions exacerbates the risks of perceived collusion between the competent authorities, and it may also threaten taxpayer's trust in the MAP. Given that the taxpayer is a stakeholder in the MAP, to address this transparency issue, it is recommended that the competent authority debrief the taxpayer after each substantial MAP discussion.[215] In addition, the BEPS Action 14 also recommends, as best practice, that jurisdictions publish agreements reached by competent authorities on difficulties or doubts arising as to the interpretation or application of their tax treaties in appropriate cases.[216]

4.3.1.1.4 Authority Rules

The authority rules specify the range of possible actions of the taxpayer and the competent authority (what they must, must not and may do) in their respective roles as MAP applicant and MAP administrator at particular points in the MAP process. The taxpayer, as a MAP applicant, may start the MAP process by making a request for MAP assistance with the relevant competent authorities.[217] The MAP applicant also has the responsibility of approving the MAP decision reached by the competent authorities at the end of the MAP process before it can be implemented.[218] In certain circumstances, the taxpayer may also be invited to submit additional information during the MAP process.

Other than that, the taxpayer does not participate in the actual MAP process.[219] It is noted that the taxpayer may choose to withdraw from MAP at any point in the process or refuse to provide the requested information to the competent authorities, in which case the MAP case would be closed.[220] This constitutes a risk of wasted resources for both the taxpayer and the competent authority. Alternatively, if no MAP agreement is reached, the taxpayer may also trigger the arbitration process under the OECD Model, if applicable, to prompt the competent authorities to issue a decision on the MAP case. This arbitration mechanism under the OECD Model is discussed in section 4.3.3.

The competent authority as the MAP administrator is responsible for conducting the MAP process from beginning to end. It either accepts or rejects the MAP request

214. *Ibid.*, at 16.
215. *Ibid.*, at 30.
216. Action 14 Peer Review Documents, *supra* n. 31, at para. 12.BP2.
217. Article 25(1) OECD Model; Art. 25(1) UN Model.
218. MEMAP, *supra* n. 22, at 46. The MEMAP recommends a timeline of one month for the taxpayer to respond to the competent authorities.
219. *Ibid.*, at 24.
220. *Ibid.*, at 31.

received from the taxpayer,[221] following which it may attempt to resolve the issue unilaterally.[222] If the competent authority is not able to arrive at a satisfactory solution on its own, the competent authority then engages with the other competent authority to endeavour to resolve the matter by mutual agreement.[223] The competent authorities will then communicate any agreement reached to the taxpayer and implement the decision through relevant adjustments in the taxpayer's returns if the taxpayer agrees to the decision. If no agreement is reached within a specified timeframe (two years under the OECD Model or three years under the UN Model), the competent authorities should still communicate the outcome to the MAP applicant for the latter to take appropriate measures (e.g., request arbitration if applicable or apply for domestic remedies).[224]

It is quite clear from the above that the decision-making powers of the taxpayer are quite restricted in the MAP process, which calls into question the balance of rights and responsibilities in the current tax treaty dispute resolution system.[225] More importantly, the fact that competent authorities are not obliged to resolve a MAP case but only need to endeavour to resolve the case in good faith exacerbates uncertainty on the part of the taxpayer regarding the effective resolution of the tax dispute.

4.3.1.1.5 Aggregation Rules

4.3.1.1.5.1 Applicable Law

Aggregation rules determine the level of control that participants in various positions may exercise in choosing a particular course of action depending on the applicable law and the administrative framework. In MAP, the applicable law includes treaty laws and principles that the two jurisdictions have in common, including the DTT between the two contracting states; any commentary, technical explanations, and specific country guidance related to that treaty; and finally, published guidance by the OECD.[226] Since the tax treaty is finalised on a bilateral basis, each treaty may include differences in the provisions, resulting in the rules being applied differently across the DTT network. For example, contracting states may decide not to include Article 9(2) of the OECD or UN Model in the treaty that provides for corresponding adjustments of income among associated enterprises,[227] in which case the relevant competent authorities may disallow the resolution of transfer pricing cases under MAP.

The OECD and UN Models also include different provisions under Article 25, which may result in a differential application of the MAP rules across jurisdictions. For

221. *Ibid.*, at 46. The MEMAP recommends a timeline of one month from the date that the opening letter was received for the other competent authority to confirm acceptance or rejection of MAP request.
222. Article 25(2) OECD Model; Art. 25(2) UN Model.
223. Article 25(2) OECD Model; Art. 25(2) UN Model.
224. MEMAP, *supra* n. 22, at 29-30.
225. Ramazan Bicer, *The Effectiveness of Mutual Agreement Procedures as a Means for Settling International Transfer Pricing Disputes*, 21 Int'l Transfer Pricing J. 76, 83 (2014).
226. MEMAP, *supra* n. 22, at 25-27.
227. *See supra* n. 58 for a definition of Art. 9(2) of the OECD or UN Model.

example, under the OECD Model, the taxpayer may submit a MAP request to the competent authority of either contracting state, even if it is not resident in that state;[228] the taxpayer may even present its case to the competent authority of both contracting parties at the same time.[229] Under the UN Model, however, the taxpayer is required to present its case to the competent authority of the state of which it is a resident.[230] Such differing treatment between the OECD and the UN Models may discourage taxpayers from developing countries that follow the UN Model provisions from requesting MAP, especially if they are from countries that do not have the necessary expertise or capacity to administer MAPs efficiently.

Although the MAP process is separate from the domestic legal framework, domestic laws may also impact the conduct of MAP by imposing certain constraints on the order in which a taxpayer may lodge a case with MAP and with the domestic court. As a general matter, most tax administrations will deal with a taxpayer's case in the MAP or in a domestic forum (usually a court), but not both at the same time; one process will be suspended or put on hold pending the outcome of the other.[231] In countries where the decision rendered by the domestic court will bind the tax administration and prevent it from providing greater relief through the MAP, the competent authority of that country may have to negotiate with the other contracting state to provide additional relief through MAP.[232] Such misalignment between domestic laws and treaty rules may give rise to unfair negotiation practices among competent authorities through power imbalances and deal-making.

There may also be situations where jurisdictions may decide not to implement a MAP agreement if the domestic statute of limitations is exceeded,[233] despite recommendations in the BEPS Action 14 to implement MAP decisions irrespective of the domestic timelines.[234] To protect the taxpayer in such situations, taxpayers are advised to protect their domestic rights by filing waivers of domestic time limits on assessments (if possible), a protective claim, or lodging an appeal, if applicable.[235]

4.3.1.1.5.2 Administrative Framework

The administrative rules may also influence the actions of taxpayers and competent authorities in the MAP process. The OECD or UN Model does not set forth rules or other guidelines for the form in which a taxpayer must present a request for MAP assistance,

228. Action 14 Peer Review Documents, *supra* n. 31, at para. 14.B2. Where the treaty does not permit a MAP request to be made to either Contracting Party (as prescribed in the UN Model) and the competent authority who received the MAP request from the taxpayer does not consider the taxpayer's objection to be justified, the competent authority should implement a bilateral consultation or notification process which allows the other competent authority to provide its views on the case.
229. Paragraph 75 OECD Model: Commentary on Article 25.
230. Article 25(1) UN Model.
231. MEMAP, *supra* n. 22, at 33.
232. *Ibid.*
233. OECD Transfer Pricing Guidelines 2022, *supra* n. 54, at paras 4.45-4.49.
234. Action 14 Peer Review Documents, *supra* n. 31, at paras 17.D2 and D3.
235. MEMAP, *supra* n. 22, at 34.

and taxpayers usually would refer to the specific rules set out by the competent authorities.[236] The structure of a competent authority is also determined administratively at the competent authority level[237] and with certain specific guidelines being specified through BEPS Action 14. For example, BEPS Action 14 prescribes specific rules to ensure that the competent authority is sufficiently resourced for officials to conduct their work independently of the approval or the direction of the tax administration personnel who made the adjustments at issue.[238] From this perspective, the effectiveness of the MAP process may be directly affected by the administrative functions of the competent authority if, for example, the officers do not have the required expertise or if they are overburdened by the number of MAP cases being received.

In fact, although the mandatory rules under BEPS Action 14 have streamlined the MAP process, based on the higher number of MAP cases being opened and closed annually (*see* Table I.1 in Appendix I), the BEPS rules were less effective in ensuring a timely resolution of MAP cases. As shown in Table I.2 in Appendix I, for example, the time period for resolving transfer pricing cases in the years 2016-2020 consistently exceeded the prescribed time limit of 24 months, averaging 30-35 months instead.

4.3.1.1.6 Scope Rules

4.3.1.1.6.1 Jurisdiction of MAP

Scope rules determine the jurisdiction and finality of the potential MAP outcomes. The MAP covers double taxation issues that are not in accordance with the treaty;[239] it also addresses doubts or difficulties arising from the interpretation or application of the treaty (e.g., *see* Article 4(3) of the OECD/UN Model regarding the dual residence of corporations) and double taxation in cases not provided for under the treaty.[240] Disputes relating to other taxes that are not generally covered under the treaty (as listed under Article 2 of the OECD and UN Models) may be excluded from the MAP, such as DSTs that are designed to operate outside the scope of tax treaties.[241] In practice, despite the BEPS Action 14 recommendations, transfer pricing cases may also be excluded from MAP in certain jurisdictions depending on the domestic legislation, as discussed in section 2.2.3.2. At this point, it is also unclear how disputes under Pillar Two (i.e., disputes relating to the implementation of a 15% minimum corporate tax regime) will be addressed through MAP, if at all. Thus, not all types of cross-border tax disputes may be eligible under the MAP, forcing taxpayers to resort to domestic remedies instead.

236. *Ibid.*, at 14-15. *See also* Action 14 Peer Review Documents, *supra* n. 31, at para. 15.B8.
237. *Ibid.*, at 39-41.
238. Action 14 Peer Review Documents, *supra* n. 31, at paras 16.C3 and C4.
239. Article 25(1) OECD Model; Art. 25(1) UN Model.
240. Article 25(3) OECD Model; Art. 25(3) UN Model.
241. *See supra* n. 61.

4.3.1.1.6.2 Finality of Outcomes

In relation to the finality of MAP outcomes, competent authority agreements or resolutions are often case and time-specific.[242] Therefore, they are not considered precedents for either the taxpayer or the tax administrations in regard to adjustments or issues relating to subsequent years or for competent authority discussions on the same issues for other taxpayers. The MAP agreement may also be rejected by the taxpayer, in which case the taxpayer may pursue other domestic redress mechanisms (appeal or court).

4.3.1.1.7 Payoff Rules

Payoff rules govern how costs and benefits are meted out in the action situation. There are no additional fees charged by the competent authorities for administering the MAP on behalf of taxpayers.[243] It is a structured and fairly rapid process (usually under the recommended 24-month period) which provides a resolution in at least 70% of the MAP cases filed (*see* Table I.3 in Appendix I). The MAP is also presumably a cheaper alternative than going to court, all of which make the MAP an attractive dispute resolution mechanism for the taxpayer.

However, although there are no additional administrative costs for requesting MAP, the taxpayer may incur legal costs when preparing a submission, especially in cases where the taxpayer is represented in the MAP by legal counsel and substantial factual information must be collected and disclosed during the process (e.g., in transfer pricing cases). Moreover, by sharing substantial amounts of financial information with the competent authorities in both contracting states, the taxpayer may face higher risks of being subjected to tax audits in the future as there is no guarantee that the information will not be used against the taxpayer if the negotiations fail.[244] The MAP may also present other costs for the taxpayer in terms of limited participation in the process, fragmented coverage of tax issues and uncertain resolution of the tax disputes (as discussed in this section 4.3.1.1).

As discussed in section 4.3.1.1.4, the competent authorities control the MAP process from beginning to end, with limited scrutiny of taxpayers or other government bodies. The negotiations through MAP do not usually require any extra costs other than the administrative costs of the exchanges between the two contracting states. While BEPS Action 14 may have imposed additional rules on competent authorities (e.g., additional MAP guidance to be issued and possibly additional staff to be recruited and trained to ensure timely resolutions) in addition to the annual IF membership fees,[245] there are no financial sanctions (fines/penalties) for non-compliance with any of the

242. MEMAP, *supra* n. 22, at 14.
243. *Ibid.*, at 15. There may be fees associated with Advance Pricing Arrangement programmes or for the rare occurrences of using independent experts or mediators, but this discussion is not within scope of this study.
244. *See* CRA MAP Report 2018, *supra* n. 49.
245. *See* OECD/G20 BEPS IF (5th meeting of the Inclusive Framework in Lima, Peru on 27-28 Jun. 2020) www.oecd.org/tax/beps/flyer-inclusive-framework-on-beps.pdf accessed 2 Oct. 2020.

Action 14 minimum standards. The competent authorities may, however, incur reputational costs if they do not comply with the recommendations made in the peer review conducted by the OECD Forum on Tax Administration MAP Forum (FTA MAP Forum).[246] Thus, while the MAP may be beneficial to taxpayers for resolving disputes, it holds even more benefits for the competent authorities as MAP administrators. This could explain why the MAP has remained largely unchanged since it was first designed in the 1920s in spite of the issues identified (as discussed in section 2.2).

4.3.1.2 Community Attributes

4.3.1.2.1 Aligned Objectives for a Simple MAP with Clear Guidelines

The analysis of the community attributes aims to identify potential trends relating to MAP based on the objectives and interests among the relevant actors, i.e., taxpayers and competent authorities. Taxpayers and competent authorities both support a MAP process that provides clear guidelines to taxpayers and tax administrators as to the interpretation and application of tax treaties to prevent future disputes within the ITR.[247] Both actors also support a quick and simple MAP procedure having limited time-value-of-money (lost interest) and risk consequences as that would entail minimal compliance costs to taxpayers[248] and minimal administrative costs to tax administrators without the need for treaty renegotiation.[249] These common objectives are reflected in the best principles with respect to MAP as recommended in the BEPS Action 14 report.[250]

4.3.1.2.2 Misaligned/Conflicted Interests

4.3.1.2.2.1 Transparency Within MAP

While competent authorities and taxpayers do share certain common objectives, they also reflect conflicting interests at various levels. Competent authorities arguably prefer

To become a member of the IF, a country or jurisdiction needs to commit to the BEPS package and pay an annual membership fee of EUR 20,800 (subject to annual adjustment for inflation).

246. The FTA members include commissioners and tax administration officials from 53 OECD and non-OECD countries including all G20 members. *See* OECD, Forum on Tax Administration www.oecd.org/tax/forum-on-tax-administration/about/ accessed 1 Nov. 2020. *See also* OECD (Assessment schedule for Stage 1 peer review and stage 2 peer monitoring) www.oecd.org/tax/beps/beps-action-14-peer-review-assessment-schedule.pdf accessed 1 Oct. 2020. In stage 1, jurisdictions' implementation of the Action 14 Minimum Standard is evaluated, and recommendations are made where jurisdictions have to improve in order to be fully compliant with the requirements under this standard.
247. *See* Action 14 Peer Review Documents, *supra* n. 31, at paras 12.BP1 – BP4 on best practices to prevent disputes.
248. Robert T. Cole et al., *Mutual Agreement: Procedure and Practice – Proceedings of the Berlin Conference,* International Fiscal Association, *Cahiers de Droit Fiscal International* Vol. 66a, 282 (1981).
249. MEMAP, *supra* n. 22, at 18.
250. Action 14 Peer Review Documents, *supra* n. 31, at paras 15.BP5-BP8, 16.BP9-BP12.

a less transparent procedure that allows them to be flexible in applying ad hoc solutions to specific taxpayer grievances without the fear that others might also demand similar treatment.[251] While some taxpayers may also benefit from such a procedure to ensure greater flexibility regarding their tax treatment, on the whole, most taxpayers would prefer a much more transparent system that reduces the perceived risks of deal-making among competent authorities at the taxpayers' expense.

4.3.1.2.2.2 Taxpayer Participation Levels and Information Disclosure

Tax administrations and competent authorities prefer a MAP process with limited taxpayer participation that arguably might slow the process down or impede a free discussion with their counterparts.[252] Conversely, some taxpayers demand full (face-to-face) participation during the MAP to ensure there is no misunderstanding of the facts and arguments that are relevant to their case.[253] Taxpayers consider that such increased involvement in the MAP would alleviate their concerns regarding potential deal-making between competent authorities at their expense.[254] While taxpayers may also prefer a system that limits disclosure to reduce the risks of leakage of confidential information and the risks of additional audits in case of retaliation by domestic and foreign tax administrations,[255] competent authorities generally require full access to the taxpayers' financial information to efficiently conduct the MAP.[256]

4.3.1.2.2.3 Intergovernmental Conflict: Short-Term Versus Long-Term Revenue Objectives

Tax administrations and competent authorities are mostly entrusted with collecting revenue, while governments have overall broader objectives that extend beyond economic rents. Thus, even though one of the objectives of government may be to secure long-term economic growth, the tax administration or the competent authorities may have a preference for much shorter-term revenue objectives.[257] This may lead to intra-governmental conflict as a result of the different functions that each department within the government is required to perform. This is especially relevant if the competent authorities engage in unfair deal-making with the competent authorities of

251. Cole et al., *supra* n. 248, at 281.
252. *See supra* n. 152 for examples of international tax scholars that argue for limited taxpayer participation. *See also* Robert T. Cole, *Competent Authority Procedure: International Tax Counsel Gives His Views* 35(8) J. Tax'n 10 (1971). (Robert T. Cole was the US Treasury's International Tax Counsel when writing his opinion).
253. OECD Transfer Pricing Guidelines 2022, *supra* n. 54, at paras 4.58-4.61.
254. Lofti Maktouf, *Resolving International Tax Disputes through Arbitration* 4 *Arb. Int'l*, 32, 42 (1988) DOI: 10.1093/arbitration/4.1.32.
255. *See* Elmer Pergament et al., *The 'Competent Authority' Rules for Section 482 Relief: An Analysis of Rev. Proc. 70-18* 35 *J. Tax'n* 2, 4-5 (1971).
256. Maktouf, *supra* n. 254, at 41. *See also* CRA MAP Report 2018, *supra* n. 49 confirming that taxpayer reluctance to disclose information is one of the main reasons for MAP failures in 2018.
257. Altman, *supra* n. 71, at 248-249.

the other contracting state to secure revenue and, in the process, worsen the international relations that the other bodies of the government are building.

To sum up, the analysis of the community attributes reveals that while there is possible consensus between the taxpayers and competent authorities for quick, simple and clear procedures under the MAP, conflicts exist with respect to the transparency and disclosure levels within the MAP and the extent to which taxpayers should be involved in the process. Also, at the intergovernmental level, since competent authorities may be more concerned with short-term revenue objectives, this could create conflict vis-à-vis other government departments that are concerned with more long-term objectives. All these objectives and interests need to be addressed when developing a new tax treaty dispute resolution system.

4.3.1.3 Physical Conditions

Based on the definitions in section 3.2.2.3, the analysis of the physical conditions relates to the public-private characteristics associated with the various functions linked with the different mechanisms.[258] The aim is to understand the economic rationale of various functions of the dispute resolution system from a collective-action perspective and their contribution to the wider field of international tax governance. There are three distinct functions associated with the MAP, including (1) dispute resolution, (2) administering of the MAP system at the state level, and (3) compliance-monitoring under BEPS Action 14.

4.3.1.3.1 Dispute Resolution Function

MAP is a private negotiation process that involves the competent authorities of the disputing states and the taxpayer whose MAP case is being dealt with. The costs are incurred by the concerned taxpayer for preparing and submitting its request for MAP to the competent authority (e.g., legal fees). If a favourable MAP agreement is reached, then the associated benefits are also enjoyed primarily by the taxpayer in question. The dispute resolution function is, therefore, an excludable process as there are strict rules that restrict the costs and benefits to the concerned taxpayer only. The confidentiality requirements of the MAP and lack of resulting case law also limit the benefits of MAP resolution to that specific taxpayer. The dispute resolution function is subtractable because the time that a competent authority spends resolving one dispute cannot be spent deciding other disputes, especially in the typically limited-resource environment of a tax administration. The MAP resolution function thus constitutes a private good that restricts costs and benefits primarily to the concerned taxpayer whose MAP case is being resolved.

258. The basis for such private-public characteristics is taken from the public goods theory in that private goods are excludable and subtractable and, therefore, incur costs and benefits primarily for the users whereas public or intermediate public goods are generally non-excludable and non-subtractable with the costs and benefits affecting not only the users but also a wider public.

4.3.1.3.2 *Administering the MAP System*

The administration of a MAP system that effectively resolves tax treaty disputes and contributes to the smooth flow of international trade may produce incidental spillover effects that are felt by a wide range of actors beyond the MAP applicant (i.e., the taxpayer in person). One of these effects is the suggestion that the MAP may be contributing to one of the main objectives of the DTT for eliminating double taxation to promote international trade and investments.[259] This effect is emphasised through the implementation of the BEPS Action 14 minimum standard that aims to standardise the MAP across the DTT network and the publication of the MAP Statistics and MAP profiles of the different IF jurisdictions, all of which aim to make the MAP more effective. As such, an effective MAP system arguably constitutes an intermediate public good as it contributes to securing the ultimate public good of enhanced economic relationships and cooperation among IF members by removing administrative barriers.

4.3.1.3.3 *Compliance Monitoring under BEPS Action 14*

In addition to mandatory MAP rules and recommended best practices, the BEPS Action 14 minimum standard also includes a robust peer review process that seeks to increase efficiencies and improve the timeliness of the resolution of double taxation disputes through the MAP.[260] All IF jurisdictions commit to a compliance-monitoring mechanism under the peer review process, the costs of which are covered by the annual IF membership fees contributed by each IF country. The compliance-monitoring function involves a review of the MAP standards, which is published through publicly available peer review reports. Countries are also required to publish guidance on their MAP practices, share their MAP profiles and report on relevant annual MAP statistics in accordance with the MAP Statistics Reporting Framework.[261] Since this information is available on the OECD website,[262] it may be considered non-subtractable and non-excludable.[263] All IF countries may access this information to improve their own MAP system and generate wider debates on the relevant best practices to be adopted within tax treaty dispute resolution. As such, the compliance monitoring function may be considered a public good.

259. *See* Preamble of the OECD Model; Preamble of the UN Model.
260. *See* Annex A of Action 14 Peer Review Documents, *supra* n. 31, at 19. The peer review process was launched in 2016 and targeted 79 jurisdictions to be reviewed over a period from 2016 to 2021. It consists of two stages: in stage 1, jurisdictions' implementation of the Action 14 minimum standard is evaluated, and recommendations are made where jurisdictions have to improve in order to be fully compliant with the requirements under this standard. The follow-up of the recommendations is measured in stage 2 of the process.
261. *See* OECD, *MAP Statistics Reporting Framework* www.oecd.org/tax/dispute/mutual-agreement-procedure-statistics-reporting-framework.pdf accessed 20 Jul. 2020.
262. OECD, *Action 14 Mutual Agreement Procedure* www.oecd.org/tax/beps/beps-actions/action14/ accessed 20 Mar. 2022.
263. Countries not part of the IF cannot access or benefit from the peer review results, however the IF comprises more than 140 countries worldwide including most countries with a tax system. For this reason, consumption of this information is considered non-excludable.

To sum up, the dispute resolution function of MAP constitutes a primarily private good as it only affects the concerned taxpayer only, whereas the administration and peer review functions represent intermediate public and public goods, respectively, due to their ability to impact parties other than the disputant parties within the ITR.

4.3.2 Action Situation 2: Voluntary Arbitration under the UN Model

4.3.2.1 Working Rules

Arbitration under the UN Model is a supplementary procedure to the MAP; therefore, the MAP working rules relating to the taxpayer and the competent authority, discussed in section 4.3.1.1 above, still apply. This section will focus mainly on the rules pertaining to the arbitration panel under the UN Model.

4.3.2.1.1 Boundary Rules

The arbitration procedure under the UN Model involves the taxpayer that submitted the initial MAP case, the competent authorities of the disputant states and an independent arbitration panel set up to review the unresolved MAP case. Under the UN Model, an arbitrator can be any person (even a government official of the contracting state) unless the arbitrator was involved in the particular case beforehand; the arbitrator is also required to provide a written statement to declare his/her independence.[264]

4.3.2.1.2 Position Rules

The taxpayer and the competent authority still assume their roles as MAP applicant and MAP administrator. The arbitration panel, for its part, usually comprises three independent arbitrators, with the first two being appointed by the competent authorities and the third arbitrator being appointed jointly by the first two arbitrators to chair the panel.[265] If they are not able to appoint the arbitrators within the required time period (three or four-month period), the arbitrator(s) will be appointed by the Chair of the UN Committee of Experts on International Cooperation in Tax Matters (UN Tax Committee) within one month.[266] If the Chair is a national or resident of one of the two countries involved in the case, the responsibility to appoint an arbitrator will fall onto the longest-serving member of that Committee who is not a national or resident of these countries.[267]

---

264. *See* UN Model: Sample Mutual Agreement on Arbitration, Annex to Commentary on paragraph 5 to Article 25 Alternative B para. 7 (UN Model: Sample Arbitration Agreement).
265. *Ibid.*, at para. 5.
266. *Ibid.*
267. *Ibid.*

4.3.2.1.3 *Information Rules*

All official communications among the arbitrators of the panel and between the panel and competent authorities and/or the taxpayer should ensure confidentiality, and in this respect, the UN Model provides that the appointed arbitrators be deemed as authorised representatives of the appointing parties as regards communication of information under Article 26 on the exchange of information. The arbitration decision reached under the independent opinion approach,[268] if agreed to by the taxpayer and both competent authorities, may be published with redacted details on the understanding that these decisions would carry no precedential value.[269] However, for the purposes of this study, no publicly available information was found regarding any MAP cases resolved through the UN arbitration mechanism.

4.3.2.1.4 *Authority Rules*

Just as with the MAP, under the UN arbitration mechanism, the taxpayer is also required to approve the arbitration decision issued by the arbitration panel before it can be implemented by the competent authorities.[270] If the taxpayer rejects the arbitration decision, then the case will be closed, and the taxpayer may proceed with domestic remedies, if possible, to seek relief for any unresolved tax issues.[271]

Under the UN Model, it is the competent authorities that decide whether to trigger the arbitration process if they were unable to reach a MAP agreement within a generally prescribed three-year time period (hence, it is a voluntary mechanism).[272] The taxpayer may request the competent authority to submit the request for arbitration, but the competent authorities have no obligation to accept.[273] This is in contrast to the OECD's arbitration mechanism, which is triggered by the taxpayer if no MAP agreement is reached within a specific time period, as discussed in section 4.3.3.1 below.

The competent authorities are required to circulate among themselves and the taxpayer a mutually agreed Terms of Reference that includes the list of questions to be addressed and the procedure to be applied (e.g., the baseball approach or the independent opinion method), including the cost-sharing allocations, etc., within three months of triggering the arbitration procedure.[274] Each competent authority is also responsible for appointing one of the three arbitrators to the three-member panel.[275]

---

268. There are two possible arbitration approaches. The default approach is the baseball arbitration where the arbitrators choose one of the submitted proposed solutions. Otherwise the panel may come to its own decision based on its own analysis of the treaty rules and the applicable domestic laws under the independent opinion approach. *See* further discussion in s. 4.3.2.1.5.2 below.
269. Paragraph 11(a) UN Model: Sample Arbitration Agreement.
270. Paragraph 77 UN Model: Commentary on Article 25(5) Alternative B.
271. *Ibid.*
272. Paragraphs 1-2 UN Model: Sample Arbitration Agreement.
273. Paragraph 63 UN Model: Commentary on Article 25(5) Alternative B.
274. Paragraph 3 UN Model: Sample Arbitration Agreement.
275. *Ibid.*, at para. 15.

The competent authorities have a period of six months to implement the arbitration decision rendered, or they may reject the decision and agree on a different solution within that six-month period (subject to the taxpayer's approval).[276]

As for the arbitrators appointed to the three-member panel, they will analyse the issues submitted by the competent authorities through the Terms of Reference and render an independent arbitration decision based on a simple majority vote of the three-member panel.[277] The third arbitrator of the panel is appointed jointly by the two arbitrators selected by the competent authorities, and he/she functions as the Chair.[278] It is important to note that the arbitrators have no say in the arbitration procedure to be applied (baseball approach or independent opinion). The two procedures are discussed in detail in section 4.3.2.1.5.2 below.

4.3.2.1.5 Aggregation Rules

4.3.2.1.5.1 Applicable Law

Just as with the MAP, the arbitration panel will render a decision in accordance with the provisions of the applicable treaty, including reference to the relevant domestic laws of the states concerned, in light of the principles of treaty interpretation under Articles 31 to 33 of the VCLT.[279] The arbitrators may also consider any other sources which the competent authorities may expressly identify in the Terms of Reference.[280]

4.3.2.1.5.2 Administrative Framework

The arbitration procedure is determined jointly by the competent authorities and set out in the Terms of Reference. The default mode of arbitration under both the UN and OECD Models is the baseball approach, where the arbitration panel chooses one of the two solutions proposed by each competent authority on the questions specified in the Terms of Reference.[281] This is also referred to as the streamlined baseball approach, and the panel will issue a decision within three months of receiving the necessary information from the competent authorities.[282]

In the alternative, the competent authorities may also prescribe an arbitration procedure based on the independent opinion method. In this case, the competent authorities will present their positions and views to the arbitration panel in writing, and the panel will reach their own decision.[283] Such procedure ensures that the competent authorities still maintain a relatively high level of control over the arbitration process, although the final decision is rendered by the arbitration panel based on a simple

276. *Ibid.*, at paras 17-18.
277. *Ibid.*, at para. 15.
278. Paragraph 5 UN Model: Sample Arbitration Agreement.
279. *Ibid.*, at para. 14.
280. *Ibid.*, at para. 14.
281. *Ibid.*, at para. 6.
282. *Ibid.*, at para. 6(b).
283. *Ibid.*, at para. 11.

majority vote. In the independent opinion method, the arbitrators will deliberate for a period of six months.[284]

Taking into consideration the differing timelines of the two procedures, the arbitration process may last over a minimum period of 13 to 16 months under the baseball approach and the independent opinion method, respectively.[285] However, more importantly, compared to the independent opinion method, the baseball approach limits the arbitrators' ability to produce and publish their own independent legal findings,[286] which may further perpetuate the lack of relevant case law in the ITR.

4.3.2.1.6 Scope Rules

4.3.2.1.6.1 Jurisdiction of UN Arbitration

Under the UN Model, only cases that were submitted to MAP under Article 25(1) can proceed to arbitration; this rule effectively prevents the arbitration of tax issues that were presented under Article 25(3), including double taxation issues in cases not provided for under the treaty and other interpretive issues, unless the competent authorities mutually agree to examine the issue.[287] Additionally, under the UN Model, the competent authority cannot make an arbitration request in cases where the amount of taxes involved in the relevant MAP case is less than a certain prescribed amount (to be determined bilaterally) unless both competent authorities agree that it is appropriate to do so (e.g., in order to resolve a question of principle).[288] Although this practice may be reasonable from a cost perspective for the competent authorities that may already be operating at maximum capacity, the MAP case of the taxpayer may remain unresolved to the detriment of the taxpayer.

The UN arbitration mechanism is also subject to various domestic legal constraints as arbitration may only be triggered if no decision on the same issues has already been rendered through domestic remedies (e.g., court or administrative tribunal in either state) as evidenced through a written statement that needs to be submitted along with the arbitration request.[289] Moreover, only the unresolved issues of a MAP case that prevent an agreement from being reached can be presented for

284. *Ibid.*, at para. 11(b).
285. *See* UN Model: Sample Arbitration Agreement. Under baseball approach, it takes 3 months to agree on Terms of Reference and circulate to taxpayer; another 3 months for competent authorities to appoint both arbitrators; 2 months for arbitrators to appoint Chair; 2 months for each competent authority to present its reply to panel following appointment of Chair; within 3 months of receiving reply, panel should notify competent authorities of arbitration decision, lasting 13 months total. The independent opinion method includes 6 months of deliberations by the arbitration panel instead of 3 months, bringing the total length of the arbitration procedure to 16 months.
286. *See* n. 269, *supra*.
287. *See* para. 73 UN Model: Commentary on Article 25(5). States may extend arbitration clause to also cover mutual agreement cases arising under Art. 25(3) i.e., double taxation issues not covered under the bilateral treaty.
288. Paragraph 1 UN Model: Sample Arbitration Agreement.
289. *Ibid.*

arbitration (not the whole case).[290] Some countries may also restrict the range of cases that may be presented for arbitration (e.g., highly factual cases such as those related to transfer pricing or the question of the existence of a PE while extending arbitration to other issues on a case-by-case basis).[291] States that are also members of the EU must coordinate the scope of their arbitration provisions with their obligations under the European Arbitration Convention (although this discussion is beyond the scope of this study).[292]

Based on the above, there seem to exist significant scope limitations for triggering the arbitration mechanism under the UN Model. This may subject disputant parties (i.e., taxpayers) across the ITR to a disadvantage depending on their jurisdiction of residence, especially if the statute of limitations is exceeded for domestic remedies in their own countries. In this way, the UN arbitration mechanism may emphasise a fragmented application of MAP rules and inequitable solutions across the ITR.

4.3.2.1.6.2 Finality of Arbitration Decision

Under the UN model, the arbitration decision is not legally binding on the competent authorities as they may agree on a different solution within the same six-month implementation period following the issuance of the arbitration decision, subject to the acceptance of the taxpayer.[293] In practice, this is likely to be more relevant for the independent opinion rather than the baseball arbitration approach. Moreover, under both the UN and OECD Models, the arbitration decision will not be binding on the contracting states if the final decision of the courts in one of the contracting states holds that the arbitration decision is invalid (because of a violation of Article 25(5) or of any other procedural rules).[294] Such constraints impact the certainty associated with the UN arbitration process for resolving a MAP case effectively and efficiently. Just as with MAP decisions, the arbitration decision has no formal precedential value, as each case is decided based on the specific situation of the taxpayer.[295]

4.3.2.1.7 Payoff Rules

Payoff rules determine how costs and benefits are distributed across the action situation. Just as in the MAP, there are no additional fees for taxpayers for triggering the UN arbitration process, except if the taxpayer or their representative participates directly in the arbitration session.[296] This makes arbitration particularly attractive for taxpayers as they are guaranteed some form of resolution of their tax issues (even if it is not the actual arbitration decision rendered) with no extra out-of-pocket costs. The

290. Paragraph 64 UN Model: Commentary on Article 25(5) Alternative B.
291. *Ibid.*, at para. 66.
292. *Ibid.*, at para. 67.
293. Paragraphs 17-18 UN Model: Sample Arbitration Agreement.
294. *Ibid.*, at para. 17.
295. This applies to decisions reached under the baseball arbitration and the independent opinion approach.
296. Paragraph 13(a) UN Model: Sample Arbitration Agreement.

costs of administering the arbitration process (e.g., travel costs and fees of arbitrators) are thus shared between the competent authorities,[297] which may explain why competent authorities may be reluctant to voluntarily trigger the arbitration mechanism under the UN Model. The surrendering of tax sovereignty to an independent panel is another deterring factor, especially for developing countries, based on their argument that many arbitration judges generally come from and have experience in tax systems in developed countries and may therefore lack familiarity with the developing country issues, leading to inequitable outcomes (*see* discussion in section 4.3.2.2.2 below).

4.3.2.2 Community Attributes

The community attributes focus on the objectives and interests of key actors (taxpayers, competent authorities and arbitrators) to identify any relevant trends in relation to the UN arbitration mechanism. In fact, the analysis of the community attributes emphasises the different perspectives that separate developing and developed countries regarding arbitration, especially with China and India fiercely rejecting the OECD's mandatory binding arbitration, as shown below.

4.3.2.2.1 Lack of Experience and Familiarity

Several developing countries have raised concerns regarding their perceived lack of experience and familiarity with arbitration compared to developed countries.[298] They argue that the lack of experience and expertise may put undue pressure on the competent authorities of developing countries to agree on inequitable MAP solutions when negotiating with their developed country counterparts in order to avoid arbitration.[299]

4.3.2.2.2 Issues of Even-Handedness

Some developing countries also have concerns in regard to the even-handedness of the arbitration process.[300] They consider that currently, there is only a small pool of possible arbitrators who can deal with complex international tax and transfer pricing issues, and most of them come from the developed world. Although this group may include academics and people having no affiliation with governments or businesses, the perception is that the thought process and understanding of international taxation of these arbitrators may be tuned to the developed world and might not be familiar with the concerns of developing countries.[301] There are also concerns that few potential

297. Paragraph 13 UN Model: Sample Arbitration Agreement.
298. UN, *Chapter 5 on MAP Arbitration of the Handbook on Avoidance and Resolution of Tax Disputes* E/C18/2020/CRP.28 para. 25 (2020) (2020 UN Secretariat Paper).
299. 2020 UN Secretariat Paper, *supra* n. 298, at para. 25.
300. *Ibid.*, at para. 27.
301. *Ibid.*

arbitrators would be fluent in the official languages of some developing countries, which might make it difficult for these arbitrators to fully understand the position of the competent authorities of these countries.[302]

4.3.2.2.3 Lack of Resources

In relation to the arbitration costs incurred by the competent authorities, some developing countries express that they may be disproportionately affected in comparison with their counterparts from developed countries through the fact that the arbitrators' fees could be payable in a foreign currency on a scale that is not proportional to the resources available to them.[303] Alternately, other countries believe that the costs associated with arbitration may actually be lower than expected owing to the limited number of cases that may go to arbitration and their limited ability to structure an efficient arbitration process, proposing accordingly to put a cap on the compensation of arbitrators (e.g., as is sometimes done in baseball arbitration).[304] In fact, a number of officials from developing countries do not rule out an eventual recourse to arbitration but consider that they are not yet ready for such a mechanism based on the negative experience of some developing countries regarding the application of the arbitration provisions to tax measures under bilateral investment agreements.[305] They also note that, in the current environment, most arbitration cases would focus on taxes collected by developing countries as opposed to taxes collected by developed countries.[306]

4.3.2.2.4 Need for Transparency

Certain developing countries have expressed that greater transparency may avoid the situation where only a small circle of arbitrators, advisors and officials from the countries directly affected would know the outcomes and make decisions accordingly, leaving the majority of countries 'out of the loop'.[307] However, although the lack of transparency within the arbitration process may be of concern, countries seem to agree generally that such transparency issues are not limited to the UN arbitration process but are also reflected in the MAP and in the OECD's mandatory and binding arbitration process.[308]

302. *Ibid.*
303. *Ibid.*, at para. 24.
304. *Ibid.*
305. *Ibid.*, at para. 26. *See also* Shruti Srivastava, *At G20 talks, India to Come out Strongly Against 'Mandatory' Arbitration for Tax* (The Indian Express, 13 Nov. 2014) http://indianexpress.com/article/business/economy/at-g20-talks-india-to-come-out-strongly-against-mandatory-arbitration-for-tax/ accessed 10 Mar. 2021.
306. 2020 UN Secretariat Paper, *supra* n. 298, at para. 26.
307. UN, *Secretariat Paper on Alternative Dispute Resolution in Taxation,* E/C.18/2015/CRP.8 para. 39 (2015) (2015 UN Secretariat Paper).
308. 2020 UN Secretariat Paper, *supra* n. 298, para. 28.

4.3.2.2.5 *Concerns on Finality of Arbitral Awards*

Some countries have also expressed concerns regarding the finality of the arbitral awards as prescribed under the UN and OECD Models. In current practice, arbitral awards present final and binding outcomes for the competent authorities who must resolve the case in accordance with the decision (unless the taxpayer rejects the decision under the OECD model or both competent authorities act together to reject the decision under the UN model). There is no possibility for review or appeal of the decision, which may negatively impact the take-up of arbitration among countries.[309] This argument may explain why the OECD arbitration mechanism has not been implemented on a wide scale among the IF countries so far.[310] However, the current developments under Pillar One indicate that developing countries may be ready to adopt mandatory and binding arbitration, especially if their requirements are taken into account.

The analysis of the community attributes under the UN arbitration mechanism reveals a clear separation between developing and developed countries based on institutional concerns (e.g., lack of expertise, lack of resources, etc.) that may lead to differential treatment for taxpayers from developing and developed countries. To obtain a more equitable resolution of cross-border tax disputes across the ITR, the institutional gaps in terms of resources and expertise between developing and developed countries need to be addressed.

4.3.2.3 *Physical Conditions*

The analysis of the physical conditions is based on the public-private characteristics of the various functions associated with the arbitration mechanism. These include dispute resolution and administration functions.

4.3.2.3.1 *Dispute Resolution*

The dispute resolution function of arbitration is excludable in that the taxpayer may access arbitration only if certain strict conditions are met. The decision to trigger arbitration depends on the competent authorities and thus can be denied to the taxpayer. In addition, only MAP cases involving taxes above a certain monetary threshold, as agreed by the competent authorities, can be submitted to arbitration. The dispute resolution function associated with the UN Model arbitration is also subtractable because competent authorities are responsible for the costs of setting up an arbitration session in each case, and this effectively reduces the available budget that can be allocated to the arbitration of other MAP cases. As with the MAP, the dispute resolution aspect of arbitration produces costs and benefits that are restricted to the

309. *See* 2015 UN Secretariat Paper, *supra* n. 307, at 39. In fact this lack of appeal mechanism has been criticised by stakeholders in other areas such as in the context of international investment arbitration.
310. *See supra* n. 27.

disputant parties only, especially if the arbitration decision is not published and thus constitutes a private good.

4.3.2.3.2 Administering the UN Arbitration Mechanism

Although the arbitration mechanism is, to a large extent, standardised under the UN Model, it is an optional procedure that is not adopted uniformly across the DTT network. The process is administered fully by the competent authorities of the disputing parties with no involvement of the taxpayer (except for approving the final decision prior to implementation). Since the costs and benefits of administering the system are restricted to the disputing parties only (i.e., the competent authorities and the taxpayer, if applicable), the administering aspect of the arbitration mechanism under the UN Model also represents a private good, that is under the control of the competent authorities.

4.3.3 Action Situation 3: Mandatory Arbitration under the OECD Model

4.3.3.1 Working Rules

This section explores the key functions of the taxpayer, the competent authorities and the arbitration panel under the OECD Model arbitration, and it also points out the differences in relation to the UN arbitration mechanism as discussed in section 4.3.2.1 above.

4.3.3.1.1 Boundary Rules

Just as with the UN Model, the actors involved in arbitration under the OECD Model include the taxpayer that submitted the MAP request, the competent authorities administering the MAP and an independent three-member panel of arbitrators. Unlike the UN Model, however, where the arbitrator may be anyone, including a government official of one of the contracting states, an arbitrator under the OECD Model should be a person with recognised competence in the fields of international tax law who may be relied upon to exercise independent judgment in the area of tax treaty disputes.[311] Additionally, the arbitrator must be independent of the competent authorities, tax administrations and ministries of finance of either contracting state, including all persons directly affected by the case.[312] Each arbitrator must also maintain his impartiality throughout the proceedings and must, for a reasonable time afterwards, avoid conduct that may damage the appearance of impartiality and independence with respect to the proceedings.[313]

311. Paragraph 3(1) OECD Model: Sample Arbitration Agreement.
312. *Ibid.*
313. *Ibid.*, at para. 17.

4.3.3.1.2 *Position Rules*

As with the UN arbitration mechanism, each competent authority selects one arbitrator to the three-member panel and the third arbitrator is appointed jointly by the first two arbitrators to chair the panel.[314] If no appointment is made within this timeline by the competent authorities, the highest-ranking official at the OECD Centre for Tax Policy and Administration (CTPA) will make the necessary appointment of the arbitrator(s).[315]

4.3.3.1.3 *Information Rules*

As with the UN mechanism, the OECD arbitration session is a private and confidential process between the disputant parties. The arbitrators appointed by competent authorities are deemed authorised representatives of the competent authorities as regards communication of information under Article 26 on the exchange of information.[316] The OECD Model adds another layer of protection by increasing the number of persons subject to confidentiality requirements: it provides that not only the arbitrators will constitute authorised representatives but also their support staff (up to three staff members per arbitrator).[317] It also requires a written statement with regard to confidentiality and non-disclosure obligations from each arbitrator and designated staff member.[318] As in the UN Model, the arbitration decision reached under the independent opinion approach may be published with redacted details if all parties agree,[319] although no information is available on the extent of its use across the countries that have implemented the OECD arbitration mechanism.

4.3.3.1.4 *Authority Rules*

Under the OECD Model, arbitration is triggered by the taxpayer (the MAP applicant) if no MAP agreement is reached between the competent authorities within a period of two years. The taxpayer sends a request for arbitration in writing to one or both of the competent authorities after the two-year deadline has passed,[320] along with a written statement that no decision on the same issues has been rendered by a court or domestic administrative tribunal.[321] This procedure is different from that of the UN Model, where arbitration is triggered by the competent authorities. The OECD Model thus attributes more control to the taxpayer for prompting a resolution of any unresolved

314. *Ibid.*, at para. 3.
315. *Ibid.*
316. *Ibid.*, at para. 6(1).
317. *Ibid.*
318. *Ibid.*, at para. 6(2).
319. *Ibid.*, at para. 5.
320. The request can be made at any point in time after a period of two years after all information was provided to both competent authorities to conduct MAP. *See* para. 7 OECD Model: Sample Arbitration Agreement.
321. Paragraph 1 OECD Model: Sample Arbitration Agreement.

MAP cases through arbitration. In turn, this may push competent authorities to make greater effort to reach a MAP agreement within prescribed timelines to avoid surrendering decision-making to an independent arbitration panel. This is discussed further as the 'prophylactic effect' of the mandatory and binding arbitration, as discussed in section 4.3.3.2.1 below. The taxpayer is also required to approve the arbitration decision reached by the arbitration panel before it can be implemented by the competent authorities, and in certain circumstances, the taxpayer may also have the option to participate in person in the proceedings to present his position (in contrast to the proceedings under the UN Model).[322]

Once the taxpayer's request for arbitration is received, the competent authorities are responsible for circulating among themselves and the taxpayer a Terms of Reference containing the questions for arbitration and other procedural requirements of the arbitration session (just as in the UN Model).[323] The competent authorities are also responsible for appointing arbitrators to the panel within a 60-day period (compared with three months under the UN Model)[324] and for implementing the arbitration decision within six months from the communication of the decision to them by reaching a mutual agreement on the case that led to the arbitration, subject to the taxpayer's acceptance.[325] This is different than in the UN Model, where the competent authorities may reject the arbitration decision and agree on a different solution within the same six-month period.[326]

The arbitrators follow the same procedure as under the UN mechanism in that they will render an arbitration decision based on a simple majority of the three-member panel in accordance with the procedure devised by the competent authorities.[327]

4.3.3.1.5 Aggregation Rules

4.3.3.1.5.1 Applicable Law

As in the UN arbitration mechanism, the competent authorities, under the OECD Model, will jointly decide on the procedural rules to be adopted for the conduct of the arbitration, including the baseball or last best offer approach (as the default mechanism)[328] and the independent opinion approach (as the optional approach).[329] The arbitration panel will decide the issues submitted in accordance with the provisions of the applicable treaty and subject to these provisions, of those of the domestic laws of the contracting states while taking into account Articles 31 to 33 of the VCLT.[330] The

322. *Ibid.*, at para. 5.2.
323. *Ibid.*, at paras 15.1-15.5.
324. *Ibid.*, at para. 3.
325. *Ibid.*, at para. 12.
326. *See supra* n. 276.
327. Paragraphs 4-5 OECD Model: Sample Arbitration Agreement.
328. Paragraph 20 OECD Model: Annex to Commentary on Article 25.
329. *Ibid.*, at paras 25-26.
330. *Ibid.*, at paras 30-31.

arbitrators will also consider any other sources which the competent authorities may expressly identify in the Terms of Reference.[331]

4.3.3.1.5.2 Administrative Framework

Under the OECD Model, the arbitration process may last between 10 and 16 months under the baseball approach and the independent opinion method, respectively,[332] which is comparable to the timelines under the UN Model of 13 and 16 months, respectively. The timeline for requesting arbitration, however, differs under the OECD and UN Model provisions. Under the OECD Model, arbitration may be triggered within two years from the start of the MAP process, whereas the UN arbitration may be triggered within three years of the MAP process. It follows that the dispute resolution process takes longer (at least one year longer) under the UN Model compared to the OECD Model. As such, although the BEPS Action 14 report recommends jurisdictions implement the arbitration decision irrespective of the domestic time limits,[333] there is a lower risk that the MAP outcome from the OECD mechanism will exceed the domestic time limits compared to the UN mechanism.

Another difference relates to taxpayer participation. Under the independent opinion procedures in the OECD and the UN Models, the taxpayer may, either directly or through its representatives, present its position to the arbitrators in writing to the same extent allowed in MAP.[334] In addition, under the OECD Model, if the competent authorities and arbitrators all agree, the taxpayer may also present its position in person during the arbitration proceedings.[335] This may give the taxpayer more incentive to use the arbitration mechanism under the OECD Model and, conversely, urge the competent authorities to reach a MAP agreement before arbitration is triggered, as they would lose control of the decisions to a third party.

4.3.3.1.6 Scope Rules

4.3.3.1.6.1 Jurisdiction of OECD Arbitration

As in the UN Model, only cases that were submitted to MAP under Article 25(1) can proceed to arbitration under the OECD Model, thus excluding the arbitration of tax issues that were presented under Article 25(3) (although the competent authorities

331. Paragraph 5(4) OECD Model: Sample Arbitration Agreement.
332. *See* OECD Model: Sample Arbitration Agreement. Under baseball approach, 60 days from receipt of arbitration request, competent authorities appoint arbitrators, another 60 days for Chair to be appointed, 60 days to circulate Terms of Reference, 60 days for competent authorities to send reply to arbitration panel, 60 days for panel to send decision in writing to competent authorities for a total of 300 days i.e., around 10 months. The independent opinion method requires panel to issue decision to competent authorities in writing 365 days from appointment of Chair of arbitration panel for a total of 16 months.
333. Article 25(2) OECD Model.
334. Paragraph 5(2) OECD Model: Sample Arbitration Agreement.
335. *Ibid.*

may agree otherwise).[336] Additionally, as under the UN Model, the scope of arbitration under the OECD Model may also be restricted by domestic legal constraints, e.g., applying arbitration to those issues for which no decision has been rendered through domestic court or restricting the range of MAP cases eligible for arbitration.[337] EU Member States may also be bound by rules under the EU Arbitration Convention. Such scope restrictions may give rise to non-uniform application of the arbitration rules across the IF jurisdictions. These issues are further exacerbated through the limited adoption of the OECD's arbitration mechanism across the ITR so far.[338]

4.3.3.1.6.2 Finality of Outcomes

Like the UN Model, the arbitration decision under the OECD Model has no formal precedential value as each case is decided based on the specific situation of the taxpayer.[339] The difference, however, is that under the OECD Model, the arbitration decision is legally binding on the competent authorities, subject to the taxpayer's acceptance (not the case under the UN Model, where competent authorities may reject the decision and opt for a different mutually agreed solution). This constitutes another factor that may urge the competent authorities to reach an agreement through MAP rather than having an arbitration decision imposed on them.

4.3.3.1.7 Payoff Rules

Under the OECD Model, as under the UN Model, the costs of the arbitration process are covered by the competent authorities at no additional costs for the taxpayer unless the latter is participating in person at the session (only possible under the OECD Model), in which case the taxpayer would have to cover its own travel and accommodation costs, if applicable. In contrast to the UN Model, however, the OECD mechanism allocates more decision-making power to the taxpayer to trigger the arbitration if no MAP agreement is reached within the prescribed time limits of two years. Additionally, the mechanism also allocates more decision-making power to the arbitration panel by implementing the arbitration decision that they issue (with the consent of the taxpayer). These procedures undeniably create a more equitable distribution of decision-making power among the different actors involved (competent authorities, arbitrators and taxpayer) despite the fact that competent authorities determine the procedural rules that the arbitrators would use (baseball or independent opinion approach). This ensures a more independent and balanced process for resolving the outstanding MAP issue.

336. Paragraphs 72-73 OECD Model, Commentary on Article 25(5).
337. *Ibid.*, at para. 74.
338. *See supra* n. 27.
339. This applies to decisions reached under the baseball arbitration and the independent opinion approach.

Thus, compared to the UN Model, arbitration under the OECD Model imposes more restrictions on the competent authorities – they have to administer the arbitration session if the taxpayer chooses that option and the arbitration decision by the panel is legally binding – which may urge them to maximise their efforts for reaching agreement through MAP as discussed in section 4.3.3.2 below.

4.3.3.2 Community Attributes

The analysis of the community attributes will focus on the objectives and interests of the various actors involved in the OECD mechanism to identify any potential trends.

4.3.3.2.1 Common Benefits of Prophylactic Effect of Mandatory Mechanism

The most significant benefit perceived by some (mostly developed) countries of the arbitration process is its 'prophylactic effect', i.e., its deterrence effect that urges disputing parties to reach some form of agreement under MAP before arbitration is invoked.[340] This characteristic of the OECD arbitration is beneficial both for taxpayers that wish to resolve their MAP cases and competent authorities that do not wish for taxpayers to trigger arbitration as it would impose a legally binding decision on them. In practice, such prophylactic effect has been observed under the Canada-United States tax treaty, which has included mandatory binding arbitration since 2010.[341]

4.3.3.2.2 Preference for Arbitration over Domestic Remedies

Although taxpayers and competent authorities may both benefit from the prophylactic effect of the OECD arbitration, the actual use of the arbitration process may also hold potential benefits for both parties. The use of mandatory arbitration with binding decisions may reinforce taxpayer faith in applying the MAP, thereby reducing reliance on sometimes inefficient and unilateral domestic remedies.[342] The alternative for the taxpayer, of bringing the case to a domestic court, may not be the best solution for the tax administration either since it might be more cost-efficient for the tax administration to go for arbitration as opposed to prolonged judicial processes.[343] Therefore, from a monetary aspect, arbitration would be more favourable to the taxpayer, given that it is essentially free of charge for the taxpayer. Although most of the costs would be borne by the competent authorities, arbitration may also present a preferable option for the competent authority, as the latter may have more control in arbitration (e.g., by setting out the procedures, etc.) rather than in a domestic court case.

340. 2020 UN Secretariat Paper, *supra* n. 298, at para. 31.
341. *Ibid.*
342. *Ibid.*, at para. 33.
343. *See supra* n. 1.

4.3.3.3 *Physical Conditions*

The OECD Model arbitration comprises similar functions as the UN mechanism, including: (1) the dispute resolution function and (2) the administration aspect with certain key institutional differences.

4.3.3.3.1 Dispute Resolution Function

As with the UN Model, arbitration under the OECD Model constitutes a private good. Although the taxpayer is in a position to trigger the arbitration mechanism if no MAP agreement is reached within a two-year period, the MAP case may still be excluded depending on the tax issues therein. The fact that arbitration decisions are not usually published also restricts the impact that such decisions may have on other taxpayers and competent authorities, making it into a private good, just as with MAP and UN arbitration. However, if the arbitration decision is published, even under a redacted format, then it may reach a wider public, increasing the public good characteristics of the dispute resolution function.

4.3.3.3.2 Administering the OECD Arbitration Mechanism

Just as with an effective MAP system that aims to eliminate double taxation and enhance economic relationships across the ITR, an effective arbitration mechanism under the OECD Model may arguably present some public good characteristics. It is different from the UN Model because it constitutes a mandatory process with a binding decision for competent authorities to implement. Even if the OECD arbitration mechanism is not triggered, the prophylactic effect associated with the mechanism prompts an effective resolution of cross-border tax disputes for ultimately securing peaceful and cooperative international relations, which constitute a public good. On this basis, the administration of the OECD arbitration mechanism across the ITR is an intermediate public good.

However, in contrast to the MAP process that is implemented and monitored on a global scale among 141 IF countries, the arbitration mechanism is currently available as an optional provision under the MAP provision and has been implemented in 31 countries only as of June 2022.[344] This limited application of the mechanism across the ITR reduces the forum for global debates on tax arbitration. In addition, the lack of case law produced (or published) arguably fails to extend the related costs and benefits beyond a small group of relevant disputing parties. This exacerbates the private good characteristics of arbitration, mitigating the intermediate public good effect of administering the costly process of arbitration.

The analysis of the public-private characteristics of the functions discussed above reveals a high potential for the OECD arbitration mechanism to display public good characteristics. However, to ensure that all IF members (developed, developing and

344. *See supra* n. 27.

emerging countries) may have access to and implement such arbitration mechanism, it is necessary to address the institutional issues that developing countries face vis-à-vis the developed countries.

4.3.4 Politico-economic Context

The analysis of the politico-economic context situates the influence of the working rules, community attributes and physical conditions within a power-centric context. As discussed in section 3.2.2.4, the emerging economic and political powers of China within the international legal order may be exerting an eastward shift in the political economy's centre of gravity (formerly controlled by the US and other western countries). This section analyses the evolving impact that China may have on the broader development of international tax regulations, including tax treaty dispute resolution.

4.3.4.1 Rapid Expansion of China's Global Tax Treaty Network to Promote Trade and Investment

At the time that provisions of the OECD Model were being negotiated in the 1920s, China had no relevant role to play, be it as a norm setter or norm taker, because it had not yet opened its economies to cross-border income and capital. The negotiations were dominated by a small group of western, developed countries led by the US. In fact, the draft provisions for eliminating double taxation developed by the League of Nations and eventually consolidated into the first draft OECD Model in 1963 reflected largely international tax regulations as advocated by the US.[345] This is exemplified in the provisions of the OECD Transfer Pricing Guidelines that were based initially on the US domestic law provisions.[346]

This situation rapidly changed, however, when China opened its borders to foreign trade and investment in the 1980s. Although China had no direct input in the design of the OECD Model (with minor input in the UN Model developed in 1980), it was quick to adopt the international tax regulations as it signed its first tax treaty with Japan in 1983.[347] Since then, China has concluded more than One hundred bilateral tax treaties based on the OECD and UN Models.[348] The Chinese tax treaty network is currently larger than that of the US and has evolved in successive phases according to China's evolving role in the global economy.[349] In fact, by 2012, China had become the world's third largest outbound investor, after the US and Japan, with an outbound

345. Baistrocchi, *supra* n. 189, at 242.
346. *Ibid.*, at 246 The provisions of the 1995 OECD Transfer Pricing Guidelines are based on the regulations of the US Internal Revenue Code (IRC) Art. 486 following the 1986 and 1994 US tax reforms.
347. Jinyan Li, *The Great Fiscal Wall of China: Tax Treaties and Their Role in Defining and Defending China's Tax Base* 66(9) Bull. Int'l Tax'n 452, 453 (2012).
348. *See* the complete list of bilateral tax treaties on China's State Taxation Administration site www.chinatax.gov.cn/eng/c101276/c101732/index.html accessed 10 Mar. 2021.
349. Li, *supra* n. 347, at 453.

direct investment (ODI) of USD 88 billion and a foreign direct investment (FDI) of USD 112 billion.[350] By 2016, China's ODI reached USD 183 billion, surging well beyond inward FDI at USD 131 billion, placing China at the ranks of the US, primarily as a capital exporter.[351]

4.3.4.2 *Structural Shift to Align with OECD and Developed Country Frameworks*

Although China initially joined the DTT regime as a developing, non-OECD country in the 1980s, it quickly and systematically aligned its international tax policies with those of the more developed OECD countries, especially since the beginning of the BEPS project in 2012 as a key partner of the OECD.[352] China also strived towards more active participation through a leadership role at both the OECD and the UN Tax Committee levels following its presidency at the G20 in 2016. To be well prepared for the involvement at the level of OECD discussion on BEPS, the Chinese State Taxation Administration (STA) set up both a Leadership Group and a Working Group on the G20 Tax Reform Project.[353] The STA also appointed its representative to the Steering Committee of the BEPS, working with other committee members on designing, supervising and reviewing the proposed BEPS actions.[354] From 2013 through 2015, the STA participated in 86 meetings relevant to the BEPS project and submitted over 1,000 pieces of position statements and proposals to the OECD, many of which have been adopted and reflected in the final BEPS package.[355]

While there have been no major new tax rule changes reflecting this structural shift in Chinese international tax policymaking, signs evidencing a shift from a 'source' country to a 'residence' country mindset are apparent. This includes the updated terms of tax treaties with countries participating in the Belt and Road Initiative,[356] pushing for much lower withholding tax (WHT) rates (e.g., Russia, Romania, Malaysia DTT updates) and the steadily increasing numbers of tax disputes facing Chinese MNEs in

350. Chris Xing et al., *China after BEPS, for Now ...* (International Tax Review, 28 Nov. 2017) www.internationaltaxreview.com/article/b1f7nb1h471zlm/china-after-beps-for-now accessed 10 Mar. 2021.
351. Xing et al., *supra* n. 350.
352. In May 2007, the OECD Council, meeting at ministerial level, invited the Secretariat to strengthen OECD cooperation with Brazil, India, Indonesia, the People's Republic of China and South Africa through 'Enhanced Engagement' programmes. These Key Partners contribute to the OECD's work in a sustained and comprehensive manner.
353. OECD, *G20 finance ministers endorse reforms to the international tax system for curbing avoidance by multinational enterprises* (9 Oct. 2015) www.oecd.org/tax/beps/g20-finance-ministers-endorse-reforms-to-the-international-tax-system-for-curbing-avoidance-by-multinational-enterprises.htm accessed 9 Mar. 2021.
354. Reuven Avi-Yonah and Haiyan Xu, *China and BEPS* 7(1) Laws 4 (2018).
355. Avi-Yonah and Xu, *supra* n. 354, at 4.
356. The BRI project comprises the land-based Silk Road Economic Belt and the 21st Century Maritime Silk Road and was proposed by Chinese President Xi Jinping in 2013 aiming to build a community of shared interests, shared destiny, and shared responsibility among all the participating countries with multilateral mechanisms. *See* Lingliang Zeng, *Conceptual Analysis of China's Belt and Road Initiative: A Road towards a Regional Community of Common Destiny* 15 Chinese J. Int'l L. 517, 518-519 (2016) DOI: 10.1093/chinesejil/jmw021.

overseas investee jurisdictions, for example, in relation to PE challenges.[357] Such an increase in cross-border tax disputes has led to increased demands on the STA to offer assistance through MAP.[358]

4.3.4.3 China's Norm-Setting Strategies in the ITR

The economic superpowers of China, as the world's leading capital exporter after the US, have arguably given a much more powerful voice to China in relation to international tax regulations at the level of the OECD and the UN Tax Committee, especially in the post-BEPS ITR. One of the most visible aspects of this positioning is China's approach to the OECD's prescribed ALP for allocating global corporate income across the various jurisdictions within which an MNE operates.[359] The ALP applies to each subsidiary of an MNE in isolation and prices transactions between them as if those same transactions were undertaken between unrelated economic actors at market prices. In contrast, China has introduced a unique approach based on the concept of LSA that includes location savings and market premiums, unique to each MNE, in the transfer pricing calculations. The Chinese position is that with more and more companies poised to conduct business as groups, economic activities are more and more likely to take place in the inner circle of MNE groups, and it is, therefore, nearly impossible to take out one piece of a value chain of an MNE group and try to match it to independent comparable transactions.[360] In spite of vocal criticism from other countries, especially the US,[361] the Chinese position was adopted in the updated 2017 OECD Model, evidencing the growing political influences of China on international tax standards.

China has adopted a less vocal but equally assertive position by rejecting the OECD's mandatory binding arbitration under BEPS Action 14. On this issue, China has sided with other developing nations like India by citing sovereignty concerns and capacity issues (*see* discussion in section 4.3.2.2), although it has subsequently agreed to the OECD's Pillar One proposals, including mandatory and binding dispute resolution mechanism.[362] With respect to dispute resolution under tax treaties, China has reported comparatively fewer MAP cases than India since 2016,[363] although there has been a steadily increasing number of tax disputes facing Chinese MNEs, especially in relation to PE challenges with neighbouring Southeast Asian countries (ASEAN).[364] In this respect, China has been one of the few countries to effectively address the recent

357. Xing et al., *supra* n. 350.
358. *Ibid.*
359. Martin Hearson and Wilson Prichard, *China's Challenge to International Tax Rules and the Implications for Global Economic Governance* 94(6) Int'l Aff. 1287, 1297 (2018) DOI: 10.1093/ia/iiy189.
360. Hearson and Prichard, *supra* n. 359, at 1297-1300.
361. *Ibid.*, at 1301.
362. *See* Statement on a Two-Pillar Solution, *supra* n. 5.
363. *See* Govind and Rao, n. 28, at 317 for a comparison of the MAP cases.
364. Diheng Xu, *Regional Tax Coordination between China and ASEAN under the Belt and Road Initiative* (2019) https://papers.ssrn.com/sol3/papers.cfm?abstract_id=3349398 accessed 10 Mar. 2021.

surge in MAP cases by speeding up the rate at which MAP cases are closed,[365] although the stage 2 peer review of BEPS Action 14 issued in October 2021 reveals that China has more work to do in this respect to ensure that cases are resolved within the 24-month deadline.[366]

Based on the above analysis of China's stance with respect to international tax regulations, including MAP, it seems that China has adopted a unique strategy of changing the rules from within the international tax frameworks of the OECD and the UN Tax Committee to benefit its own agenda and interests. It aligns with the developed nations when necessary (e.g., by renegotiating higher WHT rates in its tax treaties with developing countries) and sides with the developing nations at other times (e.g., by rejecting the implementation of the OECD arbitration provisions). China's advocacy of LSAs, in particular, appears likely to carry benefits to China, which will come at the expense of both developed OECD countries and non-OECD developing countries, revealing a novel self-interested approach within the ITR based on its growing economic market powers.

4.3.5 Discourse

As explained in section 3.3.1.5, this study applies a four-step historical discourse analysis approach with the aim of examining the evolving motivations in the ITR in relation to tax treaty dispute resolution.

4.3.5.1 Identify Discursive Event for Study

In order to study the underlying motivations that influenced the development of tax treaty dispute resolution in the ITR, the analysis will focus on the conferences held by the League of Nations and the OECD. It is through such international negotiations for developing the OECD Model that the provisions of the MAP were drafted.

4.3.5.2 Select the Texts for Study

The analysis will focus on the evolving drafts of the OECD Model and, more specifically, the formulation of MAP provisions from the point of their development in the 1920s. Since the UN Model was developed in the 1980s only and basically follows the OECD Model provisions, they will not form part of this analysis except in the post-BEPS period when some divergence was noted.

365. *See* Deloitte, Global Transfer Pricing Alert 2017-012 (6 Apr. 2017) www2.deloitte.com/content/dam/Deloitte/global/Documents/Tax/dttl-tax-global-transfer-pricing-alert-17-012-6-april-2017.pdf accessed 20 Feb. 2023. *See also* Govind and Rao, *supra* n. 28, at 317.

366. *See* EY, *OECD releases People's Republic of China Stage 2 peer review report on implementation of Action 14 minimum standard* (27 Oct. 2021) https://taxnews.ey.com/news/2021-1960-oecd-releases-peoples-republic-of-china-stage-2-peer-review-report-on-implementation-of-action-14-minimum-standard accessed 20 May 2022.

4.3.5.3 *Choose Specific Points in Time for Studying the Evolution of the Identified Texts*

The MAP provisions are studied at four different points in time, starting with their formulation in the 1927 League of Nations Report drafted by a group of technical experts on double taxation and tax evasion (1927 League of Nations Report).[367] Next, the 1963 Draft Double Taxation Convention on Income and Capital that produced Article 25 on MAP (1963 Draft OECD Model) will be studied.[368] The 2008 OECD Model Tax Convention on Income and Capital will also be studied as it added the first provision on arbitration (2008 OECD Model) to the existing MAP.[369] Finally, the 2017 updates in the OECD and UN Models (post-BEPS MAP updates) that reflect the impact of BEPS initiatives on dispute resolution will be examined.

4.3.5.4 *Analyse Content at Specific Points in Time to Uncover Patterns/Tensions*

The guiding questions at each of these four points in time will include: What is the geographical composition of the decision-making group and their views? Which mechanisms are specified under the MAP provisions? The aim is to understand how the views of the decision-makers are reflected in the treaty by analysing how the changing circumstances and composition of the decision-making group of country representatives have influenced the evolution of tax treaty dispute resolution along the timeline mentioned in section 4.3.5.3 above.

4.3.5.4.1 *The 1927 League of Nations Report*

4.3.5.4.1.1 Dispute Resolution Proposal and Group Composition

Following recommendations of the International Chamber of Commerce in the early 1920s that double taxation issues were hindering the flow of trade and investments for the reconstruction of the global economy in the post-WWI era and, in particular, the economy of the allied countries,[370] a Technical Experts Committee was set up within the League of Nations to work on a treaty-based dispute resolution mechanism. The resulting 1925 resolutions referred to a procedure that seeks an amicable settlement to a dispute between two or more of the contracting states through a technical body regarding the interpretation or application of the treaty before it is brought before the

367. League of Nations, *Report Presented by the Committee of Technical Experts on Double Taxation and Tax Evasion*, Doc. C.216.M.85.1927 II (Geneva April 1927) (League of Nations Report 1927).
368. *OECD Draft Double Taxation Convention on Income and Capital 1963* (OECD Publishing 1963).
369. *OECD Model Tax Convention on Income and on Capital 2008* (OECD Publishing 2008).
370. Bret Wells and Cym H. Lowell, *Income Tax Treaty Policy in the 21st Century: Residence vs. Source* 5(1) Colum. J. Tax L. 1, 13 (2013).

Permanent Court of International Justice or any other arbitral tribunal.[371] The resolutions also briefly considered the creation of an international organisation to settle application or interpretation issues in the case of an international tax treaty, suggesting that the organisation could undertake the duties of conciliation or voluntary and advisory arbitration between states without being given any judicial powers.[372] The procedure being recommended at the time was similar to those being included in the international conventions at the time, with the necessary modifications.[373]

The 1927 League of Nations Report represents the first attempt by the League of Nations to develop a treaty-based dispute resolution mechanism to tackle ramping double taxation and tax evasion issues. In order to prepare the draft convention in the 1927 Report, the Technical Experts Committee that worked on the prior 1925 resolutions was subsequently expanded from a group of seven government experts (from Belgium, Czechoslovakia, France, Italy, The Netherlands, Switzerland and the UK) to also include delegates from non-European countries including Argentina, Germany, Japan, Poland and the US.[374] The expanded group of negotiating countries constituted the Tax Experts Committee.

4.3.5.4.1.2 Dispute Resolution Text Adopted

Given the proposed bilateral nature of the draft treaty, the dispute resolution provision in the 1927 Report was agreed as follows:[375] First, states would attempt to settle the issue bilaterally, and if that fails, then it would be possible to seek an amicable settlement by submitting the dispute to a technical body appointed by the Council of League of Nations to obtain an advisory opinion. The advisory opinion may be considered final if both contracting states agree so prior to the opening of the procedure. In the absence of such agreement between the contracting states, they may choose instead to have recourse to any arbitral or judicial procedure, including reference to the Permanent Court of International Justice, if the matters are within the competence of that Court. The creation of an international organisation to undertake conciliation or advisory arbitration was dropped, given the bilateral mechanics of the tax treaty.

For deciding whether the convention should be multilateral (single treaty) or bilateral, the Tax Experts Committee working on the 1927 Report expressed that 'in the matter of double taxation in particular, the fiscal systems of the various countries are so fundamentally different that it seems at present practically impossible to draft a collective convention, unless it were worded in such general terms as to be of no

371. League of Nations Report 1927, *supra* n. 367, at 6.
372. League of Nations, *Double Taxation and Tax Evasion Document F.212* 30 (Geneva February 1925) (League of Nations Report 1925).
373. *Ibid.* Examples of procedures include the Convention for the Simplification of Customs Formalities signed in Geneva in November 1923 (Art. 22), the Convention on the Freedom of Communications and Transit signed in Barcelona in 1921 (Art. 13) and the Statute on the International Regime of Railways signed in Geneva in 1924 (Art. 35).
374. League of Nations Report 1927, *supra* n. 367 at 6.
375. *Ibid.*, at 12.

practical value' and '... there is no reason to delay the putting into force of bilateral convention which would immediately satisfy the legitimate interests of the taxpayers as well as those of the contracting States'.[376]

The draft MAP provision, as laid out in the 1927 Report, thus created a first level of settlement of a dispute as regards the interpretation or application of the provisions of a tax treaty by agreement between states. Further, this provision created a flexible framework where states that cannot mutually resolve a dispute may either obtain a final advisory opinion through a mandatory expert determination process[377] or obtain a non-binding expert opinion in order to aid them in resolving the dispute or may even have recourse to any other judicial or arbitral procedure. It is interesting to note that such a flexible framework was recommended even though it was a bilateral treaty. The aim was to resolve the tax disputes in a swift and effective manner for the benefit of both the contracting states and the taxpayer to encourage cross-border trade.

4.3.5.4.2 The 1963 Draft OECD Model

4.3.5.4.2.1 Context of the Negotiations

The draft treaty proposed in the 1927 Report was subsequently endorsed in October 1928 as a useful basis of discussion for the preparation of model texts by the governments of 27 countries that constituted the League of Nations.[378] A series of regional conferences were held at The Hague in April 1940 and Mexico City in June 1940 and July 1943,[379] resulting in the 1943 Mexico Model Convention that was updated in the 1946 London Model. These two Models were essentially similar in that both Models followed the principle that income might be taxed in a country when it has its source therein, except for a few differences in the London Model that reflected clauses from actual negotiated tax treaties (e.g., the UK-US treaty concluded after the 1943 conference).[380] One of the key differences was attributing the right to tax certain types of passive income, including interest, dividends, royalties, annuities and private pensions, to the country of residence of the taxpayer,[381] creating the source-residence principle on which the subsequent DTT regime was built.

376. *Ibid.*, at 8.
377. Harm Mark Pit, *Arbitration under the OECD Model Convention: Follow-Up under Double Tax Conventions – An Evaluation* 42(6-7) Intertax 445 (2014) DOI: 10.54648/taxi2014043.
378. League of Nations, *Report presented by the General Meeting of Government Experts on Double Taxation and Tax Evasion*, Doc. C.562.M.178.1928.II (Geneva October 1928) (League of Nations Report 1928).
379. The conference shifted from The Hague to Mexico as the Chairman of the Sub-Committee settled in Mexico following the bombing of Rotterdam on 10 May 1940 during WWII that broke out in September 1939. The conference included representatives of Canada, the US, Mexico, and other Latin American countries, such as Argentina, Bolivia, Chile, Colombia, Cuba, Ecuador, Uruguay, Guatemala, Mexico, Peru, and Venezuela. *See* Mitchell B. Carroll, *International Tax Law: Benefits for American Enterprises and Enterprises Abroad* 2(4) Int'l Lawyer 692, 707-708 (1968).
380. League of Nations, *London and Mexico Model Tax Conventions: Commentaries and Text*, Doc. C88.M.88.1946.II.A 9 (Geneva November 1946) (League of Nations Report 1946).
381. *Ibid.*

4.3.5.4.2.2 Updated Text of MAP Provision

In relation to the MAP provision proposed in the 1927 and 1928 draft treaties, there are some major changes that occurred as it was redrafted into the Mexico and London Models.[382] The redrafted article devised a procedure for triggering the dispute resolution process if the taxpayer had proof that the action of the tax administration from one of the contracting states had resulted in double taxation. In such cases, the taxpayer had the right to lodge a claim with the tax administration in his/her state of domicile or of which he/she is a national. If the claim was justified, the competent authorities of the contracting states would consult with each other with a view to reaching an agreement to resolve the double taxation.

It is interesting to note that the reference to an amicable settlement process for obtaining an advisory opinion from a technical body appointed by the League of Nations was removed, effectively restricting the decision-making process at the competent authority level. The responsibility for triggering the MAP procedure was also delegated to the actual taxpayer who was suffering from double taxation. The decision to adopt this simplified MAP process that is administered by the competent authorities only once the MAP request is lodged by the taxpayer may be due to the experiences of treaty negotiators and competent authorities during actual negotiations and dispute resolution processes that took place involving especially Canada and the US that were the most active international trading partners at the time.

Although the draft provisions in the Mexico and London Models underwent several other changes when the Committee of Fiscal Affairs (CFA) of the OECD (formerly the Organisation for European Economic Co-operation/OEEC) took over the work of developing a DTT after the dissolution of the League of Nations in 1946, the dispute resolution mechanism proposed in the Mexico and London Models was adopted essentially in the same format under Article 25 of the 1963 draft OECD Model. Article 25 in the 1963 OECD Model thus outlined the basic structure of the MAP.

4.3.5.4.3 The 2008 OECD Model

4.3.5.4.3.1 Role of the OECD Leading up to the 2008 Model

The MAP Article in the 1963 draft of the OECD Model remained largely unchanged throughout the subsequent updated versions of the OECD Model, although discussions regarding an arbitration procedure emerged in 1984 at the OECD level in connection with Transfer Pricing Regulations.[383] Although the OECD recognised some shortcomings of the MAP during the 1984 discussions (one of the main obstacles being that MAP did not require a final resolution of cases), it concluded at the time that the MAP was

382. *Ibid.*, at 68-69. *See* Art. 16 of the Mexico Model and Art. 17 of the London Model.
383. OECD, Transfer Pricing and Multinational Enterprises: Three taxation issues paras 34-40 (OECD Publishing 1984) (OECD three taxation issues).

'an efficient and flexible instrument in the interpretation, application and development of double taxation agreements and a suitable means for the elimination of both juridical and economic double taxation'.[384] The OECD also weighed the difficulties of using arbitration (e.g., sovereignty issues and legislative and procedural problems) against its limited benefits and further concluded that there was no urgent need for introducing an arbitration procedure as the MAP provided a solution in the majority of the MAP cases.[385] In spite of some changes to the Commentaries on Article 25 for considering supplemental dispute resolution methods such as seeking an advisory opinion from an impartial expert or the possibility of the parties obtaining an 'opinion' on the 'correct understanding' of a treaty provision from the CFA,[386] no changes were made to Article 25 until a mandatory arbitration mechanism was introduced in the 2008 Model.

4.3.5.4.3.2 Introduction of the Mandatory Arbitration Clause

The mandatory arbitration mechanism was finalised as the most appropriate supplementary dispute resolution mechanism following the 2004 progress report issued by a joint working group (JWG) at the OECD on how to improve the international tax dispute resolution.[387] As pointed out by both private sector representatives and the JWG delegates, the inability of the MAP process to provide for all steps possible to facilitate a final resolution of issues arising under treaties was one of the principal obstacles to ensuring an effective MAP.[388] It caused taxpayers to hesitate in making the resource commitment to enter into the MAP and likewise provided no incentive to competent authorities to take all steps necessary to ensure a speedy resolution of the issues involved.

The proposed mandatory arbitration mechanism introduced in 2008 clearly reflected: (1) the need of taxpayers for more certainty in regard to MAP resolution; (2) the fact that optional mechanisms included traditionally in certain tax treaties (in 2004, optional arbitration was included in 60 tax treaties) had proved useless for finalising unresolved issues as no cases were brought to arbitration; and (3) the need for a mechanism that would be supplemental to the current MAP and not replace MAP.[389] This move towards mandatory arbitration thus not only evidenced the increasing powers of the taxpayers, especially the MNEs,[390] on their governments for providing more certainty in matters of international tax dispute resolution (by ensuring a final resolution of MAP cases) but also represented an apt incentive for governments to

384. *Ibid.*
385. *Ibid.*, at paras 54-55, 59-60 and 125(c).
386. Paragraphs 46-47 OECD Model: Commentary on Article 25.
387. OECD, *Improving the Process for Resolving International Tax Disputes* (2004) www.oecd.org/ctp/treaties/33629447.pdf accessed 10 Mar. 2021. The JWG consisted of delegates from OECD Member States' tax authorities involved in the OECD Working Party 1 (Double Tax Conventions) and Working Party 6 (Transfer Pricing).
388. *Ibid.*, at 9.
389. OECD, *Improving the resolution of tax treaty disputes* (Report adopted by the Committee on Fiscal Affairs on 30 Jan. 2007) para. 12 (OECD Publishing 2007).
390. *See* Hearson and Tucker, *supra* n. 65.

ensure that the MAP process is conducted efficiently in order to avoid the necessity of triggering the arbitration procedure in the first place.[391]

4.3.5.4.4 *Post-BEPS MAP Updates*

Although there have been no substantive changes to the basic structure of Article 25 of the OECD and UN Models since the arbitration clause was introduced in 2008, the BEPS Action Plan launched in 2015 has emphasised the need for greater international cooperation and increased efficiency and effectiveness within international tax dispute resolution (through the insistence of MNEs for increased certainty and the growing needs of governments to collect tax revenue). In fact, there are some positive results from the implementation of the mandatory rules under the BEPS Action 14 minimum standard in terms of streamlining and standardising the MAP processes across IF jurisdictions, as reflected in the OECD MAP statistics.[392] The optional implementation of the mandatory arbitration mechanism offered under the MLI in BEPS Action 15,[393] on the other hand, reveals a more mitigated effect and a lack of consensus among the IF countries, as only 31 out of the 141 IF countries had opted to implement arbitration as of June 2022.[394] The points of disagreement come mostly from developing countries, as discussed in section 4.3.2.2.

Despite such mitigated effect, BEPS Action 14 provisions have brought two significant changes to tax treaty dispute resolution. It has provided a framework for all IF jurisdictions to implement a standardised MAP mechanism to ensure that both competent authorities and taxpayers across the IF may have recourse to more uniform rules. It has also opened the tax treaty dispute resolution debate to the developing countries across the IF. Through the BEPS steering group and the IF, non-OECD representatives may have a platform to participate in the decision-making process. The ongoing negotiations regarding the adoption of a mandatory and binding dispute resolution under Pillar One (discussed in section 2.3.1.3) presents yet another opportunity to develop an effective multilateral dispute resolution system for the benefit of both developed, developing and emerging countries across the ITR.

4.3.5.5 *Implications in This Study*

From its earliest formulation in the 1927 League of Nations Report to the 2008 OECD Model, the development of the MAP provision has followed a mostly pragmatic approach with the aim of providing a simple and swift resolution of the tax issue

391. *See* OECD, *Proposals for improving mechanisms for the resolution of tax treaty disputes: Public Discussion Draft 2006* 4 (OECD Publishing 2006).
392. *See* Table I.1 in Appendix I which shows the increasing number of MAP cases being opened and closed on an annual basis in the period 2016-2020, based on the OECD MAP Statistics.
393. OECD, *Multilateral Convention to Implement Tax treaty Related Measures to Prevent Base Erosion and Profit Shifting* arts 18-26 (2016) https://www.oecd.org/tax/beps/multilateral-convention-to-implement-tax-treaty-related-measures-to-prevent-BEPS.pdf accessed 20 Mar. 2022.
394. *See supra* n. 27.

between the relevant competent authorities. The bilateral structure of the MAP, as emphasised in the analysis of the 1927 Report, was a practical consequence of the bilateral nature of the tax treaty and did not represent a major point of discussion as the other substantive provisions of the bilateral treaty, e.g., source-residence principle. It was decided mostly based on the practical experience of treaty negotiators and tax officials, most of whom came from similar developed country backgrounds.

However, the implementation of the BEPS Project and the IF in 2016 has created a new negotiation framework that includes developing and emerging countries on equal footing with the developed countries. Although the aim of BEPS Action 14 was focused on improving the procedural effectiveness of the MAP through more standardisation across the DTT network, the multilateral negotiations across the BEPS steering group and the IF have also introduced a new element to the debate on tax treaties and the resolution of tax treaty disputes based on equitable processes and outcomes (through tax fairness).[395] This is evidenced through the ongoing reform of the allocation of taxing rights across the ITR under Pillar One. Although such negotiations may be subject to power dynamics through economic, technical and political disparities, the current debates across the ITR have opened doors for more equitable solutions for all parties through compromise to achieve universal consensus across the IF.

4.4 CONCLUSIONS

Action situations 1, 2 and 3 in the ITR include the MAP, UN arbitration and OECD arbitration mechanisms, respectively. The analysis of the working rules shows that although the implementation of the mandatory rules under BEPS Action 14 may have succeeded in standardising and streamlining the MAP process for both the taxpayers and the competent authorities, there are significant capacity issues threatening the MAP mechanism due to the boom in the number and complexity of MAP cases across jurisdictions. More than 80% of the disputes are resolved at the MAP level. However, for those disputes that are not resolved within a reasonable timeline, the UN arbitration is clearly unable to satisfy the needs of taxpayers in terms of guaranteeing a resolution to their case because it is the competent authorities that decide whether to initiate arbitration. As for the mandatory OECD arbitration mechanism, although it guarantees a resolution of the MAP case, it has not been adopted by the majority of the jurisdictions across the IF, thus creating uneven and unequal treatment for both taxpayers and competent authorities across the ITR.

The analysis of the community attributes reveals that taxpayers and the competent authorities that aim to resolve tax disputes on behalf of taxpayers do not necessarily share similar interests and preferences. This may generate mistrust among taxpayers in the dispute resolution process. Despite arguments relating to the surrender of tax sovereignty by competent authorities, the mandatory and binding OECD arbitration addresses such issues within the dispute resolution process by aligning, to

395. *See* remarks of Angel Gurria, Secretary-General of OECD at G20 summit (June 2018) www.oecd.org/tax/g7-fmcbg-fostering-tax-fairness-in-modern-economy-canada-june-2018.htm accessed 1 Apr. 2021.

a greater extent, the interests of the various actors. However, developing and emerging countries insist that such binding procedures would emphasise their institutional disadvantages (e.g., lack of technical expertise and negotiating skills) vis-à-vis their more developed counterparts, resulting in potentially inequitable solutions.

The analysis of the physical conditions focuses on the economic rationale of various functions associated with the dispute resolution mechanisms. It reveals that the functions reflect mostly private good characteristics in that the costs and benefits are limited to the specific user with no major contribution within the wider field of international tax governance except for the compliance-monitoring function of BEPS Action 14 associated with MAP that may constitute a public good. Thus, in its current structure, the tax treaty dispute resolution system is not conducive to cooperative endeavours among all IF jurisdictions as the processes and outcomes tend to benefit mostly users from developed countries compared to developing countries.

In relation to the politico-economic context, the creation of the IF in June 2016 has revolutionised the political landscape within the ITR by giving a voice to developing and emerging countries alongside the original group of developed countries. Although developing countries, especially low-income countries, may not be fully utilising this platform yet, China, as one of the most powerful emerging economies of the original BRICS bloc of nations, comprising Brazil, Russia, India, China, and South Africa, has been increasingly assertive in applying its own international tax rules across the IF (*see,* for example, China's push for the LSA concept in transfer pricing rules in the 2017 OECD Model despite loud criticisms from the US). This shows that there may be a significant opportunity for China to lead the next generation of changes within international tax rules and thus may be an important ally for other developing and emerging countries, although China may also follow its own agenda when it comes to international tax governance.

The discourse analysis examines the evolving text and the negotiating structures of the dispute resolution provisions at different points in their development. The analysis reveals that despite the growing user base of MAP mechanisms since the creation of the MAP in the 1920s (developing countries have increasingly used MAP), negotiators have applied a mostly pragmatic approach to improve the effectiveness of the procedure in terms of access to MAP, resolution of MAP cases and implementation of the MAP agreements. The biggest challenge, however, now is to ensure that the treatment under the tax treaty dispute resolution system applies equally to all IF users, given the differences in terms of resources and skills between developing and developed countries.

CHAPTER 5
Mapping Institutional Arrangements in the LOSC

Chapter 5 applies Step A of the methodology to the LOSC's dispute resolution system. The mapping process reveals at least six different mechanisms in the LOSC, grouped under three categories: diplomatic negotiations, conciliation and adjudicative procedures (judicial settlement and arbitration). The mechanisms are interlinked to form a flexible yet mandatory legal framework for resolving disputes under the LOSC. While priority is given to negotiations, arbitration or judicial settlement through the ITLOS or the ICJ may be imposed if no diplomatic agreement is reached. The LOSC's system thus offers an effective, predictable and equitable dispute resolution process through uniform and binding application for all treaty members. As for the politico-economic context, the influence of China as a maritime superpower, especially in the SCS, has undeniable consequences on the evolution of the provisions of the LOSC. The discourse analysis shows that the main motivation for the LOSC's dispute resolution system was an equitable and peaceful resolution of maritime disputes.

5.1 INTRODUCTION

In line with the methodology outlined in section 3.3.1, this chapter applies Step A of the pIAD analysis to the LOSC's dispute settlement system. The aim is to map out the institutional arrangements that underpin the LOSC's system using the pIAD framework to allow for a more accurate comparison with the tax treaty dispute resolution system in the ITR, given the different institutional contexts. As with the ITR in Chapter 4, the analysis is also applied in two parts. Part 1 maps out the relevant action situations under the LOSC's dispute resolution system based on the extent to which third parties can legitimately participate in determining the settlement of the dispute and, conversely, the extent to which the parties can reject a settlement proposed by the third party (i.e., whether the decision is legally binding). As shown in section 5.2 and Figure 6, the analysis reveals three separately linked action situations under the LOSC's system, consisting of diplomatic negotiations, conciliation and adjudicative procedures, respectively.

Part 2 of the analysis is addressed in section 5.3 by mapping out the internal components of each of the three relevant action situations identified in the LOSC's dispute resolution system as identified in Part 1. It analyses the five sets of contextual variables (working rules, community attributes, physical conditions, politico-economic context and discourses) that influence dispute resolution processes under the LOSC's system.

5.2 IDENTIFYING ACTION SITUATIONS

The dispute settlement mechanism of the LOSC largely builds on the commitments enshrined in the UN Charter, requiring states to settle international disputes by such means and in such a manner that international peace and security are not endangered.[396] To ensure the implementation of the provisions of the LOSC, as well as the resolution of disputes about its interpretation or application through peaceful means, a comprehensive dispute resolution system was devised in Part XV of the LOSC that consists of three main sections, as well as supplementary annexes addressing the various dispute resolution bodies referenced in the LOSC.[397]

Section 1 of Part XV of the Convention prescribes various consensual means to reach an amicable settlement of the dispute, including diplomatic negotiations, mediation or conciliation. The consensual means are not legally binding on the parties, and if no amicable settlement is reached using any such diplomatic means, then disputant parties would be subject to the adjudicative dispute resolution mechanisms under section 2 of Part XV. These include recourse to the ITLOS as elaborated under Annex VI of the LOSC (the ITLOS Statute), the ICJ, an arbitral tribunal created under Annex VII, or the creation of a special arbitral tribunal under Annex VIII for specific disputes.[398] Although the ICJ is available as a forum for states to resolve disputes under the LOSC, the workings of the ICJ are prescribed separately in the ICJ Statute.[399] The final section 3 of Part XV deals with the various limitations and exceptions allowed with respect to the application of compulsory procedures under section 2.

Based on the classification of dispute resolution mechanisms in the extent to which third parties can legitimately participate in determining the settlement and the extent to which a decision is legally binding, this study classifies the LOSC's mechanisms under three separately linked action situations for analysis. On this basis,

396. *Charter of the United Nations* (adopted 26 Jun. 1945, entered into force 24 Oct. 1945) 1 UNTS XVI Art. 33(1) (UN Charter).
397. *See* Arts 279-299 LOSC and Annexes V-VIII, dealing with conciliation, ITLOS, arbitral tribunal, and special arbitral tribunal respectively.
398. Article 287 LOSC.
399. *See supra* n. 112.

the diplomatic means in section 1 of Part XV will be categorised under two separate action situations. Action situation 1 will focus on the diplomatic negotiation process involving the concerned States parties only (no third party) as they endeavour to reach an amicable settlement of their dispute. Action situation 2 will focus on the conciliation procedures (compulsory and voluntary conciliation) involving an independent third party in the form of a conciliation commission that assists the concerned States parties in reaching an amicable settlement. Action situations 1 and 2 both constitute procedures that are not legally binding on the disputant parties, meaning that the latter may or may not reach a mutual agreement.

If no agreement is reached under non-binding procedures in action situations 1 or 2, then the disputant parties may be submitted to the compulsory procedures prescribed in section 2 of Part XV that entail a binding third-party settlement. These procedures will be analysed in action situation 3 under judicial settlement (ITLOS or the ICJ) and arbitration (arbitral tribunals under Annexes VII and VIII). The connections among the three action situations are illustrated in Figure 6.

Figure 6 pIAD Analysis of the LOSC's Dispute Resolution System

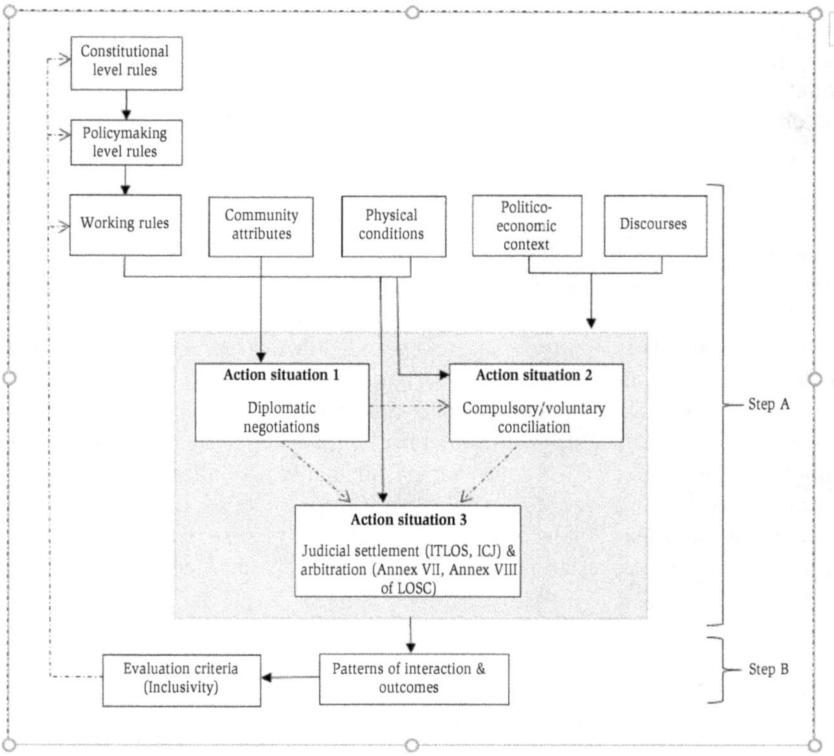

5.3 ANALYSING CONTEXTUAL VARIABLES

Similar to the pIAD analysis applied in the ITR in section 4.3, Part 2 of Step A analyses the working rules, community attributes and physical conditions for each identified action situation; the politico-economic context and relevant discourse will be analysed with respect to the LOSC's dispute resolution system as a whole.

5.3.1 Action Situation 1: Diplomatic Negotiations

Diplomatic negotiations constitute the first step of the dispute resolution process. Given the confidentiality that surrounds diplomatic negotiations, the analysis of the institutional arrangements is limited to the rules of the LOSC and applicable UN Handbooks, such as the UN Handbook on delimitation of maritime boundaries.[400]

5.3.1.1 Working Rules

5.3.1.1.1 Boundary Rules

Boundary rules specify the criteria of the participants within an action situation. Under the inter-state instrument of the LOSC, the disputant parties that take part in diplomatic negotiations comprise States parties to the LOSC, which include states and international organisations.[401] This excludes private individuals and non-State entities.

5.3.1.1.2 Position Rules

Position rules specify the roles and responsibilities that participants may assume within the action situation. In diplomatic negotiations, State negotiators act on behalf of the disputant states that constitute the disputant parties. State negotiators include experts in various fields, representing, to a practicable degree, relevant governmental agencies according to the competencies assigned to them at each of the three stages of negotiations (preparatory, agreement and drafting).[402] The negotiating team is assembled at the preparatory stage and generally includes the head of the delegation, one or more legal advisers, at least one expert on bilateral relations with the country concerned, as well as relevant technical experts responsible for the preparation of the relevant technical report.[403] More specifically, the involvement of a domestic lawyer at the preparatory stage is important to assist with the implementation of the LOSC as a

400. UN Handbook on delimitation on maritime boundaries, *supra* n. 182.
401. Article 1.2 LOSC. The definition includes self-governing associated states and territories entitled to participate in the LOSC under Art. 305 and international organisations entitled to participate in the LOSC under Annex IX.
402. UN Handbook on delimitation on maritime boundaries, *supra* n. 182, at 65.
403. *Ibid.*

matter of domestic Constitutional law.[404] This ensures that each negotiating team has specialist knowledge of the issue at hand when negotiating with the disputant team.

5.3.1.1.3 Information Rules

Information rules control the distribution of information within the action situation. To conduct negotiations, the negotiating team gathers the necessary scientific and historical data along with relevant legislation, as appropriate, at the national level. Information is also gathered, to the extent possible, on the neighbouring coastal state with which the negotiations are to be conducted.[405]

The negotiations under the LOSC are usually conducted in private, especially in light of the potentially sensitive issues that may be related to maritime issues.[406] Any agreement reached is not required to identify the considerations that led the parties to adopt a particular arrangement (cooperation or other) or even the specific methods used to reach a decision.[407] It is noted also that nothing that has been said or done by the negotiators during the negotiations has any bearing on the legal positions of the parties in the subsequent proceedings before a court or tribunal.[408] In this way, negotiations under the LOSC are similar to the exchanges between the competent authorities in the ITR during the MAP.

5.3.1.1.4 Authority Rules

Authority rules specify what a participant in a particular position must, must not or may do at a particular point. State negotiating teams assume various tasks at each stage of the negotiations. At the preparatory stage, the teams may need to perform the following tasks: discuss the state of preparedness for the negotiations; conduct a thorough review of relevant documents; consider the negotiating strategy; identify what additional documents or studies may be needed; summarise known issues about the negotiating position of the neighbouring State; and discuss issues concerning publicity.[409]

At the next stage of negotiating an agreement, the negotiators are bound by the principles of international negotiation that require negotiations to be carried out in good faith, characterised by a spirit of fairness and effectiveness.[410] They are also guided by the objective of the LOSC of reaching an agreement that is perceived by both

404. Dharshini Amaratunga, *Maritime Boundary Delimitation: Building and Preparing a Negotiating Team* 24:1-2 Commonwealth L. Bull. 516, 526 (1998) DOI: 10.1080/03050718.1998.9986500.
405. *See* UN Handbook on delimitation of maritime boundaries, *supra* n. 182, at 67 for a comprehensive list of documentation that may be useful for maritime boundary negotiations.
406. *Ibid.*, at 75.
407. *Ibid.*
408. *Ibid.*, at 74.
409. *Ibid.*, at 66.
410. *See UNGA Res 53/101*, UN Doc. A/RES/53/101 (20 Jan. 1999) on principles and guidelines for international negotiations.

sides as representing an equitable solution.[411] This objective is different from the objective of the competent authorities in the MAP, which is restricted to objectively interpreting the tax provisions.

The third and final stage involves the drafting of the agreement by the negotiators. While there might be cases of agreements concluded without any written documents or cases of a unilateral declaration with binding effect, the agreement is usually concluded as an international agreement in written form and governed by international law.[412] The negotiators may take model clauses for their draft agreement. The designation in itself (treaty, convention, agreement, exchange of letters or notes) has no bearing on the validity of the agreement.[413]

5.3.1.1.5 Aggregation Rules

5.3.1.1.5.1 Applicable Law

Aggregation rules determine how the participants at various positions in an action situation choose among the possible actions available to them based on the applicable law and the administrative framework within which they operate. Negotiators are generally bound by the principles of good faith, which implies that the parties are not allowed to engage in any conduct or activity which is contrary to their objectives of reaching an agreement.[414] Negotiators should thus refer to the LOSC and other international rules, including the law of treaties under the 1969 VCLT, especially the law of treaties regarding third States, as maritime issues may involve several countries connected through their geographic characteristics.[415] More specifically, the LOSC provides the legal basis for negotiating disputes, including negotiations among the States parties. For example, Articles 74 and 83 of the Convention apply to the delimitation of the EEZ and of the continental shelf, respectively, with specific reference to equitable considerations under Article 38 of the ICJ Statute (discussed further in section 5.3.3.1.5).

In addition, negotiators should also refer to their own national (constitutional and other) rules relevant to the negotiations, conclusion and implementation of treaties. National rules usually regulate the rules of State negotiations by specifying the authority competent to initiate the negotiations and to conclude a treaty, the authority

411. *See e.g.*, Arts 74, 83 LOSC. The provisions call in identical general terms for agreement to be reached on the basis of international law in order to achieve 'an equitable solution' in relation to the extensive national zones of the continental shelf and EEZ. Equitable considerations have also been upheld by the ICJ as one of the factors that determine maritime delimitations along with applying the more scientific rule of equidistance as explained in Art. 15 of the LOSC. *See Maritime Delimitation in the Black Sea (Romania v. Ukraine)*, Judgment (3 Feb. 2009) I.C.J. Rep 101 for an application of the three-stage approach to maritime delimitation which proceeds from (i) a provisional equidistance line, then (ii) takes into account relevant circumstances, before (iii) applying a final proportionality test. This is discussed further in s. 5.3.3.1.5.
412. UN Handbook on delimitation of maritime boundaries, *supra* n. 182, at 76.
413. *Ibid.*, at 76.
414. *Ibid.*, at 72.
415. *Ibid.*, at 73.

competent to bind the State definitively, the legal relations between the treaty and juridical acts effected under domestic law, provisions on the conditions governing the application of the treaty under domestic law, etc.[416] When deciding on the form and designation of the resulting agreement, the negotiators may first consider their own constitutional rules on the conclusion and effects of treaties.

5.3.1.1.5.2 Administrative Framework

The rules or tactics used during the negotiation process (including the issuance of full powers and determining at which stage they may be required)[417] are usually discussed among the negotiators prior to the initiation of formal negotiations. At this stage, various contacts can take place between potential parties, such as exploratory talks or soundings, the main purpose of which is to discreetly explore the degree of interest of the other party in negotiations without raising excessive expectations among the public.

Based on the implicit need to achieve an equitable solution, negotiating parties of both states are also encouraged to build trust by staging informal events.[418] With regard to the time devoted to such negotiations, the concept of a reasonable time period is usually determined by political imperatives, although ample time should be assigned to each round. Practice shows that a number of rounds might be held over several months, even years.[419] Given the emphasis on reaching an agreement through diplomatic means, the lengthy negotiation timelines may not necessarily be problematic as long as the negotiating parties are putting in their best efforts. It is important to note that contrary to the MAP, where competent authorities negotiate on behalf of the taxpayer, the negotiators under the LOSC do not act on behalf of a third party, which may explain why the process is less regulated than the MAP (e.g., in terms of timelines).

5.3.1.1.6 Scope Rules

5.3.1.1.6.1 Jurisdiction

Scope rules govern the jurisdiction of the process and the finality of the outcome. Negotiation constitutes the first step for resolving any dispute concerning the interpretation or application of the LOSC[420] after an exchange of views between the disputant parties.[421] Negotiation may be used to address any form of dispute under the LOSC.

416. *Ibid.*
417. *See* UN, *LA41TR/221/Full Powers Guidelines/2010* https://treaties.un.org/doc/source/publications/NV/2010/Full_Powers-2010.pdf accessed 10 Oct. 2021.
418. UN Handbook on delimitation of maritime boundaries, *supra* n. 182, at 76.
419. *Ibid.*
420. Articles 287.1 and 288.1 LOSC.
421. Article 283 LOSC.

5.3.1.1.6.2 Finality of Negotiation Outcomes

If a diplomatic agreement is reached through negotiations, the agreement may be finalised in the form of a treaty, convention, agreement, exchange of letters or notes, depending on the nature of the maritime dispute and will be implemented accordingly.[422] As with any treaty entered into by the UN Member States, the treaty negotiated and concluded under the LOSC will be registered as soon as possible with the UN Secretariat.[423] If no mutually agreed solution is reached, then parties may jointly decide which other means of dispute settlement they will pursue, including adjudicative measures such as judicial settlement or arbitration.

5.3.1.1.7 Payoff Rules

Payoff rules govern how costs and benefits are distributed among the actors in the action situation. Diplomatic negotiations involve State negotiators as the disputant parties. States thus retain autonomy over the rules of the negotiation process (e.g., agreed timelines and procedures), the outcome and its implementation. If the parties cannot reach a mutual agreement, they have the option of simply walking away from the negotiation (depending on the agreed procedure). Arguably, the negotiation process involves the lowest level of risk and political pressure, especially since the process is private and confidential. By favouring compromise and accommodation, negotiators may work toward a freely agreed rather than imposed solution, which is likely to preserve good long-term cooperative relations between the parties. Moreover, negotiations also hold a cost advantage compared to the alternative dispute settlement methods like conciliation or arbitration, where third parties have to be remunerated by the disputant parties (or even the ITLOS or ICJ through annual fees and often hefty legal expenses) – negotiations do not involve payments to any third-party.

However, the diplomatic negotiation process is a political endeavour between states to reach an agreement, and it inevitably involves power imbalances, which may result in less favourable outcomes for the weaker party (usually the developing country if faced with a developed country counterpart). While it may be possible for the wealthy and developed countries to apply extra-legal, political and economic pressures to achieve their goals, the developing countries may find it difficult to impose their own views on equal footing during the negotiations. This may explain the insistence of developing countries to have disputes directed into legal channels where the principle of equality before the law prevails and their overwhelming stake in the establishment and operations of the ITLOS (discussed in section 5.3.3 below).

422. UN Handbook on delimitation of maritime boundaries, *supra* n. 182, at 86.
423. Article 102 UN Charter.

5.3.1.2 *Community Attributes*

The analysis of community attributes focuses on the potential trends among the actors based on their objectives and interests. Although bilateral negotiations may be the preferred method for settling maritime boundary claims,[424] identifying the fact that negotiations are going forward is difficult as states often keep them quiet. At least 16 negotiations were identified from 1994 to 2012, some of which were successful, such as the 2003 Negotiation between Azerbaijan, Kazakhstan and the Russian Federation, the 2004 Negotiation between Australia and New Zealand and the 2008 Mauritius-Seychelles EEZ Delimitation Treaty.[425] In fact, a study focused on dispute resolution mechanisms for settling maritime boundary disputes identified 186 maritime boundary agreements achieved between 1960 and 2008, 76 of which referred to dispute resolution mechanisms, with 56 of these agreements specifying bilateral negotiation as the preferred way to settle future conflicts.[426] According to the authors, such preference is based on the lower costs and increased flexibility of the negotiation process compared to other mechanisms, such as the ITLOS, although there may be a need for more legalistic measures if costs and flexibility are not of concern.

5.3.1.3 *Physical Conditions*

The analysis of physical conditions focuses on the public-private characteristics of the various functions associated with diplomatic negotiations. There are two functions associated with negotiations: (1) dispute resolution and (2) administrative aspect for building international relations.

5.3.1.3.1 Dispute Resolution Function

The dispute resolution function of diplomatic negotiations among State negotiators is excludable as the parties need to mutually agree to engage in negotiations following an exchange of views under the LOSC.[427] It is a private and confidential process between the disputant parties, and costs incurred (e.g., for any cartographic data) are limited to the parties concerned. The process is also subtractable as a negotiating team may not handle multiple negotiations simultaneously. Therefore, the dispute resolution function of diplomatic negotiations exhibits predominantly private goods characteristics (just as the dispute resolution function of the MAP).

424. *See* Olivier Marquais, *Lalive Lecture by Professor Sean Murphy: A Rising Tide: Dispute Settlement under the Law of the Sea* (Geneva 15 Jul. 2015) www.international-arbitration-attorney.com/law-of-the-sea-dispute-settlement-mechanism accessed 11 Jul. 2021. *See also* Aslaug Asgeirsdottir and Martin Steinwand, *Dispute Settlement Mechanisms and Maritime Boundary Settlements* 10(2) Rev. Int'l Org. 119, 121-123 (2015) DOI: 10.1007/s11558-015-9217-9.

425. Marquais, *supra* n. 424.

426. Asgeirsdottir and Steinwand, *supra* n. 424, at 121.

427. Article 283.1 LOSC.

5.3.1.3.2 Administration Function: International Relations Building

Negotiation processes may also provide a strategic opportunity to build or strengthen diplomatic relations among countries by encouraging joint development initiatives. Joint development may be defined as an inter-governmental arrangement of a provisional nature between two or more countries, designed for functional purposes of joint exploration for and/or exploitation of onshore or offshore hydrocarbon resources, and it is especially crucial in areas with overlapping or disputed claims or in areas where countries have not achieved agreement on delimitation, such as in the SCS.[428] China has categorically rejected any other non-consensual means of dispute resolution prescribed under the LOSC (as discussed further in section 5.3.4.3), and instead, the Chinese government has actively engaged in diplomatic negotiations with other coastal states over the joint development of the SCS since 2017. This has resulted in China and the Philippines signing the *Memorandum of Understanding on Cooperation on Oil and Gas Development* in November 2018.

Based on the above analysis, diplomatic negotiations have a wider impact on oceans governance other than resolving disputes. They may help to promote peaceful regional relations and multilateral development incentives that may benefit all states economically and politically, thus displaying intermediate public good characteristics.

5.3.2 Action Situation 2: Compulsory/Voluntary Conciliation

The rules for voluntary and compulsory conciliation are similar, except that in the case of voluntary conciliation, the parties may choose whether to proceed with conciliation in the first place. This depends on the nature of the dispute; in the case of disputes relating to the delimitation of maritime borders, the LOSC prescribes compulsory conciliation for resolving the dispute.[429]

In 2018, the maritime boundary dispute between Timor-Leste and Australia became the first and only instance of a publicly known compulsory conciliation case under the LOSC (Timor Sea conciliation).[430] The conciliation successfully resulted in the 'Treaty on the Timor Sea Maritime Boundary' and the Timor Sea Conciliation Report (TSCR) including the Rules of Procedure (TSCR Rule of Procedure) issued by the conciliation commission were exceptionally published on the website of the Permanent Court of Arbitration (PCA) with the parties' consent.[431] These documents provide much information for analysing the institutional arrangements under a ompulsory conciliation

428. Huaigao Qi, *Joint Development in the South China Sea: China's Incentives and Policy Choices* 8(2) J. Contemp. East Asia Stud. 220, 221 (2019) DOI: 10.1080/24761028.2019.1685427.
429. *See* Arts 297.3 and 298.1 LOSC.
430. Dai Tamada, *The Timor Sea Conciliation: The Unique Mechanism of Dispute Settlement* 31(1) Eur. J. Int'l L. 321, 324 (2020) DOI: 10.1093/ejil/chaa025. It should be recalled that the 1981 Jan Mayen conciliation between Iceland and Norway had been decided on the basis of prior agreement between the disputants and, thus, it pertains to an ad hoc conciliation that is different from compulsory conciliation under the LOSC.
431. Timor Sea Conciliation (*Timor-Leste v. Australia*) (Report and Recommendations of the Compulsory Conciliation Commission between Timor-Leste and Australia on the Timor Sea) (9 May 2018) (TSCR) https://pcacases.com/web/view/132 accessed 10 Jul. 2021. *See also* Annex

process from a practical aspect. This case is also interesting because it was instituted after the two countries failed to reach an agreement regarding maritime boundary delimitation through diplomatic negotiations.[432]

5.3.2.1 Working Rules

5.3.2.1.1 Boundary Rules

The conciliation procedure is a government-government mechanism that only States parties can avail of (those that have ratified the LOSC). These include states and international organisations as defined in the Convention[433] and represented by State negotiators (as discussed in section 5.3.1.1.1).

The conciliation procedure also involves the setting up of a conciliation commission as an independent third party. The conciliators that form part of the commission are persons who enjoy the highest reputation for fairness, competence and integrity.[434] Each commission may also specify additional criteria for the conciliators. For example, the conciliation commission in the Timor Sea conciliation provided for a special procedure pertaining to the 'challenge of a conciliator' for maintaining the credibility, impartiality and independence of the conciliators[435] and required the conciliators to be skilled lawyers and negotiators. As the commission points out in the TSCR, 'effective conciliation requires that a careful mix of diplomatic and legal skills, backgrounds, and approaches be deployed in varying combinations at different stages of the process'.[436]

5.3.2.1.2 Position Rules

The conciliation procedure involves the disputing parties (represented by State negotiators as in diplomatic negotiations) and the conciliators as part of an independent conciliation commission set up specifically for the conciliation case. The conciliation commission consists of five members unless the States parties agree otherwise.[437] Four of the five members of the conciliation commission are nominated by the disputant parties, and the nominated conciliators then jointly appoint the fifth member who will act as the Chairperson of the commission.[438] The conciliators are selected from a pre-approved list of conciliators that is maintained by the UN Secretary-General, and each State party is

8 of the TSCR for the Rules of Procedure (22 Aug. 2016) (TSCR Rules of Procedure) https://pcacases.com/web/sendAttach/2357 accessed 10 Jul. 2021.

432. *See* Clive Schofield and I. Arsana, *The Delimitation of Maritime Boundaries: A Matter of Life or Death for East Timor?* in *East Timor: Beyond Independence* 67-85 (Damien Kingsbury and Michael Leach eds, Melbourne University Press 2007).
433. *See supra* n. 401.
434. Article 2 Annex V LOSC.
435. TSCR Rules of Procedure, *supra* n. 431, at Art. 7(1).
436. TSCR, *supra* n. 431, at para. 294.
437. Article 3 Annex V LOSC.
438. *Ibid.*

allowed to nominate up to four conciliators to the list.[439] Of the two conciliators appointed by each disputant party to the commission, only one may be its national.[440]

5.3.2.1.3 Information Rules

Conciliation proceedings are, in principle, confidential and not public.[441] The confidentiality rule is not provided for in the LOSC but, rather, in the rules of procedure as agreed between the parties. For example, the TSCR Rules of Procedure specify that except for several parts of proceedings that may be made public in consultation with the parties, the conciliation commission, the Registry and the parties 'shall keep confidential all matters relating to the conciliation proceedings'.[442] This practice is also reflected in the United Nations Model Rules for the Conciliation of Dispute between States (UN Conciliation Model).[443]

5.3.2.1.4 Authority Rules

In the voluntary conciliation, the disputant parties, in their role as State negotiators, have the responsibility for initiating the conciliation procedures. The claimant may send a written notification to the other party, which may or may not be accepted by the respondent.[444] If the invitation to conciliation is accepted, then both disputant parties may discuss their respective claims and objections to reach an amicable settlement, assisted by the conciliation commission.

Where a dispute falls within certain specific categories (e.g., a dispute relating to maritime boundary delimitation),[445] either party to the dispute may unilaterally submit the dispute for settlement by conciliation, triggering a compulsory conciliation procedure, as in the Timor Sea conciliation.[446] During the proceedings, the disputant parties will share their claims and objections in the presence of the conciliation

439. Article 2 Annex V LOSC.
440. Article 3 Annex V LOSC.
441. Jean-Pierre Cot, *Expectations Attached to Conciliation Reconsidered*, in *Conciliation in International Law: The OSCE Court of Conciliation and Arbitration* 9 (Christian Tomuschat et al. eds, Brill 2016); *see also* UN, *United Nations Model Rules for the Conciliation of Dispute between States Res 50/50*, UN Doc. A/RES/50/50 Arts 25-26 (29 Jan. 1996) (UN Conciliation Model) https://documents-dds-ny.un.org/doc/UNDOC/GEN/N96/762/31/PDF/N9676231.pdf?OpenElement accessed 21 Jul. 2022.
442. TSCR Rules of Procedure, *supra* n. 431, at Art. 16(7).
443. UN Conciliation Model, *supra* n. 441, at Art. 20(3). In the *Timor Sea* case, although the publication of the Report had not been stipulated in the Rules of Procedure (TSCR para. 61), the commission attempted to balance the need to respect the confidentiality of the proceedings with the need to make known to other states the implications for maritime delimitation that this settlement presents (TSCR para. 60). Consequently, the parties 'made clear their expectation that the Report would be made public' (TSCR note 38).
444. Article 1 Annex V LOSC.
445. *See* Arts 11-14 Annex V LOSC. *See also* Art. 298.1(a) LOSC. The requirement to submit the dispute to conciliation only applies to disputes relating to maritime boundary delimitations or those involving historic bays or titles.
446. *See* Arts 11-12 Annex V LOSC. Such compulsory conciliation was invoked for the first time only in April 2016 by Timor-Leste against Australia in relation to their undelimited maritime boundary.

commission, which will assist with reaching an amicable settlement.[447] If the parties reject the commission's report, they may be required to mutually agree to resolve the dispute using one of the adjudicative mechanisms available under the LOSC (discussed in section 5.3.1.1.3).

The conciliation commission determines the procedure for the conciliation session through a majority vote, with the consent of the disputant parties.[448] The commission may also invite any interested State party to make an oral or written submission of their respective views for setting out the rules of procedure if the disputant parties agree.[449] In the Timor Sea conciliation, in order to establish a flexible and informal approach that would facilitate an amicable settlement of the maritime delimitation dispute, the commission met with the disputant parties separately rather than jointly for developing the rule of procedure that comprised 26 articles[450] while the Annex V of the LOSC contains merely 14 articles in relation to conciliation.

The commission will then hear out the disputant parties, review their claims and objections and make proposals/recommendations accordingly.[451] There are two types of involvement of the commission in the conciliation proceedings: the commission may concentrate on making recommendations, leaving the parties to reach an agreement after the proceedings, or the commission may also assist the parties to reach an agreement during the conciliation process.[452] In the *Timor Sea* case, the commission assisted the parties to reach an agreement during the conciliation process.[453] All decisions and recommendations are made by a majority vote of the five members of the commission,[454] following which it presents its report to the UN Secretary-General within a period of 12 months of its constitution.[455]

5.3.2.1.5 Aggregation Rules

5.3.2.1.5.1 Applicable Law

The choice of applicable rules of conciliation normally depends on a case-by-case basis of each treaty.[456] This means that the commission, along with the parties, may decide

447. Article 6 Annex V LOSC.
448. Article 4 Annex V LOSC.
449. *Ibid. See also* Sienho Yee, *Intervention in an Arbitral Proceeding under Annex VII to the UNCLOS* 14 Chinese J. Int'l L. 79, 83-84 (2015) DOI: 10.1093/chinesejil/jmv010. The approach of third-party intervention in compulsory conciliation is prescribed under para. 3 of the Annex to the 1969 VCLT between states and international organisations or between international organisations in accordance with Art. 66 of that Convention. It also extends to voluntary conciliation under para. 10 of the Annex to the 1986 VCLT.
450. TSCR, *supra* n. 431, at paras 56, 80.
451. Articles 4-6 Annex V LOSC.
452. Tamada, *supra* n. 430, at 326.
453. TSCR, *supra* n. 431, at paras 63-64.
454. Article 4 Annex V LOSC.
455. Article 7 Annex V LOSC.
456. Roberto Lavalle, *Conciliation under the United Nations Convention on the Law of the Sea: A Critical Overview* 2(1) Austrian Rev. Int'l & Eur. L. 25, 29 (1997) DOI: 10.1163/157365197x00024.

the scope of applicable laws to be used for each case. However, there are some rules that may set the legal framework for the conciliation session. For example, in conciliation cases regarding boundary delimitation under the LOSC,[457] the applicable law may include non-LOSC and non-legal factors for reaching an equitable solution.[458] In addition, the commission has to record its conclusions on 'all questions of fact or law',[459] which suggests that the analysis may exceed the strict application of legal rules. Also, it is worth noting that while the ITLOS and the arbitral tribunals have to apply the LOSC and other rules of international law not incompatible with the LOSC, this legal constraint does not apply to conciliation, which again suggests that conciliation can consider factors that are not within the LOSC or international rules per se.[460]

For a more practical example, in the *Timor Sea* case, it is specified that 'the Commission will be guided by principles of objectivity, fairness and justice, giving consideration to, among other things, the rights and obligations of the parties and the circumstances surrounding the dispute, including any previous practices between the parties'.[461] Arguably, principles of 'objectivity, fairness and justice' may contain wider factors that are not limited to the strict application of legal rules.

5.3.2.1.5.2 Administrative Framework

The conciliation procedure involves strict timelines that allow for a swift resolution of the dispute. After the commission submits its report to the UN Secretary-General within a period of 12 months from the start of the conciliation, the report is immediately transmitted to disputant parties for their consideration.[462] The disputant parties have a period of three months to notify the UN Secretary- General of whether they accept or reject the report, following which the session is expired.[463] The conciliation procedure, therefore, lasts over a period of 15 months.

Conciliation procedures may also involve a unique characteristic that allows a separation between the commission's recommendations (i.e., the conclusions) and the background considerations (i.e., the reasons).[464] This separation may encourage parties to use conciliation as it effectively removes any legal responsibility on the part of the parties if the case proceeds to court. This mechanism was, in fact, applied in the Timor Sea conciliation, specifying that 'acceptance by a party of recommendations submitted by the commission in no way implies any admission by it of the considerations of law or of fact which may have inspired the recommendations'.[465]

457. Article 298.1(a) LOSC.
458. Articles 74 and 83 LOSC.
459. Article 7.1 Annex V LOSC.
460. *See* Art. 293.1 LOSC: 'A court or tribunal having jurisdiction under this section [s. 2 of Part XV] shall apply this Convention and other rules of international law not incompatible with this Convention.' As compulsory conciliation is stipulated in s. 3 of Part XV, it is not required to apply the Convention nor international law per se.
461. TSCR Rules of Procedure, *supra* n. 431, at Art. 18(2).
462. Article 7 Annex V LOSC.
463. Article 8 Annex V LOSC.
464. UN Conciliation Model, *supra* n. 441, at Art. 28(2).
465. TSCR Rules of Procedure, *supra* n. 431, at Art. 26(2).

5.3.2.1.6 Scope Rules

5.3.2.1.6.1 Jurisdiction

The scope of the LOSC is fixed in principle on a 'dispute concerning the interpretation or application of this Convention',[466] and the same applies to voluntary conciliation. The scope of compulsory conciliation, on the other hand, is restricted to disputes relating to marine scientific research and fisheries within the EEZ[467] and disputes relating to sea boundary delimitations (under Articles 15, 74 and 83) or involving historic bays or titles where either party has made a declaration to exclude the dispute from adjudication (discussed in section 5.3.3.1.5.2.2 further below).[468]

5.3.2.1.6.2 Finality of Conciliation Outcome

The conciliation report issued by the commission is not legally binding on the parties.[469] If accepted by the parties, the recommendations will be implemented accordingly. If rejected, then the parties must exchange views on whether to proceed to adjudicative procedures under the LOSC or go back to negotiations to resolve the dispute.[470]

5.3.2.1.7 Payoff Rules

Payoff rules determine how costs and benefits are distributed among the actors involved. The fees and expenses for setting up the conciliation commission are borne equally by the disputing parties.[471] The benefits of the conciliation procedure are also shared among the disputing parties as both need to mutually agree on the rules of procedure, thereby giving equal control to both parties. In addition, the parties may also rely on the independent recommendations of the conciliation commission to achieve an equitable solution to their disputes. In situations of power imbalances, the recommendations of the commission may be more beneficial to the weaker party (e.g., a developing country with less negotiation expertise) by helping the latter to assert its own interest and objectives vis-a-via the more powerful party. The *Timor Sea* conciliation case involving Timor-Leste and Australia is a fitting example since Australia had been reluctant to reach an agreement during the preceding negotiation stage.[472]

466. Articles 287.1 and 288.1 LOSC.
467. Articles 297.2(b) and 297.3(b) LOSC.
468. Article 298.1(a)(i) LOSC.
469. Article 7.2 Annex V LOSC.
470. Article 298.1(a)(ii) LOSC.
471. Article 9 Annex V LOSC.
472. *See supra* n. 432.

5.3.2.2 *Community Attributes*

Community attributes examine the potential trends based on the interests and objectives of the various actors. First, the objective of the conciliation procedure is not to settle a dispute by applying law per se but rather to bring the disputant parties to an agreement by way of negotiation and compromise. Even where the choice of applicable rules of conciliation normally depends on a case-by-case basis,[473] the relevant provisions of the Convention allow the consideration of non-LOSC and non-legal factors, which may strengthen the arguments of both parties (as discussed in section 5.3.2.1.5 above). Second, although the rules of procedure are usually devised by an independent conciliation commission, the disputant parties are still afforded much initiative in deciding the applicable rules of the conciliation proceedings along with the conciliators.[474] There is also greater interaction and collaboration between the commission and the parties through discussion on the report, suggestions by the parties, and many occasions of meetings as indicated in the published Rules of Procedure of the *Timor-Leste* case.[475] Thus, the proceedings and the final result of the conciliation are transparent to the disputing parties. Third, since the parties have to share the costs of the conciliation, they are more likely to make maximum efforts to achieve an amicable settlement and accept the final report of the commission. Thus, arguably, conciliation contributes to a levelling of the playing field among the various parties.

Voluntary conciliation has not been in popular usage between disputing states, and presumably, it is because once states have agreed to relinquish control over the process by involving a third party, they would rather have recourse to binding third-party settlement.[476] In addition, so far, there is only one publicly known instance of compulsory conciliation. It is, therefore, unclear whether there have been more compulsory conciliation cases carried out which are not made public or whether the *Timor Sea* case is a unique instance of compulsory conciliation. However, if there is one aspect that the Timor Sea conciliation proceedings make clear is that compulsory conciliation provides an automatic legal basis for dispute resolution for developing countries (i.e., Timor-Leste) to achieve an equitable solution to a disagreement with developed countries (i.e., Australia) that may be reluctant to reach a solution in negotiations or other judicial measures.[477] Thus, this procedure, although it is non-binding, may be useful to developing countries that may have less technical or negotiation expertise compared to more developed economies for achieving an equitable outcome.

473. Lavalle, *supra* n. 456, at 29.
474. Article 4 Annex V LOSC. The procedure is determined by the conciliation commission with the consent of the parties who may submit their views orally or in writing.
475. *See* TSCR Rules of Procedure, *supra* n. 431, at Arts 18 and 20.
476. Ted L. McDorman, *Ocean Dispute Settlement in the Baltic Sea*, in *The Baltic Sea: New Developments in National Policies and International Co-operation* 189, 197 (Renate Platzöder and Philomene Verlaan eds, Martinus Nijhoff Publishers 1996).
477. Tamada, *supra* n. 430, at 324.

5.3.2.3 Physical Conditions

There are two functions associated with conciliation: (1) dispute resolution and (2) administering of the conciliation mechanism.

5.3.2.3.1 Dispute Resolution Function

Conciliation usually involves the disputant parties and the conciliation commission set up specifically to address the dispute at hand, although relevant States parties may be consulted if the disputant parties agree.[478] The confidentiality of the process is determined through the rules of procedure as agreed among the disputant parties and the conciliation commission. In fact, several elements of the only known compulsory conciliation case (i.e., the Rules of Procedure and the Report of the conciliation commission in the *Timor Sea* conciliation case) were made public for States parties and other interested users to learn from.[479] For this reason, the dispute resolution process may be considered to exhibit intermediate public good characteristics despite the fact that the costs are shared by the disputant parties only.

5.3.2.3.2 Administering the Conciliation Procedure

Maritime boundary disputes exist on all continents, and although the figures concerning the total number of maritime boundary disputes may vary across different sources, it is clear that fewer than half of the potential disputes have been agreed so far.[480] Ambiguous and undefined sea borders arguably lead to increased risks of conflict among states over commercial, economic, and security interests[481] (e.g., China's military operations in the SCS discussed in section 5.3.4.2 below). This would suggest that in the interest of maintaining peaceful and cooperative relations, establishing boundary delimitations may not only be desirable but also a necessity. Since compulsory conciliation is the default dispute resolution mechanism for resolving disputes on maritime boundary limitations (if disputant parties have opted for such disputes to be excluded from adjudication),[482] it has a significant role to play in ensuring peaceful resolution of maritime disputes among countries. As such, the administering of compulsory conciliation may be considered an intermediate public good for maintaining peace under the LOSC.

478. *See supra* n. 449.
479. *See supra* n. 431.
480. *See* Andreas Osthagen, *Maritime Boundary Disputes: What Are They and Why Do They Matter?* 120 Marine Pol'y 6 (2020) DOI: 10.1016/j.marpol.2020.104118.
481. Michael Sutherland and Susan Nichols, *Maritime Boundary Delimitation for Ocean Governance,* in *FIG Technical Program Proceedings, XXII FIG International Congress* 7 (Washington DC 2002).
482. *See* Arts 297.3 and 298.1(a) LOSC.

5.3.3 Action Situation 3: Judicial Settlement and Arbitration Mechanisms

Action situation 3 comprises four different types of third-party dispute settlement procedures under the LOSC, including recourse to the ITLOS (explained under Annex VI of the LOSC) and the ICJ that constitute judicial settlement and arbitral tribunals under Annexes VII and VIII of the LOSC that constitute arbitration.[483] Disputant states are subject to such compulsory and legally binding procedures (considering specific exceptions) if they are unable to reach an amicable settlement using the non-binding procedures discussed in action situations 1 and 2.

This section will analyse the influence of the contextual variables on the four different mechanisms that constitute action situation 3. Although the authority of the ICJ is recognised under the LOSC and disputes regarding the law of the sea have been brought before the international court, the ICJ constitutes an external body to the LOSC and is governed separately by the ICJ Statute as 'the principal judicial organ of the United Nations'.[484] For this reason, the working rules of the ICJ will be analysed only in relation to the functioning of the ITLOS to emphasise the differences between the two judicial bodies and their respective contribution to dispute settlement under the LOSC.

It is also worth noting that while the ICJ handled maritime cases before the LOSC was designed, the ITLOS created through the LOSC has administered 29 cases under the LOSC since it started operating in 1996; the PCA has served as registry for 14 arbitration cases under Annex VII and one compulsory conciliation case (Timor Sea conciliation as discussed in section 5.3.2 above).

5.3.3.1 Working Rules

5.3.3.1.1 Boundary Rules

5.3.3.1.1.1 Disputant Parties

5.3.3.1.1.1.1 ITLOS

As discussed in action situations 1 and 2, dispute resolution under the LOSC is a government-government procedure that involves states and international organisations[485] represented by State negotiators. In regard to the functioning of the ITLOS, however, these criteria are expanded to include natural or juridical persons that seek the prompt release of a vessel and its crew when detained by a coastal state, though

483. Judicial settlement and arbitration are two methods included under Art. 33(1) of the UN Charter for the peaceful settlement of international disputes.

484. Article 92 UN Charter.

485. *See supra* n. 401. *For e.g.*, the European Union has appeared as a party in Conservation and Sustainable Exploitation of Swordfish Stocks in the South-Eastern Pacific Ocean *(Chile/European Union)*, ITLOS Case No. 7 (25 Jul. 2021).

they only do so on behalf of the flag State of the detained vessel (and therefore must first receive authorisation from that state).[486]

The ITLOS includes the SDC that exclusively hears disputes between states relating to activities in the seabed 'Area'[487] involving two entities created by the LOSC—the International Seabed Authority (ISA) and the Enterprise.[488] In certain circumstances, natural or juridical persons and prospective contractors may also participate in the SDC proceedings with respect to activities in the Area.[489] Finally, as will be discussed in section 5.3.3.1.6.1 further below, the ITLOS may have jurisdiction to hear cases brought consensually under agreements other than the LOSC, effectively extending access more generally to non-State actors.[490]

5.3.3.1.1.1.2 ICJ

In contrast to the ITLOS, only states may participate in contentious cases before the ICJ (excluding international organisations, non-governmental organisations, transnational corporations, or individuals).[491] Since the UN Charter prescribes that all UN Member States are parties to the ICJ Statute,[492] all 193 UN Member States are parties to the ICJ Statute and thus capable of appearing before the Court in contentious maritime cases.[493]

5.3.3.1.1.1.3 Arbitration under Annexes VII and VIII

The disputant parties in arbitration under Annexes VII and VIII may include States parties to the LOSC as defined by the Convention (i.e., states and international organisations). In addition, given that Annex VII arbitration is the default dispute resolution mechanism under the LOSC (discussed in section 5.3.3.1.5.2.1 further below), it may also be used by states that have not ratified the LOSC (i.e., non-States parties).[494]

5.3.3.1.1.2 Members of Tribunal/Court/Arbitration Panel

5.3.3.1.1.2.1 ITLOS/ICJ

For both the ITLOS and the ICJ, the judges are elected or appointed based on their independence, character, and expertise, in addition to representing the principle legal

486. Article 292.2 LOSC.
487. Articles 15 and 17 Annex VI LOSC.
488. *See* s. 4 of Part IX of the LOSC. The International Seabed Authority administers the resources of the deep seabed area and the Enterprise will serve as the Authority's mining operator.
489. Article 187 LOSC.
490. *See* Arts 20 and 21 Annex VI LOSC and Arts 291(2) and 308 LOSC. *See also* Alan E. Boyle, *Dispute Settlement and the Law of the Sea Convention: Problems of Fragmentation and Jurisdiction* 46 Int'l & Comp. L.Q. 37, 47-54 (1997) DOI: 10.1017/s0020589300060103.
491. Article 34(1) ICJ Statute.
492. Articles 92-93(1) UN Charter.
493. States that are not UN members are able to adhere to the court's statute if they so choose. *See* Art. 35(2) ICJ Statute.
494. Article 13 Annex VII LOSC.

systems of the world.[495] Under the ITLOS, the judges are elected from a preapproved list of persons nominated by each State party to the LOSC.[496] Two persons of the same nationality would not be elected or appointed to serve on the judicial body simultaneously, and the selection processes are designed to ensure broad geographic representation.[497] While judges or members are precluded from sitting in a case in which they were previously involved as counsel, they are not prevented from sitting in a case simply because it involves a state of the judge's or member's nationality.[498] Moreover, if a state has no judge of its nationality on the ICJ or the ITLOS, then it may appoint a judge ad hoc for the purposes of that case.[499]

The judges of the ITLOS are paid international civil servants; they receive no pay and take no instructions from governments, and they cannot be recalled or dismissed by the governments of their nationalities.[500] However, a Tribunal judge may not participate in the decision of any case in which he has previously taken part as agent, counsel or advocate for one of the parties, or as a member of a national or international court or tribunal, or in any other capacity.[501] The judge is also precluded from exercising any political or administrative function or having any financial interests in any enterprise concerned with the exploitation of the sea or the seabed.[502] If the judge no longer fulfils the required conditions in the unanimous opinion of the other members, he/she may be relieved of its functions by the President of the Tribunal.[503]

5.3.3.1.1.2.2 Arbitration panel

The potential judges under Annexes VII and VIII are persons experienced in maritime affairs and who enjoy the highest reputation for fairness, competence and integrity.[504] In the case of the special arbitral tribunal under Annex VIII, the judges are also expected to have specific competence in the legal, scientific or technical aspects of each of the four fields included within the jurisdiction of the special arbitral tribunal. These include (1) fisheries; (2) protection and preservation of the marine environment; (3) marine scientific research; and (4) navigation, including pollution from vessels and by dumping.[505]

---

495. Article 2 Annex VI LOSC.
496. Article 4 Annex VI LOSC. Each State Party may nominate not more than two persons having the qualifications prescribed in Art. 2 of this Annex.
497. Articles 3-4 Annex VI LOSC.
498. Article 17 Annex VI LOSC.
499. Articles 17.2 and 17.3 Annex VI LOSC; *see also* Art. 31(2) and (3) ICJ Statute.
500. Sean D. Murphy, *International Judicial Bodies for Resolving Disputes Between States*, in *The Oxford Handbook of International Adjudication* 185 (Cesare P.R. Romano, Karen J. Alter and Yuval Shany eds, Oxford University Press 2013).
501. Article 8 Annex VI LOSC.
502. Article 7 Annex VI LOSC.
503. Article 9 Annex VI LOSC.
504. *See* Art. 2 Annex VII LOSC and Art. 2 Annex VIII LOSC.
505. Article 2 Annex VIII LOSC.

5.3.3.1.2 Position Rules

5.3.3.1.2.1 Applicants/Respondents

The disputant parties assume the role of applicants and respondents (as opposed to State negotiators in action situations 1 and 2) when lodging cases with the ITLOS, the ICJ and the arbitral tribunals. Legally binding decisions are imposed on the disputant parties.

5.3.3.1.2.2 Adjudicating Third Party

5.3.3.1.2.2.1 ITLOS/ICJ

The judges or members who sit on these judicial bodies (ITLOS or ICJ) are not permanent, but they are elected or appointed for relatively long terms, during which they participate in a large number of cases, again reinforcing a culture of continuity as well as reliance on past decision-making.[506] The ITLOS comprises 21 judges elected by secret ballot of the States parties to the LOSC for renewable, nine-year terms, with seven judges of the ITLOS being elected every three years to allow continuity of membership even amidst change, with no term limits.[507] The ITLOS judges may sit in special chambers,[508] including the SDC that hears disputes between states as to the interpretation or application of Part XI of the LOSC (i.e., activities in the seabed Area).[509] The SDC consists of 11 of the ITLOS judges selected by majority vote, but when hearing a dispute among states, it may form an ad hoc chamber composed of three of its members.[510]

The ICJ consists of 15 respected jurists from across the globe, also elected for nine-year terms by the UN General Assembly and UN Security Council.[511] Like the ITLOS, the ICJ terms are staggered so that one-third of the judges' terms expire every three years.[512] The Court may also sit in special chambers if requested by the parties appearing before it.[513]

5.3.3.1.2.2.2 Arbitration panel

The arbitral tribunal constituted under both Annexes VII and VIII comprises five judges that are appointed by the parties to the dispute,[514] preferably from a preapproved list of arbitrators and experts that was drawn up by the States parties of the LOSC.[515] Under

506. *See* Erik Voeten, *The Politics of International Judicial Appointments* 9(2) Chi. J. Int'l L. 387 (2009).
507. Article 5 Annex VI LOSC.
508. Article 188.1 LOSC.
509. Articles 15 and 17 Annex VI LOSC.
510. Article 36 Annex VI LOSC.
511. Articles 3-4 and 13 ICJ Statute.
512. Article 13 ICJ Statute.
513. Murphy, *supra* n. 500, at 185.
514. Article 3(a) Annex VII LOSC and Art. 3(a) Annex VIII LOSC.
515. Article 2 Annex VII LOSC and Art. 2 Annex VIII LOSC.

Annex VII, the preapproved list comprises four potential arbitrators nominated by each State party and maintained by the Secretary-General of the UN.[516] Each disputant party will appoint one arbitrator (who may be its national), preferably from the list and will agree jointly on the appointment of the remaining three members of the arbitration tribunal, also from the preapproved list, although the three arbitrators jointly appointed will be nationals of third States unless the parties otherwise agree.[517] If the parties are unable to reach an agreement on the appointment of one or more of the members of the arbitral tribunal within a set time period, the remaining appointment or appointments will be made by the President of the ITLOS within a two-week period from the request made by one of the disputant parties.[518]

Under Annex VIII special arbitration, there are four different lists of experts drawn up and maintained by specific international organisations in four areas of competence: (1) fisheries, (2) protection and preservation of the marine environment, (3) marine scientific research, and (4) navigation, including pollution from vessels and by dumping and maintained by the appropriate organisation concerned with each function.[519] Each State party is required to nominate two experts to each of the four lists.[520] To constitute the special arbitral tribunal, each disputant party will appoint two experts from the appropriate lists, one of whom may be its national.[521] The disputant parties will then jointly appoint the President of the special arbitral tribunal, who will be the national of a third State. If the parties are unable to reach an agreement, then the UN Secretary-General will make the necessary appointment within a specific time period from the receipt of the request by one of the parties to the dispute.[522] If there are more than two disputant parties, they may jointly agree on the appointment of the arbitrators if they have similar interests and if not, then they may each appoint one arbitrator to the panel.[523]

5.3.3.1.3 Information Rules

5.3.3.1.3.1 ITLOS/ICJ

The hearings through the ITLOS and the ICJ are generally public unless the Tribunal or Court decides otherwise or unless the parties demand that the public not be

516. Article 2 Annex VII LOSC.
517. Article 3 Annex VII LOSC.
518. Article 3(e) Annex VII LOSC.
519. *See* Art. 2 Annex VIII LOSC. The lists are maintained by the Food and Agriculture Organisation of the United Nations in the field of fisheries; the United Nations Environment Programme in the field of protection and preservation of the marine environment, the Intergovernmental Oceanographic Commission in the field of marine scientific research and the International Maritime Organisation in the field of navigation, including pollution from vessels and by dumping.
520. Article 2.3 Annex VIII LOSC.
521. Article 3 Annex VIII LOSC.
522. Article 3(e) Annex VIII LOSC.
523. Article 3(g)-(h) Annex VIII LOSC.

admitted.[524] In addition, both the ITLOS and the ICJ confer general consent to third-party intervention in proceedings.[525] The ITLOS also includes on its website as one of the key tasks of its Registrar to ensure that information regarding the 'Tribunal and its activities is accessible to Governments, the highest national courts of justice, professional and learned societies, legal faculties and schools of law and public information media.'[526] The relevant disclosures are published in the adjudicating body's official gazette, a specific series created for disclosures of a certain type,[527] and published and archived on the website of the institution.

5.3.3.1.3.2 Arbitration

As opposed to judicial settlement through the ITLOS or the ICJ, there is no legal requirement for the arbitration procedures under Annexes VII and VIII to be public. Pursuant to the parties' agreement, the rules of procedure established on a case-by-case basis by the arbitral tribunal will usually set out the extent to which basic information about the case, including procedural orders, rules of procedure, written pleadings and transcripts of oral hearings may be published.[528] In fact, the PCA has administered all but one of the Annex VII arbitrations to date, and the relevant proceedings are published on the PCA's website, suggesting that, in practice, arbitral tribunals tend to be public mechanisms.[529]

5.3.3.1.4 Authority Rules

5.3.3.1.4.1 Disputing Parties

5.3.3.1.4.1.1 ITLOS/ICJ

Any one of the disputant parties may institute proceedings with the ITLOS or the ICJ either by notification of a special agreement or by written application addressed to the Registrar (i.e., the UN Secretary-General) that will in turn notify all States Parties or ICJ members, respectively.[530] The parties may also request for disputes to be heard by special chambers of the ITLOS (e.g., the SDC)[531] or the ICJ[532] for dealing with particular categories of cases; for example, labour cases and cases relating to transit and

524. Article 26 Annex VI LOSC; Art. 46 ICJ Statute.
525. *See* Arts 31-32 Annex VI LOSC; Arts 62-63 ICJ Statute. *See also* Yee, *supra* n. 449, at 84.
526. *See* ITLOS Registry www.itlos.org/en/main/the-registry/the-registrar/ accessed 25 Jul. 2021.
527. *See e.g.*, the ICJ Reports www.icj-cij.org/en/annual-reports accessed 20 Mar. 2022. For a list of ITLOS cases, *see* www.itlos.org/en/main/cases/list-of-cases/ accessed 20 Jul. 2021.
528. *See e.g.*, Rules of Procedure of Arbitral Tribunal Constituted under Annex VII of the LOSC for The South China Sea Arbitration (*The Republic of the Philippines v. The People's Republic of China)*, PCA Case No. 2013-19 Art. 16 (27 Aug. 2013) (Rules of Procedure of The South China Sea Arbitration).
529. *See* list of LOSC Annex VII cases administered under the PCA: https://pca-cpa.org/en/services/arbitration-services/unclos/ accessed 18 Oct. 2021.
530. *See* Art. 24 Annex VI LOSC; Art. 40 ICJ Statute.
531. Article 15 Annex VI LOSC.
532. Articles 26 and 29 ICJ Statute.

communications may be heard at the ICJ. A disputant party may unilaterally lodge a case with the ITLOS or the ICJ without the explicit consent of the other dispute party.[533]

The disputant parties submit written pleadings containing detailed statements of fact and law, followed by oral proceedings.[534] The written proceedings may vary in duration depending on the complexity of the case and whether the disputant parties request long time limits and extensions of the time limits fixed. The length of the oral proceedings also depends on the parties, which may explain the long duration of a pending case.[535] The disputant parties are generally represented in their role as applicant and respondent by an agent or counsel.[536]

5.3.3.1.4.1.2 Arbitration

Any one of the disputant parties may institute arbitral proceedings either under Annex VII (covering all provisions of the Convention) or Annex VIII (regarding specific provisions of the Convention) by sending a written notification directly to the other party or parties to the dispute.[537] In contrast to the judicial mechanisms under ITLOS or ICJ, the disputant parties are also responsible for appointing the arbitrators of the arbitral tribunal (as discussed in section 5.3.3.1.2.2.2 above).

Although the arbitration decision will be rendered through a majority vote of the five-member arbitration panel under both Annexes VII and VIII, the disputant parties may also participate in the arbitration session in accordance with their law to facilitate the work of the arbitral tribunal by providing the relevant documents and information and even assisting the arbitral tribunal with gathering the necessary evidence from witnesses or experts as the case relates.[538] Compared to the ITLOS or the ICJ, the disputant parties thus have more control over the dispute resolution process in arbitration.

5.3.3.1.4.2 Adjudicating Third Party

5.3.3.1.4.2.1 ITLOS/ICJ

The ITLOS will make orders for the conduct of the case, decide the form and time in which each party must conclude its arguments, and make all arrangements connected with the taking of evidence.[539] The members present will decide all questions through a majority vote, and the President will have a casting vote in the event of an equality of votes.[540] The Tribunal may also form special chambers, composed of three or more

533. Article 286 LOSC; Art. 53 ICJ Statute.
534. *See* Art. 24 Annex VI LOSC; Art. 43 ICJ Statute.
535. *See* Art. 27 Annex VI LOSC; Art. 43 ICJ Statute. *See also* UN Handbook on delimitation of maritime boundaries, *supra* n. 182, at 98.
536. *See* ITLOS, *A guide to proceedings before the International Tribunal for the Law of the Sea* 20 (2016) (ITLOS Guide) www.itlos.org/fileadmin/itlos/documents/guide/1605-22024_Itlos_Guide_En.pdf accessed 20 Mar. 2022. *See also* Art. 42 ICJ Statute.
537. Article 1 Annex VII LOSC; Art. 1 Annex VIII LOSC.
538. Article 6 Annex VII LOSC; Art. 6 Annex VIII LOSC.
539. Article 27 Annex VI LOSC.
540. Article 29 Annex VI LOSC.

of its elected members, as it considers necessary for dealing with particular categories of disputes.[541] The Tribunal will also form annually a chamber composed of five of its elected members, which may hear and determine disputes by summary procedure to speed up the deliberations.[542] There is a similar process at the ICJ for deciding the conduct of the case and the deliberation of the judges.[543]

5.3.3.1.4.2.2 Arbitration

The five-member arbitration panel constituted under Annex VII or Annex VIII determines its own procedure with the approval of the disputant parties, ensuring that each party has a full opportunity to be heard and to present its case.[544] The rules of procedure will provide for the seat of the arbitration but may also provide that hearings may be held in other locations.[545] Under both annexes, decisions of the arbitral tribunal will be taken by a majority vote of its members and in the event of an equality of votes, the President will have a casting vote.[546]

5.3.3.1.5 Aggregation Rules

5.3.3.1.5.1 Applicable Law

5.3.3.1.5.1.1 ITLOS/ICJ

Both the ITLOS and the ICJ apply the Convention and other rules of international law to resolve a dispute under the LOSC's dispute settlement mechanism.[547] These may include customary international law, general principles of law and judicial decisions, and the teachings of the 'most highly qualified publicists of the various nations.[548] With the consent of the parties, the case may also be decided according to what is reasonable and fair on the basis (*ex aequo et bono*), which would exceed the strict application of existing rules of international law.[549]

In practice, the ICJ has not used the *ex aequo et bono* provision so far, focusing instead on the general principles of law, the equitable principles of international law or interpreting existing law in an equitable manner as discussed in the 1969 ICJ ruling in the *North Sea Continental Shelf* case.[550] In the latter case dealing with boundary delimitations of the continental shelf, the ICJ emphasised notions of equity by taking

541. Articles 13 and 38 Annex VI LOSC.
542. Article 15 Annex VI LOSC.
543. *See* Arts 48-58 ICJ Statute.
544. Article 5 Annex VII LOSC; Art. 5 Annex VIII LOSC.
545. The PCA at The Hague administered all but one of the UNCLOS Annex VII arbitrations to date. *See supra* n. 529 for the list of Annex VII arbitration cases and rules of procedure on the PCA website.
546. Article 8 Annex VII LOSC; Art. 4 Annex VIII LOSC.
547. Article 293.1 LOSC; Art. 38(1) ICJ Statute.
548. Article 38(1) ICJ Statute.
549. Article 293.2 LOSC; Art. 38(2) ICJ Statute.
550. North Sea Continental Shelf *(Germany v. Netherlands)*, Judgment, 20 Feb. 1969, ICJ Reports 1 (1969); *see also* The International Court of Justice: Handbook (ICJ Handbook) 98 www.icj-cij.org/public/files/publications/handbook-of-the-court-en.pdf accessed 29 Mar. 2022.

into account all relevant circumstances, including historical, political, economic or strategic considerations (i.e., non-legal factors). These included the appurtenance of the shelf to the countries in front of whose coastlines it lies (natural prolongation), the unity of any deposits, and the need for a reasonable degree of proportionality between the length of the respective coastlines and the extent of the shelf appertaining to the states concerned.[551] It is noted, however, that the ICJ's subsequent ruling on establishing maritime borders in the *Black Sea* (2009) requires an equidistant line to be calculated before considering other relevant circumstances that may influence the position of that line. This evolution within case law shows the potential power of the ICJ (and even the ITLOS) in shaping international law (discussed further in section 5.3.3.3.2.1).

5.3.3.1.5.1.2 Arbitration

The Annexes VII and VIII tribunals also apply the rules laid down in the LOSC and other rules of international law not incompatible with the Convention,[552] although the rules of procedure decided by the panel and the disputant parties may specify additional sources of law. In fact, the Chagos[553] and SCS[554] Awards are significant in the way in which they applied the provisions of the LOSC that referentially incorporate other international legal norms into the LOSC.[555] These include provisions of international agreements and generally accepted international rules and standards developed by other bodies such as the International Maritime Organization.[556] Such practice further strengthens the case law issued through arbitration under the law of the sea regime.

5.3.3.1.5.2 Administrative Framework

5.3.3.1.5.2.1 Choice of adjudicative procedure and default mechanism

States parties to the LOSC are free to declare which of the four available modes of adjudication (ITLOS, ICJ, Annexes VII and VIII arbitration) they wish to apply when they ratify or accede to the Convention or at any time thereafter (subject to the exceptions discussed below).[557] The adjudication procedure would apply if no amicable settlement is reached. If the disputant parties have both declared the same

551. *See* Lapidoth, *supra* n. 92, at 142.
552. *See* Art. 293.1 LOSC: 'A court or tribunal having jurisdiction under this section [s. 2] shall apply this Convention and other rules of international law not incompatible with this Convention.' Arbitration under Annexes VII and VIII are included in s. 2 of Part XV of the Convention.
553. Chagos Marine Protected Area Arbitration *(Mauritius v. United Kingdom)*, Awards (2015) (Chagos Award) https://pca-cpa.org/en/cases/11/ accessed 20 Mar. 2021.
554. The South China Sea Arbitration *(The Republic of Philippines v. The People's Republic of China)*, Merits (2016) (South China Sea Arbitration) https://pcacases.com/web/sendAttach/2086 accessed 20 Jul. 2021.
555. Øystein Jensen and Nigel Bankes, *Compulsory and Binding Dispute Resolution under the United Nations Convention on the Law of the Sea: Introduction* 48 (3-4) Ocean Dev. & Int'l L. 209, 214 (2017).
556. *Ibid.*, at 214. *See e.g.*, the reference to the 1995 UN Fish Stock Agreement in the Chagos Award, *supra* n. 553, at paras 253-256.
557. *See* Art. 287 LOSC.

adjudicative procedure, then that procedure would apply unless the parties agree otherwise.[558] For example, the ITLOS or the ICJ may be used when the two disputing states have both selected either the ITLOS or the ICJ or decide ad hoc to avail themselves of those mechanisms.

If the disputant parties made different declarations or none at all under Article 287 of the LOSC, then the dispute will be submitted to arbitration in accordance with Annex VII as the default procedure.[559] Since Annex VII arbitration may be triggered unilaterally by any disputant party,[560] and the absence or failure of the other party to defend its position does not constitute a bar to the proceedings,[561] the arbitral tribunal may proceed to issue a final legally binding decision, even in the absence of one disputant party. In practice, however, both parties have to be politically willing to implement the decision rendered, failing which, no further sanctions may be taken under the LOSC. *See*, for example, the 2016 arbitration case between the Philippines and China, where China did not attend any of the proceedings but also rejected the ruling that was largely favourable to the Philippines (discussion in section 5.3.4.2 below).[562]

5.3.3.1.5.2.2 Exceptions to application of judicial settlement or arbitration

Some categories of disputes may be excluded from adjudication procedures (i.e., judicial settlement and arbitration).[563] There are three automatic exceptions expressly mentioned under Article 297, which include, for example, disputes related to the marine conservation measures or fishing rights within the EEZ, in which case, disputant parties are required to reach a diplomatic agreement through compulsory conciliation.[564] The general exceptions under Article 297 were originally drafted to restrict the application of adjudication procedures in disputes that involve coastal states' exercise of their sovereign rights or jurisdiction.[565] Unless a dispute falls within these three exceptions, it would be submitted to adjudication, as confirmed through the arbitral tribunal's ruling in the 2015 Chagos Award.[566]

States may also opt to exclude, by a declaration in writing, any of the adjudicative procedures with respect to certain specific disputes under Article 298. These include (i) disputes relating to sea boundaries, historic bays or titles;[567] (ii) disputes concerning military activities and law enforcement activities concerning marine scientific research or fisheries in the EEZ;[568] and (iii) disputes in respect of which the Security Council of

558. Article 287.4 LOSC.
559. Article 287.3 and 287.5 LOSC.
560. Article 1 Annex VII.
561. Article 9 Annex VII.
562. *See* South China Sea Arbitration, *supra* n. 554.
563. Articles 297-298 LOSC.
564. *See* Art. 297.3(b) LOSC.
565. Churchill and Lowe, *supra* n. 17, at 455.
566. Chagos Award, *supra* n. 553, at paras 307-14 and 317. The ruling extended the scope for the exercise of adjudication in cases that were not expressly mentioned in Art. 297(1).
567. Article 298.1(a) LOSC.
568. Article 298.1(b) LOSC.

the UN is exercising functions assigned to it by the UN Charter.[569] If one of the disputant parties has made such a declaration under Article 298 regarding maritime border delimitation, it would have to accept submission to compulsory conciliation under Annex V at the request of the other disputant party.[570] If no agreement is reached through conciliation, then the parties would have to agree on a different forum to settle the disputes.[571]

Arguably, such exclusionary clauses reflect a compromise among the negotiating states to achieve universal acceptance.[572] If there were no such provisions, countries might hesitate to ratify the LOSC based on the notion that certain outcomes of exerting sovereign rights, 'especially those concerning the exercise of discretion, should not be subject to challenge in any form of adjudication'.[573] Thus, rather than allowing all disputes of interpretation and application of the Convention to be submitted to adjudication, the LOSC's system was designed to protect the primary interests at stake for each issue area.[574] However, the LOSC requires disputant parties that have elected to apply such exclusions to resolve any outstanding disputes through diplomatic means, including negotiation or conciliation, to ensure some form of resolution to all maritime disputes.

5.3.3.1.5.2.3 Mechanism of last resort

The LOSC gives full freedom to the disputant parties to settle a dispute in any peaceful manner of their choosing.[575] If no agreement is reached through a mechanism of their own choice, then the LOSC dispute resolution provisions would apply to seek a resolution of the dispute.[576] In addition, where a general, regional or bilateral agreement exists for submitting a dispute to a procedure entailing binding decisions, such procedure should be applied instead of the LOSC's dispute settlement mechanisms.[577] This means that if the States parties are not willing to follow the LOSC dispute settlement procedures, it can be avoided by an agreement that they made ahead as a precaution. Thus, it can be argued that even without being invoked, the LOSC may play a strategic role in reinforcing diplomatic ties among states by encouraging the creation of bilateral or regional agreements or treaties. In this way, the LOSC is an instrument to be applied as a last resort for resolving disputes.

569. Article 298.1(c) LOSC.
570. Article 298.1(a)(i) LOSC.
571. Article 298.1(a)(i) and (ii) LOSC.
572. John G. Merrills, *International Dispute Settlement* 182 (Cambridge University Press 2017).
573. *Ibid*. For example, Art. 297(2) prescribes that marine scientific research and fishery disputes are supposed to be submitted to conciliation under Annex V. Since they are primarily a matter for bilateral negotiation, they should thus be left at this scale. The optional exceptions under Art. 298 in regard to sea boundary delimitations, military activities and matters involving the UN Security Council also reflect the sensitive issues that states may rather deal with using diplomatic means.
574. Natalie Klein, *Dispute Settlement in the UN Convention on the Law of the Sea* 27 (Cambridge University Press 2009).
575. Article 280 LOSC.
576. Article 281 LOSC.
577. Article 282 LOSC.

5.3.3.1.6 Scope Rules

5.3.3.1.6.1 Jurisdiction

5.3.3.1.6.1.1 ITLOS/ICJ

The jurisdiction of the ITLOS comprises all disputes and all applications submitted to it in accordance with the LOSC and all matters specifically provided for in any other agreement which confers jurisdiction on the Tribunal.[578] In this respect, the website of the ITLOS provides a non-exhaustive list of 16 multilateral agreements and 8 bilateral agreements that confer jurisdiction on the Tribunal.[579] An example includes the advisory opinion delivered by the ITLOS to the Sub-Regional Fisheries Commission (SRFC) on 2 April 2015 on a series of questions related to the fishing activities of the Member States of the SRFC under the Convention on the Determination of the Minimal Conditions for Access and Exploitation of Marine Resources within the Maritime Areas under Jurisdiction of the Member States of the SRFC (MCA Convention).[580] The Tribunal established that it had advisory jurisdiction to assess matters that fall under the framework of the MCA Convention based on the wordings of Article 21 of Annex VI of the LOSC that extends the Tribunal's jurisdiction to 'all matters specially provided for in any other agreement which confers jurisdiction on the Tribunal' and not only to disputes. Conversely, the SDC under the ITLOS may only hear disputes relating to activities in the seabed Area as specified in Article 14 of Annex VI of the LOSC.

The ICJ, however, constitutes the highest court in the world. As such, it has both general and universal jurisdiction, which means that it may entertain any question of international law. The ICJ shares jurisdiction with the ITLOS for deciding on cases concerning 'pure' maritime delimitation issues, such as the 2009 case *Maritime Delimitation in the Black Sea* and the more recent 2021 case *Maritime Delimitation in the Indian Ocean*.[581] However, the ICJ may also decide on cases where the question of territorial title is anterior to the issue of maritime delimitation, such as Sovereignty over *Pedra Branca/Pulau Batu Puteh, Middle Rocks and South Ledge (Malaysia/Singapore)* in 2008 and *Territorial and Maritime Dispute (Nicaragua v. Columbia)* in 2012.[582] These questions are beyond the sovereignty of the ITLOS. In any case, the ITLOS and the ICJ both refer to each other's judgments and awards to ensure consistency under international law and the law of the sea, thus countering criticisms of fragmentation

578. Articles 21 and 22 Annex VI LOSC.
579. *See* ITLOS www.itlos.org/en/main/jurisdiction/international-agreements-conferring-jurisdiction-on-the-tribunal/ accessed 20 Feb. 2022.
580. *See Request for an Advisory Opinion submitted by the Sub-Regional Fisheries Commission* Case No. 21 (SRFC), www.itlos.org/en/main/cases/list-of-cases/case-no-21/. accessed 20 Mar. 2022. The SRFC is a regional fisheries organisation composed of seven Member States: Cabo Verde, the Gambia, Guinea, Guinea-Bissau, Mauritania, Senegal and Sierra Leone.
581. *Maritime Delimitation in the Black Sea (Romania v. Ukraine)* ICJ Reports 61 (2009); *Maritime Delimitation in the Indian Ocean* (*Somalia v. Kenya*) ICJ Reports 206 (2021).
582. Bernardo Sepulveda Amor, *The International Court of Justice and the Law of the Sea* (2012) www.corteidh.or.cr/tablas/r29686.pdf accessed 30 Mar. 2022.

under international law.[583] It is also noted that the ITLOS or the ICJ may only have jurisdiction if both disputant parties have made the same declaration under Article 287 or if they mutually agree to use either forum (as discussed in section 5.3.3.1.5.2.1 above).

5.3.3.1.6.1.2 Arbitration

The jurisdiction of the arbitral tribunal under Annex VII comprises all disputes and applications submitted under the LOSC. In contrast, the special arbitral tribunal constituted under Annex VIII is limited to carrying out an inquiry for establishing the facts giving rise to disputes relating to (l) fisheries, (2) protection and preservation of the marine environment, (3) marine scientific research, or (4) navigation, including pollution from vessels and by dumping.[584]

5.3.3.1.6.2 Finality of Outcomes

5.3.3.1.6.2.1 ITLOS/ICJ

Any decision rendered by the ITLOS or the ICJ will be final and will have to be complied with by all the parties to the dispute, although any such decision will be binding on the parties only.[585] The LOSC, however, does not compel enforcement of ITLOS decisions through national courts, except with respect to disputes relating to the deep seabed. For those disputes, any LOSC DSB decision concerning 'the rights and obligations of the Authority and of the contractor shall be enforceable in the territory of each State Party'[586] and decisions of the SDC are 'enforceable in the territories of the States parties in the same manner as judgments or orders of the highest court of the State party in whose territory the enforcement is sought'.[587]

Although the doctrine of precedent does not apply in international law, the Court or Tribunal may often cite its previous rulings or those of its predecessor to maintain a certain consistency in its decisions (international judges under the LOSC also refer to the past decisions of the ICJ).[588] It may also decide to depart from a line of reasoning adopted in a previous case, although it would only do so on serious grounds, such as subsequent developments in international law.[589] An example would be the calculation

583. *See* Judge Jin-Hyun Paik, *Statement at the 30th Annual Informal Meeting of Legal Advisers in New York* (29 Oct. 2019) www.itlos.org/fileadmin/itlos/documents/statements_of_president/paik/20191029_Paik_UN_Judicial_dialogue_en.pdf accessed 3 Jul. 2022; Judge Joan E. Donoghue, *Speech at the United Nations General Assembly* (29 Apr. 2022) www.icj-cij.org/public/files/press-releases/0/000-20220429-STA-01-00-EN.pdf accessed 3 Jul. 2022.
584. Article 5.1 Annex VIII LOSC.
585. Article 296 LOSC; Arts 59-60 ICJ Statute.
586. Article 21.2 Annex III LOSC.
587. Article 39 Annex VI LOSC.
588. *See* Shabtai Rosenne, *The Law and Practice of the International Court* 612 (vol. 2, A W Sijthoff 1965); Boleslaw A. Boczek, *International Law: A Dictionary* xxii (Scarecrow Press 2005); Gilbert Guillaume, *The Use of Precedence by International Judges and Arbitrators* 2(1) J. Int'l Disp. Settlement 5 (2011).
589. ICJ Handbook, *supra* n. 550, at 77.

of maritime boundary delimitation through evolving ICJ case law, as discussed in section 5.3.3.3.2.1 further below.

5.3.3.1.6.2.2 Arbitration

The award of the arbitral tribunal under Annex VII will be confined to the subject-matter of the dispute (i.e., it has no precedential value) and will be legally binding on the parties,[590] while the special arbitral tribunal under Annex VIII may also establish a finding of facts that will be considered as conclusive (binding) between the parties.[591] Additionally, under Annex VIII, the special arbitral tribunal may be requested to formulate non-binding recommendations for further review by the disputant parties.[592] Any controversy which may arise between the parties to the dispute regarding the interpretation or manner of implementation of the award maybe submitted by either party for decision to the arbitral tribunal which made the award or to another court or tribunal by agreement of all the parties to the dispute.[593]

5.3.3.1.7 Payoff Rules

Payoff rules determine how costs and benefits are distributed across an action situation. Under the judicial mechanisms of the ITLOS and the ICJ, judges are remunerated by the States parties and the specific parties to the dispute do not have to compensate them when bringing a case to the Tribunal or Court.[594] However, the disputant parties are required to bear the cost of presenting their arguments at the Tribunal or Court (advocates' fees, production of their written pleadings, agent fees, etc.),[595] raising the costs associated with such judicial settlement procedures.

Other constraints, such as the inability to select judges or exercise control on the decision and proceedings or the long resolution times (usually between 4 and 15 years),[596] may also make recourse to international courts less attractive, especially for low-income countries. However, the public nature of judicial settlement through such reputed international courts, in terms of process and publication of decisions, may focus much global political attention on specific issues. This represents a crucial aspect for developing countries, especially for exercising pressure on more advanced countries that may be reluctant to implement decisions that are not in their favour. An example is the UK's reluctance to implement decisions issued by the ICJ, the ITLOS and the arbitral tribunal under Annex VII that deny the UK's claim of sovereignty on the Chagos archipelago in favour of Mauritius.[597]

590. Articles 10-11 Annex VII LOSC.
591. Article 5(2) Annex VIII LOSC.
592. Article 5(3) Annex VIII LOSC.
593. Article 12 Annex VII LOSC; Art. 4 Annex VIII LOSC.
594. Article 18 Annex VI LOSC; Art. 32 ICJ Statute.
595. Article 34 Annex VI LOSC; ICJ Handbook, *supra* n. 550, at 32, 46.
596. *See* list of ICJ cases: www.icj-cij.org/en/list-of-all-cases accessed 18 Oct. 2021.
597. *See* Library of Congress, *International Tribunal for the Law of the Sea Confirms Sovereignty of Mauritius over Chagos Archipelago* (23 Feb. 2021) www.loc.gov/item/global-legal-monitor/

In relation to arbitration, the costs of the arbitral tribunals set up under both Annexes VII and VIII, including the remuneration of the judges, are generally shared equally by the parties to the dispute.[598] Despite such out-of-pocket costs for the parties, arbitration under Annex VII (no Annex VIII tribunal has been instituted so far)[599] may provide several benefits, including confidentiality of procedures and decisions, control over the selection of judges and over the rules of procedure (the rules are decided by the arbitral tribunal in consultation with the dispute parties). In addition, all eight arbitration cases administered by the PCA for which an award was rendered so far were completed within a period of six years, with 4 of them under three years.[600] This is relatively fast in comparison to judicial settlement procedures.

5.3.3.2 Community Attributes

Community attributes, in this context, refer to the norms and potential trends among actors using adjudication measures under the LOSC. Although negotiation remains the most popular means of settling international disputes peacefully,[601] international adjudication continues to occupy a prominent place in the world,[602] and the LOSC system is no exception. As of 31 July 2019, 168 countries had become parties to the LOSC by the process of ratification, accession or succession.[603] Out of these 168 countries, 63 countries in total have made definitive declarations under Article 287 of the Convention for choosing one of the four available dispute settlement forums (*see* Table II.1 in Appendix II); 39 countries chose the ITLOS as the preferred procedure while only 21 countries chose the ICJ, although some overlap is noted as several countries have indicated both the ITLOS and the ICJ (and even arbitration) as equally preferred procedures.[604] For the remaining 105 States parties that have not made a specific declaration under Article 287, arbitration under Annex VII applies as the default mechanism for settling disputes unless they mutually agree on a different forum.[605] Accordingly, both the ITLOS and arbitration under Annex VII may play increasingly significant roles in the future.

2021-02-23/international-international-tribunal-for-the-law-of-the-sea-confirms-sovereignty-of-mauritius-over-chagos-archipelago/ accessed 30 Mar. 2022.

598. Article 7 Annex VII LOSC; Art. 4 Annex VIII LOSC.
599. Robin Churchill, *Compulsory Dispute Settlement under the United Nations Convention on the Law of the Sea – How Has It Operated? Pt. 1* (9 Jun. 2016) www.jus.uio.no/pluricourts/english/blog/guests/2016-06-09-churchill-unclos-pt-1.html accessed 20 Jul. 2021.
600. *See supra* n. 529 for the list of LOSC Annex VII cases administered under the PCA.
601. *See* Marquais, *supra* n. 424.
602. Eric A. Posner and John C. Yoo, *A Theory of International Adjudication*, U. Chi. L. & Econ., Olin Working Paper No. 206 (2004) DOI: 10.2139/ssrn.507003; Eric A. Posner and John C. Yoo, *Judicial Independence in International Tribunals* 93 Cal. L. Rev. 1 (2005).
603. *See* UN Division for Ocean Affairs and the Law of the sea (DOALOS) www.un.org/Depts/los/index.htm accessed 31 Jul. 2021.
604. *Ibid.* Table II.1 in Appendix II summarises the declarations made by the States parties under Art. 287.
605. Article 287.3 LOSC.

Interestingly, 25 of the 39 countries that chose the ITLOS under Article 287 are developing/emerging countries.[606] This may not be much of a surprise since developing countries are the ones that pushed for the establishment of the ITLOS during the UNCLOS III negotiations in the late 1970s. This was a consequence of their discontent towards the ICJ following its judgment on the South West African cases lodged in 1962 by Ethiopia and Liberia against British-ruled South Africa for violating its obligations under the mandate system.[607]

An analysis of the number of cases lodged through these various mechanisms also reveals an increasing preference for the ITLOS among developing countries based on the fact that 24 of the 29 cases in the docket of the ITLOS (which started operating in 1996) involve developing countries.[608] It should be mentioned, however, that the ITLOS has sole jurisdiction over prompt release cases, which may explain the high number of cases lodged with the ITLOS. The ICJ, on the other hand, in the period 1945 to 2019, had adjudicated 28 out of a total of 150 contentious cases that dealt with the law of the sea matters.[609] These results suggest that law of the sea disputes are increasingly being handled by the ITLOS rather than the ICJ, although the ICJ remains a leading source of case law and precedents for such maritime disputes, as discussed in section 5.3.3.3.2.1 below.

With respect to arbitration, there are 14 arbitration cases under Annex VII that have been administered by the PCA to date.[610] Since no information was available regarding any Annex VIII arbitration case, this study assumes that no Annex VIII proceeding has been instituted so far (if there was any, it was not made public). As the default dispute resolution mechanism under the LOSC, arbitration under Annex VII

606. In this thesis, developing/emerging countries are those that are not included on the list of developed economies according to the UN country classification in the World Economic Situation and Prospects (WESP) Report. *See* Table II.2 in Appendix II for a list of developed countries. Table II.1 in Appendix II lists 25 developing/emerging countries including Algeria, Angola, Argentina, Bangladesh, Belarus, Cabo Verde, Chile, Cuba, Democratic Republic of Congo, Ecuador, Fiji, Madagascar, Mexico, Montenegro, Oman, Panama, Russian Federation, Saint Vincent, Timor-Leste, Togo, Trinidad & Tobago, Tunisia, Ukraine, United Republic of Tanzania and Uruguay.

607. *See* Andronico O. Adede, *Settlement of Disputes Arising under the Law of the Sea Convention* 69 AJIL 798, 818 (1975) DOI: 10.2307/2200624. The mandate system was established by the League of Nations in the aftermath of WWI for ex-enemy territories to be governed by individual states for promoting the material and moral well-being and social progress of the inhabitants and report periodically to the League. *See also* Rosalyn Higgins, *The International Court and Southwest Africa* 42(4) Int'l Aff. 573-578 (1966). Even after issuing an advisory opinion that South Africa (as a British colony) should continue to honour its legal obligations as a Mandatory over SWA territory in 1950, a preliminary judgment on the validity of the case in 1962 and four years of pleadings, the ICJ declined to adjudicate on the merits of the case in 1966 by referring to an 'antecedent' question of legal interest which apparently Ethiopia and Liberia did not have and hence could not have recourse to the Court.

608. *See supra* n. 527 for ITLOS case list.

609. UN, *The ICJ and the ITLOS: Is there a place for juridical dialogue between them?* (29 Oct. 2019) https://www.un.org/en/ga/sixth/74/pdfs/29_october_2019_2_concept_note.pdf accessed 13 May 2022.

610. The PCA administered all but one of the UNCLOS Annex VII arbitrations to date. *See supra* n. 529.

constitutes a crucial forum for addressing maritime disputes and developing international law under the law of the sea. This is shown through the tribunal's key decision in the 2015 Chagos Award to extend the scope of the application of adjudication under Article 297 beyond the three categories of disputes expressly mentioned thereunder.[611]

5.3.3.3 Physical Conditions

The adjudicative measures under action situation 3 comprise a dispute resolution function and an administrative function, as discussed below.

5.3.3.3.1 Dispute Resolution Function

The LOSC currently comprises 168 States parties eligible to use the various dispute resolution mechanisms available under the Convention. In addition, the ITLOS and the arbitral tribunal under Annex VII also allow non-States parties to participate, which further increases the user base of the LOSC's dispute resolution system. The rulings under the ITLOS and the ICJ are generally public. Although there is no legal requirement for Annex VII arbitration to be public, all but one of the Annex VII arbitration cases have been published on the PCA website, making it available to all States parties as well as non-parties to access and learn from when lodging future cases. Arguably, such practice helps to spread knowledge to a wider public in relation to the law of the sea and improves legal order within the governance of the oceans. Accordingly, the dispute resolution function of the LOSC's mechanisms is considered non-excludable. The dispute resolution process is also non-subtractable, assuming that there is capacity to institute all requests received for adjudicative measures (since only a limited number of cases are lodged on a yearly basis as shown through the list of cases under the ITLOS, ICJ and the PCA that administers Annex VII arbitrations).[612] It follows, therefore, that for the purposes of this study, the dispute resolution function of the LOSC's system constitutes a public good.

5.3.3.3.2 Administering the Adjudicative Forums under the LOSC

5.3.3.3.2.1 Clarifying Interpretations of Equity under the Law of the Sea

Judicial settlements through the ITLOS or the ICJ are generally public procedures where the decisions are legally binding on the parties. Although there is no precedence established as in domestic court, the rulings usually constitute a case law that judges abide by in subsequent proceedings. Depending on the nature of the case, emergent decisions, advice, suggestions or findings could shape oceans governance on national,

---

611. *See supra* n. 566. *See also* Stefan Talmon, *The Chagos Marine Protected Area Arbitration: A Case Study of the Creeping Expansion of the Jurisdiction of UNCLOS Part XV Courts and Tribunals* 65 Int'l & Compar. L. Q. 927, 932 (2016) DOI: 10.1017/s0020589316000403.
612. *See e.g.*, the list of cases lodged in 2019 at *supra* n. 127.

regional or international levels through successive decisions or interpretations of the Convention.[613] This is clearly exemplified in the evolving rulings of the ICJ in regard to the definition and importance of equitable considerations in the delimitation of maritime boundaries. In the *North Sea Continental Shelf* cases (1969), the ICJ's judgment established equity as the controlling factor of maritime delimitation and rejected the customary value of the equidistance/relevant circumstances principle, which had been adopted in the 1958 Convention on the Continental Shelf.[614] However, the definition of equity was unclear, ambiguous and subjective, bringing legal uncertainty to the judicial system. In order to make maritime delimitation more predictable, the ICJ rulings progressively reintroduced equidistance/relevant circumstances as the preferred method of maritime delimitation.

Consequently, in *Jan Mayen* (1993)[615] and in the case concerning *Maritime Delimitation and Territorial Questions Between Qatar and Bahrain* (2001),[616] the ICJ noted that the rule of an equitable solution in relation to the delimitation of the continental shelf and of the EEZ[617] was 'closely interrelated' to the one applicable to the territorial sea,[618] which specifically refers to equidistance/special circumstances. In the subsequent case concerning *Territorial and Maritime Dispute Between Nicaragua and Honduras* (2007), the Court then stated that even if special circumstances did not allow the application of the principle of equidistance, the latter remained the general rule.[619] In the *Black Sea* case (2009) that followed, the ICJ made a deliberate decision to close the circle of uncertainty opened in the *North Sea Continental Shelf* ruling by adopting what is now known as the 'three-stage approach'.[620] This approach provides a well-defined three-step process for achieving an equitable solution in relation to the delimitation of borders, which starts with (i) tracing a provisional equidistance line, then (ii) taking into account relevant circumstances before (iii) applying a final proportionality test for determining maritime delimitations. Such practice reveals the ability of the judicial mechanisms under the LOSC to develop international law and contribute to more predictable and peaceful oceans governance, thus making the administration of the LOSC's mechanisms into an intermediate public good.

---

613. *See* generally Anthony Mason, *International Law as a Source of Domestic Law* in *International Law and Australian Federalism* 210 (Brian R. Opeskin and Donald R. Rothwell eds, Melbourne University Press 1997); Ivan A. Shearer, *The Relationship Between International Law and Domestic Law* in *International Law and Australian Federalism* 34 (Brian R. Opeskin and Donald R. Rothwell eds, Melbourne University 1997).
614. *United Nations Convention on the Continental Shelf* (1958) 499 UNTS 311.
615. *Maritime Delimitation in the Area between Greenland and Jan Mayen (Denmark v. Norway)* ICJ Reports 38, 62 (1993).
616. *Maritime Delimitation and Territorial Questions between Qatar and Bahrain (Qatar v. Bahrain)* (Merits) ICJ Reports 40, 111 (2001).
617. *See* Arts 74 and 83 LOSC, both of which refer explicitly to the consideration of equitable principles, with no mention of equidistance.
618. Article 15 LOSC.
619. Territorial and Maritime Dispute between Nicaragua and Honduras in the Caribbean Sea *(Nicaragua v. Honduras)* ICJ Reports 443 (2007).
620. *Maritime Delimitation in the Black Sea (Romania v. Ukraine)* ICJ Reports 61 (2009).

5.3.3.3.2.2 Contributing to Environmental and Marine Protection

The SDC that operates under the ITLOS hears disputes which may involve the ISA and mining operators and contractors regarding activities in the seabed Area.[621] The ISA, created under the LOSC, has the authority to issue orders to prevent serious harm to the marine environment arising from activities in the Area and disapprove areas for exploitation where a significant risk of harm to the environment exists, although these decisions may be challenged.[622] In such cases, if the SDC finds the ISA's decisions reasonable and justified, it could uphold such environmental decisions and, in the process, augment marine environmental protection as well as strengthen the ISA's stance. Thus, by settling disputes centring on environmental protection between states, the SDC can contribute to marine environmental protection and preservation, which is essential for a sustainable oceans governance. It is noted, however, that as of 2016, although 24 exploration contracts had already been signed, commercial seabed mining in the Area had not yet started, which may explain why such marine protection mechanisms are not yet in use.[623]

In a similar vein, given the wider jurisdiction of the ITLOS to litigate disputes occurring under agreements other than the LOSC (as discussed in the scope rules in section 5.3.1.1.3), the ITLOS was successful in regulating whale populations by instituting unilateral action under the International Whaling Commission's regulations.[624] It is noted that fish stocks completely within a state's jurisdiction do not give rise to international disputes; however, since a substantial part of the world's fish stocks are shared among states either in the EEZs or high seas, the chances of interstate distributional disputes are quite high.[625] The ITLOS may thus have an important role in developing standards for regulating fish resources, contributing to the fisheries governance and, more widely, to the oceans governance. Thus, adjudication mechanisms under the SDC and the ITLOS for protecting the marine environment also constitute intermediate public goods.

5.3.4 Politico-economic Context

In the context of this study, the analysis of the political and economic context will focus on the effects of the eastward shift in the centre of gravity of the political economy through the rise of China as a global superpower in relation to the US. This section will explore China's relationship with the LOSC and its dispute settlement system and the role of the LOSC in preserving peace and security in relation to SCS disputes.

621. Articles 156-157 LOSC.
622. *See* Arts 162.2(w), (x) and 187(c)(ii) LOSC.
623. Churchill, *supra* n. 599.
624. Howard S. Schiffman, *The Protection of Whales in International Law: A Perspective for the Next Century* 22 Brook J. Int'l L. 303, 359 (1996).
625. Alf H. Hoel and Ingrid Kvalvik, *The Allocation of Scarce Natural Resources: The Case of Fisheries* 30(4) Marine Pol'y 347 (2006) DOI: 10.1016/j.marpol.2005.04.003.

5.3.4.1 *China's Implementation of the LOSC*

UNCLOS III was the first multilateral legislation activity that China had taken part in after restoring its seat at the UN in 1971 from the Republic of China (ROC or Taiwan).[626] Although, at the time, China had little involvement and less expertise on the modern law of the sea matters,[627] it quickly familiarised itself with the LOSC when it implemented 'open-door' economic policy reforms and adopted diplomatic pragmatism in the early 1980s.[628] In order to demonstrate its commitment to the new maritime regime under the LOSC, China implemented various laws that gave effect to the LOSC after it ratified the Convention in 1996. For example, China successively enacted the Law on the Territorial Sea in 1997 and the Contiguous Zone and Law on the Exclusive Economic Zone and the Continental Shelf in 1998 to establish maritime zoning regulations in domestic law.[629]

With respect to the right to control over 'security' issues in the contiguous zone,[630] the UNCLOS III negotiations had resulted in the compromised view that the LOSC should not contain any explicit rule in this regard, but implied recognition should be given to states' reasonable security concerns; China formulated the Law on the Territorial Sea and the Contiguous Zone in 1992 to regulate the right to control over security issues in its contiguous zones, in accordance with the spirit of the United Nations Convention on the Law of the Sea (UNCLOS).[631] With respect to the innocent passage by foreign warships in the territorial sea, although the Convention does not contain explicit rules, China referred to relevant State practices and prescribed in its Law on the Territorial Sea and the Contiguous Zone that foreign ships for military purposes shall be subject to approval by the Chinese government for entering the territorial sea of China.[632] China also enacted or revised a series of laws and regulations in the fields of marine environmental protection, marine scientific research, shipping, fisheries, deep sea resources, navigation safety and so on to comply with the provisions of the LOSC.[633]

626. Xinmin Ma, *China and the UNCLOS: Practices and Policies* 5 Chinese J. Glob. Governance 1, 2 (2019) DOI: 10.1163/23525207-12340036.
627. *See* Edward L. Miles, *Global Ocean Politics: The Decision Process at the Third United Nations Conference on the Law of the Sea 1973-1982* 24-25 (Brill Nijhoff 1998). According to Miles, initially, China's strategy was limited to criticising the two China-perceived superpowers (the former Soviet Union and the US) and accusing them of hegemonism in the global ocean order rather than constructing the necessary provisions for China's national interests.
628. Keyuan Zou, *Implementation of the United Nations Law of the Sea Convention in China* in *Asia-Pacific and the Implementation of the Law of the Sea* 15 (Seokwoo Lee and Warwick Gullet eds, Maritime Cooperation in East Asia Series: Vol. 1, Brill Nijhoff 2016).
629. *See* Keyuan Zou, *International Law in the Chinese Domestic Context* 44(3) Valparaiso U. L. Rev. 935, 937 (2010).
630. Ma, *supra* n. 626, at 5. During the UNCLOS III, 30 countries, including China, had proposed to include 'security' as another justification to exercise control in addition to customs, finance, immigration and sanitation reasons.
631. *See* Art. 21 LOSC.
632. Ma, *supra* n. 626 at 5.
633. *Ibid.*

5.3.4.2 *Parallel Application of the LOSC and General International Law*

With respect to all matters concerning maritime rights and obligations not explicitly regulated by the LOSC, China insists that principles of general international law will be applied in line with the Preamble to the Convention.[634] One of the most salient examples of such exclusions under the LOSC that directly impacts China involves the principle of historic rights. In this regard, China's Law on the EEZ and the Continental Shelf enacted in 1998 stipulates that 'the provisions of this Law shall not affect the historic rights enjoyed by the People's Republic of China'.[635] Accordingly, China claimed territorial sovereignty rights in the SCS by unilaterally tracing a 'nine-dash line' covering most of the SCS.[636] Such practice was not in line with the LOSC, however, and the Philippines initiated the SCS Arbitration under Annex VII in 2013 to counter China's territorial claims that interfered with the Philippines's rights and freedoms within its own EEZ (e.g., by preventing Philippine fishing around Scarborough Shoal). In 2016, the arbitral tribunal ruled that to the extent that China's nine-dash is a claim of historic rights to the waters of the SCS, it was invalid as whatever historic rights China may have had were extinguished when the LOSC was adopted to the extent those rights were incompatible with the LOSC.[637]

Interestingly, however, there is no explicit provision in the LOSC prohibiting the preservation of such rights or nullifying them.[638] In fact, there is some indication from international jurisprudence that international courts and tribunals have accepted the preservation of historic rights in parallel to the jurisdictional regime established by the LOSC. For example, in the case concerning the Continental Shelf between Tunisia and Libya, the ICJ stated that 'historic titles must enjoy respect and be reserved as they have always been by long usage'.[639] In addition, the Annex VII tribunal case *of Maritime Delimitation between Eritrea and Yemen* clearly accepted the relevance and applicability of historic rights despite the advent of the LOSC and the adoption of the relevant maritime zones by advocating that historic rights are not contradictory but complementary to the LOSC.[640] The tribunal also emphasised that historic rights have been accepted in international law with the view to preserving an existing regime for the

634. *Ibid.*, at 16-17.
635. For an unofficial English version of the law, *see* Keyuan Zou, *China's Marine Legal System and the Law of the Sea* 342 (Martinus Nijhoff 2005).
636. *See* Keyuan Zou, *The South China Sea* in *The Oxford Handbook of the Law of the Sea* 635 (Donald R. Rothwell et al. eds, Oxford University Press 2015).
637. South China Sea Arbitration, *supra* n. 554, at paras 276-278.
638. *See Arbitration between Barbados and the Republic of Trinidad and Tobago, Relating to the Delimitation of the Exclusive Economic Zone and the Continental Shelf Between Them* (Decision of 11 Apr. 2006) UN Reports of International Arbitral Awards, Vol XXVII paras 138, 140: 'it would be contrary to established methods of interpretation of treaties to read into a treaty an intention to extinguish pre-existing rights in the absence of express words to that effect' and that acquired rights such as historic rights 'survive unless explicitly terminated'.
639. Case concerning the Continental Shelf (*Tunisia/Libyan Arab Jamahiriya*) ICJ Reports, para. 100 (1982).
640. *Second Stage of the Proceedings between Eritrea and Yemen (Maritime Delimitation)* (Award of 17 Dec. 1999) UN Reports of International Arbitration Awards, Vol. XXII para. 109.

sake of stability.[641] This shows that despite the controversies surrounding China's application of the historic rights principle in the SCS, there may be valid case law in favour of China's position.[642] Arguably, such contradictory outcomes may fuel existing criticisms that the wide range of mechanisms under the LOSC exacerbate fragmentation under international law and the law of the sea through competing interpretations and inconsistent decisions of different tribunals, each having a different jurisdictional scope and expertise.[643]

5.3.4.3 LOSC's Dispute Resolution System in China

With respect to the settlement of maritime disputes, China holds that each state should settle disputes peacefully through negotiations and consultations on the basis of respecting historical facts and general international law.[644] Moreover, when dealing with disputes relating to the entitlement of the maritime features, China considers that the territorial sovereignty of the relevant features should be decided upon first, after which the maritime entitlements could be decided in accordance with the LOSC.[645] Since its founding in 1949, China has successfully resolved land boundary disputes with 12 out of its 14 neighbours except India and Bhutan; China and Vietnam also have delimited their maritime boundary in the Gulf of Tonkin through negotiations and consultations in 2000.[646] This position of China, based on its long history of resorting to negotiations as a preferred means of dispute resolution (conferred under international law), may explain why China has excluded maritime boundary disputes from the application of adjudicative procedures.[647] In this respect, China considers that the SCS arbitration under Annex VII instituted by the Philippines and the subsequent ruling, discussed in section 5.3.4.2 above, to be in bad faith and invalid.

The fact that the LOSC rejects the notion of historic rights makes it largely lacking in addressing disputes in the SCS, according to China. This situation is further complicated by the fact that a number of claimant states, including Brunei and Malaysia, have relied on the provisions of the LOSC relating to the EEZ to make claims

641. *Territorial Sovereignty and Scope of the Dispute (Eritrea/Yemen)* (Award of 9 Oct. 1998) UN Reports of International Arbitration Awards, Vol. XXII para. 126.
642. For an analysis of historic rights alongside the LOSC, *see* Sophia Kopela, *Historic Titles and Historic Rights in the Law of the Sea in the Light of the South China Sea Arbitration* (Lancaster University Law School) https://eprints.lancs.ac.uk/id/eprint/84981/1/Historic_titles_and_historic_rights_ODIL.pdf accessed 6 Jul. 2022.
643. *See e.g.*, Judge Gilbert Guillaume, President of the International Court of Justice (Address to the United Nations General Assembly, 27 Oct. 2000) www.icj-cij.org/public/files/press-releases/1/3001.pdf accessed 3 Jul. 2022. It is noted that some of the most strident criticism was directed towards the proposed ITLOS which ICJ judges saw as a judicial competitor to the ICJ and an unnecessary and unhelpful addition to the proliferation of international tribunals.
644. Ma, *supra* n. 626, at 16.
645. *Ibid.*
646. *See* Keyuan Zou, *The Sino-Vietnamese Agreement on Maritime Boundary Delimitation in the Gulf of Tonkin* 36 Ocean Dev. & Int'l L. 13 (2005) DOI: 10.1080/00908320590904920.
647. China has not made a declaration under Art. 287 of the LOSC regarding the choice of adjudicative procedure which means that arbitration under Annex VII would automatically apply. However, in 2006, China made a declaration under Art. 298 to exclude maritime boundary disputes from adjudication.

over reefs in the SCS.[648] To resolve conflicts and promote a peaceful, friendly and more harmonious environment in the SCS, China and the ASEAN have instead signed the 'Declaration on the Conduct of the Parties in the South China Sea' (Declaration) in 2002.[649] The Declaration makes reference to the LOSC (e.g., Article 123)[650] as well as the whole body of general international law, including customary international law in connection with dispute settlement in the SCS. It also emphasises the commitment of China to work with State neighbours to promote maritime cooperation, leading to continuous progress in cooperation in traditional and non-traditional fields through joint development initiatives.[651] This is reflected in the 'Memorandum of Understanding on Cooperation on Oil and Gas Development' signed between China and the Philippines in November 2018.[652]

To sum up, China has evolved quickly to become a significant player within the law of the sea regime since it ratified the LOSC in the 1990s. While China may be complying with the existing provisions of the LOSC, it also applies general principles of international law to address gaps under the LOSC, evidenced by the diplomatic strategies used to resolve the existing conflicts in the SCS. It is thus clear that China is using its growing economic and political powers to devise its own rules of the game (e.g., by applying historic rights principle to claim sovereignty) as it evolves from a norm-taker to a norm-maker, especially in relation to the SCS.

5.3.5 Discourse

A four-step historical discourse analysis approach is applied, as defined in section 3.3.1.5 (and also applied in the context of the ITR in section 4.3.5). The aim is to examine the motivations underlying the development of the dispute resolution system in the LOSC.

5.3.5.1 Identify Discursive Event for Study

To study the development of dispute resolution under the LOSC, the analysis focused on the UNCLOS III sessions held between 1973 and 1982 that produced the LOSC, including the dispute resolution provisions under Part XV of the Convention.[653] There were almost 160 delegates that participated in the UNCLOS III conference through a

648. Yann- Huei Song and Stein Tønnesson, *The Impact of the Law of the Sea Convention on Conflict and Conflict Management in the South China Sea* 44 Ocean Dev. & Int'l L. 235 (2013) DOI: 10.1080/00908320.2013.808935.
649. ASEAN Secretariat, *Declaration in the Conduct of Parties in the South China Sea* (14 May 2012) https://asean.org/declaration-on-the-conduct-of-parties-in-the-south-china-sea-2/ accessed 10 May 2022.
650. According to Art. 123 of the LOSC, states bordering an enclosed or semi-enclosed sea should cooperate with each other in the exercise of their rights and in the performance of their duties.
651. Keyuan Zou, *Implementing the United Nations Convention on the Law of the Sea in East Asia: Issues and Trends* 9 Singapore Y.B. Int'l L. & Contributors 37, 52 (2005).
652. Qi, *supra* n. 428, at 221.
653. *Third United Nations Conference on the Law of the Sea* (1973-1982) (UNCLOS III) https://legal.un.org/diplomaticconferences/1973_los/ accessed 10 Jan. 2022.

total of 11 sessions. During the first session, the Conference set up a General Committee, three Main Committees, a Drafting Committee and a Credentials Committee.[654] Each of the three Main Committees was entrusted with drafting a specific part relating to the law of the sea, including a discussion of the settlement of disputes in the extent to which it was relevant to their topic[655] (discussed further in section 5.3.5.4.2). Each of these three parts was drafted as parts I, II and III of an informal single negotiating text (ISNT). The dispute resolution provisions pertaining to each topic were subsequently amalgamated under Part IV of the ISNT by the President of the Conference, which were later combined into an informal composite negotiating text (ICNT) through the concerted efforts of the 'Collegium' prior to being finalised in Part XV of the LOSC.[656]

5.3.5.2 Select the Texts for Study

The analysis focused on the UNCLOS III conference documents, including the working papers and the summary records of the Plenary, especially those involving the discussion of the dispute resolution mechanisms. These were obtained from the publications division of the UNCLOS III website.[657]

5.3.5.3 Choose Specific Points in Time for Studying the Evolution of the Identified Texts

The text of the dispute resolution provisions was examined at four specific points of the drafting process, starting with the original presentation of the provisions in a working paper to the plenary of UNCLOS III in 1974.[658] Next, the draft provisions in Parts I, II and III of ISNT presented by the Chairmen of the three Main committees in 1975 were studied.[659] The third text studied comprised the consolidated dispute resolution provisions presented under Part IV of the ISNT as prepared by the President of the Conference in 1976.[660] Finally, the dispute resolution provisions integrated into the ICNT by the Collegium in 1977 were studied.[661]

654. UNCLOS III UN Doc. A/CONF.62/SR.2 (7 Dec. 1973).
655. UNCLOS III UN Doc. A/CONF.62/29 (21 Jun. 1974).
656. The Collegium includes the President of the Conference, the Chairmen of the three Main Committees, the Chairman of the Drafting Committee and the Rapporteur-General and was responsible for drafting and revising progressive drafts of the ISTN. *See* Albert W. Koers, *The Third United Nations Conference on the Law of the Sea: Some Remarks on Its Contribution Towards the Making of International Law* in *International Law and Its Sources: Liber Amicorum Maarten Bos* 29 (Wybo P. Heere ed., T.M.C. Asser Institute 1989).
657. *See supra* n. 653.
658. UNCLOS III UN Doc. A/CONF.62/L.7 (27 Aug. 1974).
659. UNCLOS III (17 Mar. to 9 May 1975) UN Doc. A/CONF.62/WP.8/Part I (Part I); UN Doc. A/CONF.62/WP.8/Part II (Part II); UN Doc. A/CONF.62/WP.8/Part III (Part III).
660. UNCLOS III (15 Mar. to 7 May 1976) UN Doc. A/CONF.62/WP.9; UN Doc. A/CONF.62/WP.9/Rev.1.
661. UNCLOS III UN Doc. A/CONF.62/WP.9/L.20 (28 Jun. 1977).

5.3.5.4 *Analyse Content at Specific Points in Time to Uncover Patterns/Tensions*

The guiding questions at each of these four points in time include: What is the geographical composition of the decision-making group and their views? Which dispute resolution mechanisms are proposed? The aim is to understand how the views of the negotiators are reflected in the treaty by analysing how the changing circumstances and composition of the group of treaty drafters have influenced the evolution of dispute resolution under the LOSC in accordance with the timeline identified in section 5.3.5.3 above.

5.3.5.4.1 Working Paper on Dispute Resolution Presented in 1974

5.3.5.4.1.1 Group Composition

The representatives of a number of countries held informal consultations on issues connected with the settlement of disputes which may arise under the LOSC and presented the first working paper resulting from those discussions to the Conference at the second session held on 27 August 1974.[662] The working paper set out 10 general dispute settlement provisions, including various possible alternatives, together with notes indicating relevant precedents.[663] According to the El Salvador delegate, Galindo Pohl, the working paper was an attempt to combine the results of informal consultations held by some 30 delegations representing all geographical groups and all levels of development.[664]

5.3.5.4.1.2 Guiding Principles Underpinning Dispute Resolution System

The working paper reflected four fundamental premises on which further negotiations should be based, subject to their acceptance by all delegates.[665] First, disputes should be settled by legal, effective means in order to avoid political and economic pressures (although some developing countries have already expressed reticence in relation to the application of obligatory dispute settlement procedures). Second, the interpretation of the future convention should be subject to some form of uniformity. Third, the recognition that obligatory settlement of disputes offered some distinct advantages, taking into account some exceptions which had to be determined with the greatest care (e.g., the delimitation of maritime boundaries to respect the sovereignty rights of states). Fourth, if a future convention were to be signed and ratified, then the dispute settlement system must be an integral part of that convention (given the failure of the

662. *See supra* n. 658. The group of nine countries included Australia, Belgium, Bolivia, Colombia, El Salvador, Luxembourg, The Netherlands, Singapore and the US.
663. *Ibid.*
664. UNCLOS III UN Doc. A/CONF.62/SR.51 paras 7-13 (29 Aug. 1974).
665. *See supra* n. 664, at para. 9. *See also* Louis B. Sohn, *Settlement of Disputes Arising Out of the Law of the Sea Convention* 12 San Diego L. Rev. 495, 516 (1975).

dispute settlement system under the optional protocol of the 1958 Geneva Convention). The aim of a dispute settlement system under the LOSC was thus based on a strict principle of legality (rule of law) for regulating international relations while preserving the equality of States, regardless of their political, economic and military might.

5.3.5.4.2 Draft Dispute Resolution Provisions in the ISNT

The Chairmen of each of the three Main Committees of UNCLOS III had been entrusted with the responsibility of drafting a separate part of the ISNT that was released at the third session of the Conference in May 1975.[666] Each of the three parts of the ISNT dealt with a separate area of the law of the sea, including a proposed dispute resolution method. Part I of the ISNT dealt with topics of the deep-seabed regime and accordingly recommended the establishment of the ITLOS and its special chambers for addressing disputes related to the deep-seabed regime.[667] Recourse to the ITLOS was proposed as a supplementary mechanism if no amicable settlement was reached dispute through consensual means, including consultation, negotiation, conciliation or other such means of their own choice within a set time period.[668] The proposed dispute resolution provisions also allowed the parties to mutually agree to have recourse to arbitration, composed of three independent arbitrators, instead of the ITLOS.[669]

In Part II of the ISNT covering the traditional topics under the law of the sea, the Chairman of the second Committee, Galindo Pohl, made it clear when presenting the text that due to the sheer volume of proposals received, he had to amalgamate some of the alternative formulations and in other cases, it had been necessary to choose between conflicting proposals and in some cases, a middle course was adopted. As a result, the text did not necessarily reflect the views of the delegates.[670] With respect to dispute resolution provisions, Part II does not present any specific procedures, referring instead to general dispute resolution procedures if no amicable settlement can be reached.[671]

Part III of the ISNT regarding the protection and preservation of the marine environment seems to endorse much more cooperative approaches.[672] Dispute settlement provisions in part III are set out separately in relation to the protection of the marine environment and marine scientific research. Similar to Part II, this part also recommends general dispute resolution procedures if no amicable settlement is reached.[673] In relation to marine scientific research specifically, the provisions specify recourse to negotiations before being submitted by either disputant party to compulsory measures.[674] Such measures taken by the drafters of the LOSC ensured that

666. *See supra* n. 659.
667. Part I, *supra* n. 659, at Art. 57.
668. *Ibid.*
669. *Ibid.*, at Art. 63.
670. Part II, *supra* n. 659.
671. *Ibid.*, at Arts 70(2) and 137.
672. Part III, *supra* n. 659, at Art. 41(3).
673. Part III, *supra* n. 622, at Art. 44 for the protection of the marine environment.
674. *Ibid.*, at Arts 20, 36 and 37 for the conduct of marine research.

potential disputes in all areas of the law of the sea were captured under the treaty and addressed through some form of dispute resolution mechanism. More importantly, these measures ensured that the views of all delegates were reflected in the proposals.

5.3.5.4.3 Consolidation of Dispute Resolution Provisions under Part IV of ISNT

At the fourth session of UNCLOS III, which started in March 1976, the Chairmen of the Main Committees presented revised versions of the existing Parts I, II and III of the ISNT that reflected the result of the informal negotiations that had taken place since the ISNT was released a year earlier. Part I of the revised ISNT did not include any substantive changes to the dispute resolution provisions.[675] In Part II, although more than 3,700 interventions and over 1,000 proposals were made by delegates, there were no substantive changes made to the dispute resolution provisions under the new chairmanship of Andres Aguilar.[676] Also, no substantial revisions were made to the dispute resolution provisions in part III regarding the protection of the marine environment and marine scientific research.[677] However, the process was clarified to require that disputant parties resort to diplomatic means, including negotiations or voluntary conciliation, involving experts in the field of marine scientific research as conciliators.[678]

Since the Chairmen of the second and third Main Committees had not made any special provisions in Parts II and III of the ISNT for the settlement of disputes, the President of the Conference took it upon himself to summarise and add to the dispute settlement provisions in a separate part IV of the ISNT.[679] Part IV comprised 18 Articles and 7 Annexes providing detailed procedures for conciliation, arbitration, the functioning of the ITLOS, special procedures in the fields of fisheries, pollution and marine scientific research and information and consultation procedures.[680] The detailed elaboration under Part IV was meant to generate a more effective discussion and evaluation of the complete dispute settlement system being proposed under the Convention.[681] In fact, the provision to exclude certain types of disputes regarding maritime sovereignty issues (e.g., disputes relating to the EEZ) from the application of adjudicative procedures as proposed by certain groups of coastal states[682] reflected one

675. UNCLOS III UN Doc. A/CONF.62/WP.8/Rev.1/Part I para. 6(b) (6 May 1976).
676. UNCLOS III UN Doc. A/CONF.62/WP.8/Rev.1/Part II Art. 131 (6 May 1976). Although no substantial changes were made to the dispute resolution provisions, significant non-dispute resolution revisions were made with the aim of making the text conform more to the views of delegations, as expressed during discussion in the second Committee, *see* paras 4-5.
677. UNCLOS III UN Doc. A/CONF.62/WP.8/Rev.1/Part III Arts 47 and 76 (6 May 1976).
678. *See supra* n. 677, at Art. 76.
679. UNCLOS III UN Doc. A/CONF.62/WP.9/Add.1 paras 4-5 (31 Mar. 1976).
680. *Ibid.*, at para. 8.
681. *See supra* n. 679, at paras 9 and 16.
682. *Ibid.*, at para. 31. Two proposals were brought before the Seabed Committee: one presented by Ecuador, Panama and Peru and the second one presented by Canada, India, Kenya, Madagascar, Senegal and Sri Lanka proposing that disputes within this zone be dealt with exclusively by the authorities of the coastal state.

of the most controversial points in Part IV for further negotiation among delegates to achieve a compromise.[683]

5.3.5.4.4 Integration of Dispute Resolution Provisions in the ICNT

In June 1977, the Conference authorised the Collegium to integrate all four parts of the ISNT to form the ICNT.[684] Under such a collegiate method, it was agreed that the President would supervise and would also have a veto right on the changes being made by the Chairmen in their respective topics.[685] Although the ICNT had the same informal status as the ISNT, it constituted a prototype of the draft Convention and allowed delegates to have a snapshot of the mutual concessions and compromises needed to facilitate the attainment of a consensus.[686] In regard to the dispute settlement system proposed under Part XV of the ICNT, the provisions were based on the four guiding principles discussed in the 1974 working paper including (1) freedom of choice of court or tribunal; (2) the agreement of the parties to the dispute on the choice of court or tribunal; (3) the securement of finality in the form of a binding and conclusive settlement; and (4) the application of a specific procedure where the parties to the dispute fail to agree on the compulsory dispute settlement method.[687]

Moreover, seven issue-specific negotiating groups were also formed to address any remaining contentious issues in the ICNT.[688] By April 1980, following intensive negotiations, general consensus was achieved for the majority of the dispute resolution provisions under Part XV, although outstanding issues remained regarding the settlement of disputes in relation to the seabed area (in Part XI), marine scientific research and the delimitation of maritime boundaries.[689] Consensus was achieved in relation to these contentious issues through compromises in the form of provisions that either exclude or limit the application of compulsory measures in specific situations. Although such exclusions have been criticised by some commentators as undermining the effectiveness of the LOSC's dispute resolution system, others have pointed out the exceptional nature of the LOSC in achieving universal acceptance.[690]

683. *Ibid.*, at paras 31-34.
684. *See supra* n. 656; *see also* UNCLOS III UN Doc. A/CONF.62/SR.78 (28 Jun. 1977).
685. UNCLOS III UN Doc. A/CONF.62/WP.10/Add.1 (22 Jul. 1977).
686. UNCLOS III UN Doc. A/CONF.62/L.20 (28 Jun. 1977).
687. *See supra* n. 685, at 70.
688. UNCLOS III UN Doc. A/CONF.62/62 (13 Apr. 1978). Seven negotiating groups were formed to address the hardcore issues remaining in the ICNT. Negotiating Groups 1-3 were involved in the deep-seabed regime issues; Negotiating Group 4 dealt with the right of access of land-locked countries to the living resources in the EEZ; Negotiating Group 5 dealt with the settlement of disputes relating to the exercise of the sovereign rights of coastal states in the EEZ; Negotiating Group 6 dealt with issues regarding the definition and exploitation of the continental shelf; Negotiating Group 7 dealt with maritime boundary issues and settlement of related disputes.
689. UNCLOS III UN Doc. A/CONF.62/WP.9/L.52 + Add.1 (29 Mar. and 1 Apr. 1980).
690. *See e.g.*, Jonathan Charney, *The Impact of the International Legal System of the Growth of International Courts and Tribunals* 31 N.Y.U. J. Int'l L. & Pol'y 697 (1999); Pierre Marie Dupuy, *The Danger of Fragmentation or Unification of the International Legal System and the International Court of Justice* 31 N.Y.U. J Int'l L. & Pol'y 791 (1999); Martti Koskenniemi and

5.3.5.5 *Implications in This Study*

The above discourse analysis reveals quite clearly that the guiding principles for developing a dispute resolution system under the LOSC based on a strict application of the rule of law to preserve the equality of States, regardless of their political, economic and military powers, were emphasised throughout the negotiations. At every stage of UNCLOS III, innovative arrangements were put in place to ensure that the views of all parties (especially developing countries) were reflected to produce an effective yet equitable dispute resolution system through compromise. In fact, if no consensus was reached on the dispute resolution mechanisms, the LOSC may not have been finalised, which reveals the crucial role that the dispute resolution system played in developing the multilateral treaty. This view is reflected in the speech of the US Ambassador John Stevenson at the UNCLOS III in 1974, that '[...] a system of peaceful and compulsory third-party settlement of disputes is in the end perhaps the most significant justification for the accommodations we are all being asked to make'.[691] Such motivations are in sharp contrast to the MAP that was designed on a largely pragmatic basis by a restricted number of mostly developed countries (that constituted the main trading partners in the early twentieth century) to ensure a simple and swift dispute resolution procedure for their own benefit.

5.4 CONCLUSIONS

Action situations 1, 2 and 3 under the LOSC's dispute resolution system include diplomatic negotiations, conciliation and four different adjudicative procedures (ICJ, ITLOS, and arbitration under Annexes VII and VIII), respectively. The analysis of the working rules across the various separately linked action situations reveals that the mechanisms have been designed to form a mandatory yet flexible legal framework that ensures a peaceful resolution of all types of maritime disputes. The system also gives primacy to diplomacy among the LOSC States parties by requiring parties to engage in diplomatic negotiations or conciliation (consensual means) before proceeding to adjudication for resolving disputes.

The analysis of the community attributes shows that although diplomatic negotiations may afford the highest control to the parties engaged in the dispute in terms of decision-making, setting timelines, etc., it may be more advantageous for the developing and emerging countries to have recourse to third party settlement methods such as the ITLOS that applies the rule of law or conciliation that provides independent third party recommendations. As such, third-party settlement may be useful for achieving a level playing field that may provide more equitable solutions, although costs and flexibility requirements remain important considerations, especially for low-income, developing countries.

Paivi Leino, *Fragmentation in International Law? Postmodern Anxieties* 15 Leiden J. Int'l L. 553 (2002) DOI: 10.1017/s0922156502000262.

691. John R. Stevenson, *Address to the Plenary Session of the Law of the Sea Conference* (11 Jul. 1974) US Dep. of State Press Release 301.

The examination of the physical conditions in terms of the economic rationale of the various functions associated with the different mechanisms shows that with the exception of dispute resolution under diplomatic negotiations, all other functions exhibit intermediate public good and public good features. This finding suggests that the institutional arrangements underpinning the LOSC's dispute resolution system may present many opportunities for strategic and collaborative relations among the States parties to achieve common goals within the wider field of oceans governance. For example, the rulings of the SDC under the ITLOS are intended to develop international law regarding the extent of activities in the seabed Area, which may help states coordinate their efforts to avoid future conflict and also develop common rules to ensure environmental marine protection.

As for the politico-economic context under the LOSC, the influence of China as a maritime superpower, especially in the SCS, has undeniable consequences on the evolution of the provisions of the LOSC. Although China is largely compliant with the LOSC, China also maintains that states should settle disputes peacefully through negotiations and consultations on the basis of respecting historical facts and general international law when the matter is not explicitly addressed under the LOSC. In this respect, China pursues its own national policies for building diplomatic relations with its SCS neighbours, even if it means outrightly rejecting the outcome of the China-Philippines arbitration under Annex VII, which, according to China, ignored the Chinese declaration to exclude adjudication in matters of border delimitation. This suggests that China may be evolving into a norm-maker (as opposed to a norm-taker) under the law of the sea regime by applying general international law principles to strengthen its position as a maritime superpower under the LOSC.

Finally, the discourse analysis shows quite clearly that the main underlying motivation of the negotiators of the LOSC during the various stages of the UNCLOS III negotiations (spanning nine years from 1973 to 1982) was to achieve a universally accepted comprehensive legal framework to address all matters relating to the seas in a peaceful manner. This was based on a compromised and consensus-based approach between developing and developed countries to ensure an equitable resolution of all types of disputes while emphasising peaceful and cooperative international relations among nations.

Chapter 6

Comparing Patterns of Interaction and Inclusivity

Chapter 6 explores Step B of the methodology by comparing the patterns of interaction and inclusivity (participation) levels across the two systems with the aim of identifying relevant aspects of the LOSC's system for addressing the issues of capacity, uncertainty and inequitable solutions affecting the current MAP system. At the operational level, the MAP may benefit from a flexible yet mandatory application of diplomatic and adjudicative procedures to enhance the effectiveness and predictability of the dispute resolution process. At the policymaking level, consensus-building techniques used during LOSC negotiations may be applied within context to facilitate the negotiation of reforms across the IF. These include integrating the dispute resolution provisions within a multilateral treaty, which would be drafted without a model text to ensure that all views are represented. At the constitutional level, a more unified decision-making structure may be proposed instead of the dual OECD/UN platforms and formal and informal clustering strategies may be applied to achieve a level playing field between developing and developed countries for more equitable solutions.

6.1 INTRODUCTION

As outlined in Chapter 3, this research thesis is based on a three-step methodology. Step A maps out the institutional arrangements (rules, norms and strategies) that underpin dispute resolution in the ITR and the LOSC, as explored in Chapters 4 and 5, respectively. Subsequently, Step B of the methodology, as laid out in this present chapter, comprises two parts. In the first part, it compares the patterns of interaction generated from these institutional arrangements at the operational level and in the second part, it compares the inclusivity (participation) levels across the two dispute resolution systems at the policymaking and constitutional levels. The aim of this comparative analysis is to identify aspects of the LOSC's system that may be relevant for improving tax treaty dispute resolution by addressing the issues of capacity, uncertainty and inequitable solutions that affect the current system (discussed earlier in section 2.2). The analysis in Step B thus aims to answer the second research question posed in this study.

Section 6.2 will first integrate the analysis of the institutional arrangements across the different action situations in the ITR and the LOSC to map out the relevant patterns of interaction in each system. Section 6.3 will then compare the patterns to identify relevant aspects of the LOSC's system for addressing operational-level issues identified in the ITR. Section 6.4 will assess the inclusivity levels across the two dispute resolution systems at the policymaking and constitutional levels of decision-making to identify relevant techniques to facilitate the implementation of any proposed reforms in the ITR before concluding in section 6.5.

6.2 INTEGRATING THE ANALYSIS OF INSTITUTIONAL ARRANGEMENTS

This section applies the first part of Step B analysis. It integrates the analysis of the institutional arrangements (rules, norms and strategies) across the three action situations identified in the ITR (Chapter 4) and the LOSC (Chapter 5) to compare the patterns of interaction generated within the two systems at the operational level.

Rules refer to the seven working rules identified in each action situation that control/limit decisions of relevant actors. Norms refer to potential trends among actors identified through the analysis of the community attributes (e.g., based on their interests and objectives). Strategies refer to the impact of the various dispute resolution mechanisms across the wider field of international tax and oceans governance[692] based on the analysis of the physical conditions (i.e., the public-private characteristics of the functions associated with each mechanism). The present analysis also takes into consideration the politico-economic context and discourse underlying both regimes.

6.2.1 ITR

6.2.1.1 Rules

Table 2 summarises the seven working rules analysed within each of the three action situations identified in the ITR (MAP, UN Model arbitration and OECD Model arbitration).[693] As explained below, the underlying rules structure across the three action situations reveals distinct patterns of interaction that may account for the issues of uncertainty and inequitable solutions in the ITR.

---

692. *See supra* n. 188 for a definition of oceans governance.

693. *See* ss 4.3.1.1, 4.3.2.1 and 4.3.3.1 for analysis of working rules in action situations 1, 2 and 3 respectively.

Table 2 Rules Governing Tax Treaty Dispute Resolution

	Action Situation 1: MAP	*Action Situation 2: UN Model Arbitration*	*Action Situation 3: OECD Model Arbitration*
Boundary rules	- Taxpayer resident in one of the two contracting States - Competent authority	- Taxpayer resident in one of the two contracting States - Competent authority - Independent arbitrator	- Taxpayer resident in one of the two contracting States - Competent authority - Independent arbitrator (more rigorous selection criteria than under UN arbitration)
Position rules	- MAP applicant: under the OECD Model, taxpayer may request MAP in either contracting State; under the UN Model, request MAP in resident State only - MAP administrator	- MAP applicant (same taxpayer as in MAP) - MAP administrator (same competent authority as in MAP) - 3-member arbitration panel appointed by competent authorities	- MAP applicant (same taxpayer as in MAP) - MAP administrator (same competent authority as in MAP) - 3-member arbitration panel appointed by competent authorities
Information rules	- Private/confidential	- Private/confidential. - Arbitration decision may be published in redacted form if agreed by parties (no known published decision)	- Private/confidential. - Arbitration decision may be published in redacted form if agreed by parties (no known published decision)
Authority rules	- Competent authorities accept/reject MAP request, negotiate on behalf of taxpayer to endeavour to reach agreement	- Competent authorities and taxpayer have the same responsibilities as in MAP	- Competent authorities and taxpayer have the same responsibilities as in MAP - As opposed to UN arbitration, taxpayer may trigger arbitration if no MAP agreement is reached within 24 months of MAP negotiations

	Action Situation 1: MAP	*Action Situation 2: UN Model Arbitration*	*Action Situation 3: OECD Model Arbitration*
	- Taxpayer makes MAP request, provides information as requested and must approve/reject MAP agreement prior to implementation. Taxpayer does not participate in MAP negotiations	- In addition, competent authorities may initiate arbitration if no MAP agreement is reached within three years of negotiations - Competent authorities jointly decide rules of procedure for arbitration (baseball approach or independent opinion method) and appoint arbitrators - Competent authorities may choose to implement arbitration decision or agree on a different solution - Taxpayer does not participate in arbitration – must approve/reject final MAP agreement proposed by competent authorities- Arbitrators apply arbitration procedure and issue decisions through a simple majority vote	- Competent authorities jointly decide rules of procedure for arbitration (baseball approach or independent opinion method) and appoint arbitrators - As opposed to UN arbitration, competent authorities must implement arbitration decision - Taxpayer may participate in arbitration and must approve/reject final MAP agreement proposed by competent authorities - Arbitrators apply arbitration procedure and issue decisions through a simple majority vote
Aggregation rules	- Applicable law: applicable bilateral tax treaty rules, VCLT rules of interpretation, domestic law (e.g., for resolving dual residence issues)	- Applicable law: same as in MAP as prescribed in treaty	- Applicable law: same as in MAP as prescribed in treaty

	Action Situation 1: MAP	*Action Situation 2: UN Model Arbitration*	*Action Situation 3: OECD Model Arbitration*
Scope rules	- Administrative framework: mandatory rules under BEPS Action 14 minimum standard (e.g., MAP filing requirements) - Jurisdiction: double taxation issues brought under Article 25(1) of tax treaty; doubts on interpretation and application of treaty and double taxation not covered under treaty brought under Article 25(3) - Finality of outcomes: non-binding MAP agreement; if not accepted by taxpayer, taxpayer may have recourse to domestic remedies if still available	- Administrative framework: procedural rules for arbitration devised by competent authorities (not subject to BEPS Action 14 minimum standard) - Jurisdiction: double taxation issues brought to MAP under Article 25(1), although issues under Article 25(3) may also be subject to arbitration if competent authorities agree - Finality of outcomes: non-binding arbitration decision – competent authorities may mutually agree on a different solution. Taxpayer may accept/reject decision	- Administrative framework: procedural rules for arbitration devised by competent authorities (not subject to BEPS Action 14 minimum standard) - Jurisdiction: double taxation issues brought to MAP under Article 25(1), although issues under Article 25(3) may also be subject to arbitration if competent authorities agree - Finality of outcomes: legally binding arbitration decision – competent authorities must implement decision if taxpayer accepts arbitration decision
Payoff rules	- No fees for taxpayer to request MAP - More flexibility for competent authorities through diplomatic negotiations	- No additional fees for taxpayer if arbitration is initiated by competent authorities - Arbitration costs incurred jointly by competent authorities	- No additional fees for taxpayer to trigger arbitration - Costs incurred jointly by competent authorities except for taxpayer's costs for attending in-person

	Action Situation 1: MAP	*Action Situation 2: UN Model Arbitration*	*Action Situation 3: OECD Model Arbitration*
	- BEPS Action 14 minimum standard ensures a more standardised and streamlined procedure which benefits both taxpayers and competent authorities	- Competent authorities maintain control over the arbitration process - Limited rights for taxpayers	- Competent authorities surrender decision-making to arbitrators - Prophylactic effect of binding arbitration procedure makes OECD arbitration more attractive to taxpayers

6.2.1.1.1 Lack of Effective Dispute Resolution under International Law

6.2.1.1.1.1 Indeterminacy Perpetuated Through Lack of Transparency and Relevant Case Law

The MAP and the arbitration procedures under the OECD and UN Models all constitute dispute resolution mechanisms under international law, operating through a bilateral treaty network. However, the analysis of the information rules reveals the lack of transparency perpetuated across all three mechanisms since the MAP is private and confidential, and there is limited or no publication of arbitration decisions in the ITR (the default baseball arbitration approach does not allow publication). Such opacity across the current tax treaty dispute resolution system emphasises the lack of scrutiny over competent authority transactions and their adherence to the good faith principle. Also, more importantly, it restricts the development of relevant case law in the ITR for addressing the issues of indeterminacy in interpreting increasingly complex international tax regulations, thus perpetuating tax uncertainty across the ITR.[694]

6.2.1.1.1.2 Lack of Legally Binding Processes and Outcomes

The problem of indeterminacy in the ITR is further exacerbated by the lack of legally binding processes and decisions across the MAP and existing arbitration procedures, as shown through the analysis of the scope rules. Although the taxpayer may have the final word on whether to implement the MAP agreement or not, the taxpayer is not able to force a resolution on the part of the competent authorities (they are only required to exercise their best efforts to arrive at an agreement under Article 25(2) of the applicable treaty) except by triggering the mandatory and binding OECD arbitration mechanism if no MAP agreement is reached within 24 months of negotiation. In the latter case, an

694. *See* s. 2.2.2.2.

arbitration decision will be imposed on the competent authorities to implement accordingly, further to the taxpayer's approval.

Even if the OECD mechanism is not triggered, the prophylactic effect associated with the arbitration procedure may urge competent authorities to reach an agreement through MAP to avoid surrendering decision-making to an independent panel of arbitrators.[695] Thus, the OECD mechanism may effectively resolve the tax issue for the taxpayer, although the main issue at this point is that OECD arbitration has only been adopted in 31 of the 141 IF jurisdictions[696] and developing countries generally oppose the OECD's mandatory and binding arbitration based on arguments of institutional disparities that would negatively affect developing countries compared to developed countries.[697] The lack of legally binding processes and outcomes across an increasingly multilateral ITR further increases uncertainty regarding the effective resolution of tax disputes and may also result in unequal treatment across different jurisdictions through lack of common interpretative rules.

6.2.1.1.1.3 Delayed Resolution Timelines for Transfer Pricing Cases

As shown through the aggregation rules and the MAP resolution timelines in Table I.2 in Appendix I, despite the implementation of the BEPS Action 14 rules for making MAP more effective, the average time for closing transfer pricing cases under MAP for the period 2016-2020 was 30-35 months, exceeding the prescribed timeline of 24 months under BEPS Action 14. This could be explained by the fact that transfer pricing and non-transfer pricing cases are all handled through the MAP. Since transfer pricing cases tend to be more fact-intensive compared to non-transfer pricing cases, it arguably raises resource allocation issues at the competent authority level, which may potentially compromise the ability of the competent authorities to resolve MAP cases in an effective and timely manner (within 24 months). Such administrative pressures, along with rapidly increasing MAP requests, may also explain potential bottlenecks within the MAP leading to a build-up of outstanding MAP cases, especially in the absence of effective arbitration procedures (some jurisdictions may disallow transfer pricing disputes from arbitration[698]). In fact, the OECD MAP Statistics summarised in Table I.3 in Appendix I shows that the number of unresolved MAP cases has doubled from 2016 to 2020 (11% to 22%), especially with respect to transfer pricing cases, exacerbating capacity issues across the current MAP system.

6.2.1.1.2 Excessive Control of Competent Authorities over Dispute Resolution Process

As shown through the authority rules in Table 2, the competent authorities that administer the MAP have control over the entire process. They decide whether to accept or reject the MAP request from taxpayers, negotiate (on behalf of the taxpayer) on a good

695. *See* s. 4.3.3.2.1.
696. *See supra* n. 27.
697. *See* s. 4.3.2.2.
698. *See* s. 2.2.3.2.

faith basis to endeavour to resolve the tax issue (there is no legal requirement to resolve a dispute) and implement the MAP agreement reached, subject to the taxpayer's acceptance. Even if arbitration shifts decision-making from competent authorities to an independent arbitrational panel, the competent authorities under both the UN and OECD Models still retain control over the process in terms of selecting the applicable procedure (i.e., baseball approach or independent opinion method), deciding the questions to be addressed and appointing the arbitrators of the panel. In the UN arbitration process, not only can the competent authorities decide whether to trigger arbitration, but they may even reject the arbitrators' decision and agree instead on another decision that may be more to their mutual benefit at the expense of the taxpayer.

Thus, the current MAP and arbitration procedures maximise the control that competent authorities hold over the MAP process from beginning to end. It limits the participation of the taxpayers, although they constitute a major stakeholder in the process and may also limit the law-making capabilities of the arbitration judges (by applying the baseball arbitration approach as the default mechanism and restricting the publication of relevant arbitration decisions through the independent opinion method). Arguably, these rules exacerbate an unbalanced allocation of decision-making powers across the tax treaty dispute resolution process, which may lead to mistrust among taxpayers and impact the effectiveness of the transactions between taxpayers and competent authorities (e.g., taxpayers may refuse to disclose relevant financial information to competent authorities under fear of being audited in the future).[699] Such unbalanced decision-making arguably leads to uncertainty on the part of taxpayers, resulting in ineffective resolution of disputes.

6.2.1.1.3 *Fragmented Dispute Resolution Framework*

The scope rules reveal another shortcoming of the current system that compromises the effective resolution of tax treaty disputes through a non-uniform application of dispute resolution rules across the DTT network. Although the MAP covers most cross-border tax issues under Articles 25(1) and 25(3) of the OECD and UN Models, there are taxes which jurisdictions may unilaterally choose to include under MAP (e.g., the UK adding the UK Diverted Profits Tax under MAP).[700] Jurisdictions may also restrict access to MAP for transfer pricing disputes through domestic legislation in certain cases.[701] Such fragmented application of the MAP across the ITR may arguably create uncertainty among taxpayers regarding the resolution of tax treaty disputes despite the positive impact of the BEPS Action 14 minimum standard on certain aspects of the MAP.

More importantly, the scope rules also show that tax disputes brought under Article 25(3) (i.e., doubts relating to the interpretation of the treaty and double tax issues not covered under the treaty) may be excluded from arbitration under the OECD and the UN Model unless the competent authorities mutually agree to resolve through MAP).[702]

699. *See* s. 2.2.2.3.
700. *See supra* n. 62.
701. *See* s. 2.2.3.2.
702. *See supra* n. 287 and n. 336 for the UN and OECD Models respectively.

Such exclusions that rely on the discretion of competent authorities may not only reduce the effectiveness and predictability of the tax treaty dispute resolution system but also create a fragmented system that separates contracting States that extend the application of arbitration under Article 25(3) and those that do not. This may lead to unequal treatment for taxpayers in different jurisdictions, resulting in inequitable solutions across the ITR.

The aggregation rules show that domestic laws may also impact the uniform application of the MAP across the ITR despite recommendations under the BEPS Action 14 to that effect. For example, although jurisdictions are required to implement the MAP agreement irrespective of domestic time limits,[703] some jurisdictions may still reserve their position on this point and consequently deny relief under MAP in cases where the statute of limitation has run out.[704] Moreover, in countries where the decision rendered by the domestic court will bind the tax administration and prevent it from providing greater relief through the MAP, the competent authority of that country may have to negotiate to obtain relief from the other contracting State through MAP.[705] Such differentiated procedures may lead to opportunistic behaviours among competent authorities for negotiating MAP cases, exacerbating power disparities across the tax treaty dispute resolution system.

In fact, all jurisdictions that reported not being involved in any MAP cases in 2019 involve developing economies and China as an emerging economy.[706] This may either suggest that all tax issues are resolved at the audit stage by the tax authorities with no need for MAP in the first place or that taxpayers may not be willing to initiate MAP in such jurisdictions. In the latter case, the only option for taxpayers would be to bring their case to a domestic court for settlement or its functional equivalent in countries without independent judiciary, like China. In contrast, the top ten countries having the highest MAP caseloads consistently since 2016 include all developed countries except for India in 2019.[707] Thus, the unequal processes and outcomes generated through the differences between domestic laws and even the UN and OECD Model provisions may largely impact the use of MAP by taxpayers across the DTT network, creating a gap between the developing and developed countries. This may exacerbate the risks of inequitable solutions for taxpayers from developing countries, especially in the absence of arbitration mechanisms in the bilateral treaties.

6.2.1.2 Norms

Table 3 summarises the potential trends identified in each of the three action situations in the ITR in the analysis of the community attributes.[708] The community attributes focus on the alignment of interests and objectives among the relevant actors.

703. Action 14 Peer Review Documents, *supra* n. 31, at para. 17.D3.
704. OECD Transfer Pricing Guidelines 2022, *supra* n. 54, at paras 4.45-4.49.
705. MEMAP, *supra* n. 22, at 33.
706. OECD, *2019 MAP Statistics*, *supra* n. 128.
707. *Ibid.*
708. *See* ss 4.3.1.2, 4.3.2.2 and 4.3.3.2 for analysis of community attributes in action situations 1, 2 and 3 respectively.

Table 3 Norms Underpinning Tax Treaty Dispute Resolution

	Action Situation 1: MAP	*Action Situation 2: UN Model Arbitration*	*Action Situation 3: OECD Model Arbitration*
Community attributes	- Both taxpayers and competent authorities prefer simple and streamlined MAP, resulting in an increasing number of MAP cases being opened and closed since 2016 - Taxpayers would prefer increased transparency, participation and disclosure requirements in the MAP process, but competent authorities maintain control over the entire MAP. This results in conflicting interests between taxpayers and competent authorities.	- Lack of alignment between taxpayers and competent authorities based on excessive control of competent authorities over the arbitration process (e.g., only competent authorities may initiate arbitration) - Lack of alignment between competent authorities from developed and developing countries also based on distinct institutional issues that separate developed and developing countries (e.g., lack of familiarity with arbitration, issues of even-handedness, lack of resources, etc.) - Voluntary arbitration is generally not popular among competent authorities (unwilling to surrender tax sovereignty)	- Increased alignment between taxpayers and competent authorities based on more balanced decision-making (e.g., taxpayers may trigger arbitration to ensure resolution of dispute) - More alignment between taxpayers and competent authorities also due to prophylactic effect of mandatory arbitration - Arbitration is less costly than litigation in domestic courts for both taxpayers and competent authorities, which may increase their preference for arbitration in relation to court litigation

6.2.1.2.1 Increasing Taxpayer Preference for MAP

Despite certain important issues, such as lack of transparency and limited participation, the MAP is the preferred mode of dispute resolution for taxpayers compared to domestic remedies (e.g., bringing a case to a tax court).[709] The MAP is a relatively straightforward procedure for handling tax treaty disputes, and more importantly, there are time limits and other conditions in place that regulate the exchanges between the competent authorities on behalf of the taxpayer through the BEPS Action 14 rules (e.g., independence requirements at the level of the competent authority). Since domestic remedies may involve longer processing periods and may inevitably be more costly than MAP,[710] most taxpayers seem to be opting for the MAP, as evidenced by the increasing number of MAP cases being opened since 2016 (*see* Table I.1 of Appendix I).

6.2.1.2.2 Reluctance of Developing Countries Towards OECD's Mandatory and Binding Arbitration

As discussed in section 6.2.1.1 above, although the MAP provisions under the OECD and UN Models are largely standardised across IF countries through the adoption of the BEPS Action 14 minimum standard,[711] arbitration mechanisms under the two Models present procedural differences that separate developing countries that usually apply the UN Model and developed countries that apply the OECD Model. This dual arbitration structure is emphasised through institutional differences (e.g., lack of experience with arbitration, arbitrators being more familiar with developed country systems, lack of resources, etc.),[712] which developing countries insist would put them at a disadvantage compared to developed countries when negotiating MAP agreements. Such differences may explain the reluctance of developing countries towards adopting mandatory and binding arbitration. It is important to note, however, that the interests of taxpayers and competent authorities are aligned to a greater extent under the OECD Model than the UN Model, as there is a more balanced allocation of decision-making under the OECD arbitration mechanism (e.g., the taxpayer may participate in person in arbitration and also taxpayer may trigger arbitration if no MAP agreement is reached within a prescribed timeline).[713] The prophylactic role of the OECD arbitration mechanism also aligns the interests and objectives of taxpayers and competent authorities to a large extent.

709. *See* s. 4.3.1.2.
710. *See* s. 3.5.2.
711. Noted exceptions include the timeline of three years versus two years for triggering arbitration under the OECD and UN Models respectively.
712. *See* s. 4.3.2.2.
713. *Ibid.*

6.2.1.3 Strategies

6.2.1.3.1 *Public-Private Good Characteristics of Mechanisms*

As discussed through the analysis of the physical conditions, the functions associated with each of the three dispute resolution mechanisms in the ITR have different public-private good characteristics, as summarised in Table 4.[714] The aim of this analysis is to understand the degree to which the different mechanisms contribute to the wider field of international tax governance.

Table 4 Public-Private Good Characteristics Within the Tax Treaty Dispute Resolution System

	Action Situation 1: MAP			*Action Situation 2: UN Model Arbitration*			*Action Situation 3: OECD Model Arbitration*		
	Dispute Resolution	*Admin*	*BEPS Peer Review*	*Dispute Resolution*	*Admin*	*BEPS Peer Review*	*Dispute Resolution*	*Admin*	*BEPS Peer Review*
Private good	X			X	X		X		
Intermediate public good		X						X	
Public good			X			N/A			N/A

N/A: Not applicable.

The public-private good characteristics of the various functions largely affect the distribution of their costs and benefits across the system.[715] In the ITR, the dispute resolution function of all three mechanisms constitutes a private good as it affects only the disputant parties based on the private and confidential nature of the process and its outcome. However, the administration and peer review functions of the MAP under BEPS Action 14 increase its public good characteristics by extending the benefits and costs of the MAP to actors other than the disputant parties.[716] The UN arbitration mechanism, however, represents an entirely private good as both the dispute resolution and administrative functions are restricted to the disputant parties only (the BEPS peer review function is not applicable (N/A) for arbitration under either the UN or the OECD Model). The OECD arbitration mechanism – although it is implemented on a limited scale in only 31 of the 141 IF countries as of June 2022 – represents an

714. *See* ss 4.3.1.3, 4.3.2.3 and 4.3.3.3 for analysis of physical conditions in action situations 1, 2 and 3 respectively.
715. *See* s. 3.3.1.3.
716. *See* s. 4.3.1.3.3.

intermediate public good based on its administrative function. Arguably, it allows for a more balanced distribution of power among the concerned parties, i.e., the taxpayer, competent authorities and arbitrators, and its distinctly prophylactic effect leads to a more predictable and trustworthy legal system, which may be considered a public good.[717]

6.2.1.3.2 Implications

Based on the above analysis of the public-private goods characteristics, the MAP, despite its bilateral mechanism, has put in place a multilateral strategy through its administration and peer review under BEPS Action 14 to promote cooperation among the IF countries. Through the publication of the MAP profile and the OECD MAP Statistics, all IF members can mutually benefit when engaging in disputes. Taxpayers are also better informed about the procedures through published MAP guidelines.[718] Thus, the MAP has a crucial role to play in international tax governance by not only resolving the majority of cross-border tax disputes in a swift and less costly manner (compared to arbitration or domestic remedies) but also introducing a more multilateral framework among the competent authorities across the DTT network for resolving tax treaty disputes.

In contrast, the UN arbitration mechanism does not encourage cooperation at the multilateral level; the OECD arbitration mechanism shows more potential as an effective means of dispute resolution among countries based on a more balanced allocation of decision-making powers (although institutional differences need to be taken into account to ensure equitable solutions for both developed and developing countries).

6.2.2 LOSC

6.2.2.1 Rules

Table 5 summarises the seven working rules analysed within each of the three action situations identified under the LOSC.[719]

717. *See* s. 3.3.1.3.
718. *See* s. 4.3.1.3.2.
719. *See* ss 5.3.1.1, 5.3.2.1 and 5.3.3.1 for analysis of working rules in action situations 1, 2 and 3 respectively.

Table 5 Rules Governing LOSC's Dispute Resolution System

	Action Situation 1: Diplomatic Negotiations	*Action Situation 2: Conciliation*	*Action Situation 3: Adjudication*
Boundary rules	- States parties under LOSC	- States parties under LOSC - Independent conciliators	- ITLOS: States parties and non-States parties (private individuals through SDC), ITLOS judges - ICJ: States only, ICJ judges - Annex VII arbitration: States and non-States parties, arbitrators - Annex VIII arbitration: States parties, arbitrators
Position rules	- State negotiators as disputant parties	- State negotiators as disputant parties - Five-member conciliation commission appointed by State negotiators from a pre-approved list	- ITLOS/ICJ: respondents and applicants as disputant parties and judges elected by LOSC/UN members - Annexes VII and VIII arbitration: arbitrators selected by disputant parties from pre-approved lists to form a five-member arbitral tribunal
Information rules	- Private/confidential	- Private conciliation session	- ITLOS/ICJ: public

	Action Situation 1: Diplomatic Negotiations	*Action Situation 2: Conciliation*	*Action Situation 3: Adjudication*
		- Publication of rules and decisions decided through rules of procedure determined by disputant parties and conciliation commission - Only one known case of compulsory conciliation (Timor Sea conciliation) is published on PCA website	- Annexes VII and VIII arbitration: arbitration decision may be published as decided in rules of procedure decided by disputant parties and arbitrators - All but one arbitration case under Annex VII published on PCA website (no publicly known arbitration case under Annex VIII)
Authority rules	- Rules of procedure determined through mutual agreement between State negotiators	- Rules of procedure determined jointly by State negotiators and conciliation commission	- ITLOS/ICJ: judicial procedures set by Tribunal/Court - Annexes VII and VIII arbitration: procedural rules determined jointly by disputant parties and arbitrators
Aggregation rules	- Applicable law: LOSC, customary international law, domestic law - Administrative framework: negotiation rules decided by State negotiators in line with their respective constitutional rules	- Applicable law: LOSC and any additional sources of law as determined by disputant parties and conciliators - Administrative framework: rules of procedure determined by disputant parties and conciliation commission	- Applicable law: LOSC, general principles of international law, VCLT reference to international standards developed by other international bodies (e.g., International Maritime Organization)

	Action Situation 1: Diplomatic Negotiations	*Action Situation 2: Conciliation*	*Action Situation 3: Adjudication*
	– The negotiated agreement may be finalised in the form of a treaty or convention, etc.	– Conciliation may be voluntary or compulsory depending on the nature of the dispute (e.g., disputes regarding maritime border delimitation involves compulsory conciliation)	– Administrative framework: ITLOS/ICJ rules of procedure; Annexes VII and VIII arbitration rules determined by disputant parties and arbitration tribunal – States parties free to choose one of the four adjudication mechanisms under Art. 287 of LOSC – Arbitration under Annex VII is default mechanism
Scope rules	– Jurisdiction: disputes under LOSC – Finality of outcomes: non-binding process. – Negotiation is the first step for resolving any dispute; if no diplomatic solution is reached through negotiation, then parties would proceed to conciliation or adjudication (ITLOS/ICJ/arbitration under Annex VII or VIII) as per declaration under Art. 287 until dispute is resolved	– Jurisdiction: disputes under LOSC (for certain categories of disputes compulsory conciliation; otherwise voluntary conciliation) – Finality of outcomes: non-binding. If parties do not agree with recommendation by the conciliation commission, then parties would have to agree on alternative dispute resolution mechanism to resolve dispute	– Jurisdiction: ITLOS – LOSC and any other agreement that confers jurisdiction to ITLOS; ICJ – LOSC; arbitration under Annex VII – LOSC; arbitration under Annex VIII – four categories of disputes under LOSC (fisheries, protection and preservation of the marine environment, marine scientific research, or navigation, including pollution from vessels and by dumping)

	Action Situation 1: Diplomatic Negotiations	Action Situation 2: Conciliation	Action Situation 3: Adjudication
			- Finality of outcomes: ITLOS/ICJ ruling and arbitration decisions legally binding on disputant parties; non-binding recommendations report may also be requested under Annex VIII arbitration
Payoff rules	- State negotiators bear their own costs - No third-party fees - Flexible procedure - Power disparities may affect weaker negotiating party	- Fees to set up conciliation commission shared among disputant parties - Independent conciliation report may be especially useful for weaker party to negotiate a win-win outcome (e.g., as in *Timor Sea* conciliation case)	- No additional fees for bringing case to ITLOS/ICJ as all members pay annual fees (legal costs incurred for preparing case) - International focus may throw light on issue to gather political support - Additional fees for setting up arbitral tribunal under Annexes VII and VIII shared among disputant parties

6.2.2.1.1 *Flexible Yet Mandatory Application of Dispute Resolution Mechanisms to Ensure Resolution*

As shown in Table 5, States parties under the LOSC may have recourse to at least six (inter-linked) dispute resolution mechanisms for resolving maritime disputes: diplomatic negotiations, conciliation, ITLOS, ICJ and arbitration under Annexes VII and VIII. The analysis of the aggregation rules reveals that the LOSC's system not only presents States parties with a wide range of dispute resolution mechanisms, but it also gives parties the freedom to declare their preferred means of adjudication, which are triggered if no diplomatic solution is reached within a reasonable time period (in accordance with the negotiation rules determined by both parties).[720] If the disputant parties have made different declarations or none at all, then the dispute would be submitted to arbitration under Annex VII (as the default mechanism) unless they mutually agree on a different forum. Judicial settlement or arbitration would not apply, however, if the dispute falls under a limitation in Article 297 (e.g., disputes relating to fishing rights in the EEZ) or if at least one of the parties has made an optional declaration under Article 298 to exclude the dispute from adjudication (e.g., disputes relating to maritime border delimitation).[721] If the limitation or exclusion applies, the dispute would be submitted to compulsory conciliation under Annex V of the LOSC for resolution, failing which, the parties would have to agree to any other dispute resolution mechanism until the dispute is resolved.[722]

In spite of specific exclusions from adjudication under Articles 297 and 298, the LOSC's dispute resolution system is structured with the aim of guaranteeing some form of resolution for all disputes under the LOSC through a flexible yet mandatory application of the rules. There is a wide array of adjudicative mechanisms available which parties may mutually agree to use in the absence of diplomatic solutions, irrespective of the declarations they made under Article 287 when ratifying the treaty. In addition, this flexibility aspect is also emphasised through the use of the LOSC's dispute resolution system as a last resort mechanism, as the LOSC gives priority to other dispute resolution mechanisms under other bilateral or regional treaties that states may be bound under.[723]

6.2.2.1.2 Balanced Allocation of Decision-Making Powers

The authority rules in Table 5 reveal a balanced allocation of decision-making powers across the different dispute resolution mechanisms of the LOSC to achieve equitable solutions. The diplomatic negotiation process allows disputant parties to set their own procedures through mutual agreement. In the conciliation process, disputant parties may still negotiate among themselves through a conciliation commission that sets out the rules of procedure jointly with the parties. If no solution is reached through such consensual means, then disputant parties submit the dispute to judicial settlement or arbitration, where decision-making is shifted to an independent third party. Under the ICJ or the ITLOS, the decision-making power is entirely relinquished to an independently appointed panel of judges, although disputant parties may still retain some

720. *See* s. 5.3.3.1.5.2.
721. *See* s. 5.3.3.1.5.2.
722. *See* s. 5.3.3.1.5.2.2.
723. *See* s. 5.3.3.1.5.2.3.

control over the procedures in the arbitration proceedings (e.g., by selecting arbitrators or approving the rules of procedure devised by the arbitrators). In this way, decision-making powers are distributed across the dispute resolution system to ensure that the rule of law can be applied effectively, although primacy is given to diplomatic negotiations.

The scope rules across the LOSC's system also show balance in terms of finality of outcomes between the non-binding diplomatic mechanisms that respect principles of sovereignty of the States parties and the legally binding judicial and arbitration rulings that operate under the rule of law. The LOSC's dispute resolution system recognises that although negotiations may be the preferred mode of dispute resolution,[724] it is not without fault as it may also exacerbate the power disparities between the disputant parties. Conciliation introduces a neutral third party that may mitigate the effects of such power disparities by assisting the weaker parties (usually developing countries) to negotiate an equitable agreement while avoiding the pressures and constraints of legally binding procedures. The conciliation procedure may thus constitute an alternative to and/or supplemental means to the ITLOS, the ICJ and the Annex VII tribunal as an effective compromise between diplomatic negotiations and adjudication through court and tribunals, as shown through the payoff rules in the case of *Timor Sea* compulsory conciliation case.[725]

6.2.2.1.3 Participation of States and Non-States Parties

Although the LOSC's dispute resolution mechanism is predominantly an interstate instrument, the analysis of the boundary rules across the three action situations shows that the LOSC's system allows access to not only States parties (states and international organisations) but also non-States parties through some of its specific provisions.[726] For instance, in case of disputes, a State party may initiate an arbitration proceeding under Annex VII against a non-State party. The ITLOS may also hear cases that are brought under agreements other than the LOSC that involve non-States parties. The SDC under the ITLOS is also capable of hearing disputes with respect to activities in the seabed Area involving States parties, the ISA or the Enterprise, State enterprises and natural or juridical persons such as individual contractors involved in mining contracts in the seabed Area (there is no need for the government of those persons to bring a claim on their behalf). The participation of non-States parties on equal footing with States parties allows all parties to be subject to equal rules and, hence, more equitable solutions across the law of the sea regime. In addition, the participation of juridical persons through the SDC ensures that their views and circumstances are accurately taken into consideration, given that they are directly involved in the disputes.

724. *See supra* n. 424.
725. *See* s. 5.3.2.1.7.
726. *See* s. 5.3.3.1.1.

6.2.2.2 Norms

Table 6 summarises the potential trends identified in each of the three action situations under the LOSC based on the analysis of community attributes.[727] The analysis examines the extent to which the various dispute resolution mechanisms are applied under the law of the sea regime.

Table 6 Norms Underpinning LOSC's Dispute Resolution System

	Action Situation 1: Diplomatic Negotiations	*Action Situation 2: Conciliation*	*Action Situation 3: Adjudication*
Community attributes	- Preferred method of dispute resolution (lower costs, flexible, less political pressure) - May perpetuate power disparities between disputant parties (State negotiators) - 186 maritime boundary agreements achieved between 1960 and 2008, 76 of which referred to dispute resolution mechanisms, with 56 of these agreements (i.e., 73 %) specifying bilateral negotiation as the preferred way to settle future conflicts.	- May provide a more level playing field, especially for weaker State negotiators - Voluntary conciliation not popular and only one publicly known case of compulsory conciliation (*Timor Sea* conciliation)	- Increasing preference for ITLOS (especially for developing countries) - Out of 63 countries that made a declaration under Article 287, 39 countries chose the ITLOS as the preferred procedure; 21 countries chose the ICJ - By 2019, ITLOS had adjudicated 29 cases; ICJ had heard 28 contentious cases on matters governed by the law of the sea - 14 Annex VII arbitration cases through the PCA and no publicly known case under Annex VIII

727. *See* ss 5.3.1.2, 5.3.2.2 and 5.3.3.2 for analysis of community attributes in action situations 1, 2 and 3 respectively.

6.2.2.2.1 *Preference for Negotiations and ITLOS among Developing Countries*

As shown in Table 6, there is a clear preference for diplomatic negotiations as the preferred mode of dispute resolution among States parties, as specified in more than 70% (56 out of 76 agreements) of the maritime boundary agreements finalised between 1960 and 2008 (that referred to dispute resolution). There is also an increasingly important role for adjudication, especially through the ITLOS. Out of 63 States parties that made definitive declarations under Article 287, 62% (39 states) have chosen the ITLOS, while only 33% (21 states) have chosen the ICJ; 60% of States that have selected the ITLOS constitute developing and emerging countries.[728] This signals an increasing preference among developing countries for the jurisdiction of the ITLOS. In fact, the ITLOS has adjudicated 29 cases by 2019, most of which involved at least one developing country.[729] As of 2019, the ICJ had adjudicated 28 cases relating to the law of the sea regime, while the PCA has administered 14 Annex VII cases.[730] There are no known arbitration cases under Annex VIII, and the reasons for this are not clear, although it is possible that they are not being made public. It is noted, however, that only 7 States parties have selected Annex VIII arbitration as their preferred means of dispute resolution (*see* Table II.1 in Appendix II).

6.2.2.2.2 *Limited Application of Conciliation*

In spite of the advantages that conciliation may offer in terms of flexibility (parties may select conciliators, approve the conciliation procedures devised by the commission and even reject the recommendations issued by the commission),[731] voluntary conciliation is rarely used under the LOSC's dispute resolution system.[732] Moreover, the Timor Sea conciliation comprises the only publicly known compulsory conciliation case, which suggests that States parties may be applying other mechanisms like negotiations or even adjudication instead of conciliation to resolve maritime disputes unless the conciliation case is kept private. However, these results may, in fact, support the presumption that once states have agreed to relinquish control by involving a third party, they would rather have recourse to binding third-party settlement.[733]

6.2.2.3 Strategies

6.2.2.3.1 *Public-Private Good Characteristics of LOSC Mechanisms*

The analysis of the physical conditions focuses on the public-private good characteristics of the various functions associated with each of the three action situations

728. *See* s. 5.3.3.2.
729. *See supra* n. 527 for the list of ITLOS cases.
730. *See supra* n. 529 for the list of LOSC Annex VII cases administered under the PCA.
731. *See* s. 5.3.2.1.4.
732. *See supra* n. 476.
733. *See* s. 5.3.2.2.

identified under the LOSC (diplomatic negotiations, conciliation and adjudicative measures) as summarised in Table 7.[734] The aim of this analysis is to understand the degree to which the different mechanisms contribute to the wider field of oceans governance.

Table 7 Public-Private Good Characteristics Within the LOSC's Dispute Settlement System

	Action Situation 1: Diplomatic Negotiations		*Action Situation 2: Conciliation*		*Action Situation 3: Judicial Settlement & Arbitration*	
	Dispute Resolution	*Admin*	*Dispute Resolution*	*Admin*	*Dispute Resolution*	*Admin*
Private good	X					
Intermediate public good		X	X	X		
Public good					X	X

As shown above, the dispute resolution function associated with the diplomatic negotiations constitutes the only private good with respect to the dispute resolution mechanisms under the LOSC. However, negotiations also have an important administrative function of international relations-building, which represents an intermediate public good (as it promotes peace among countries). The compulsory conciliation procedure also represents an intermediate public good as it is the only prescribed mechanism for resolving border delimitation disputes that are exempt from adjudication under Article 298 of the LOSC to establish peace. More importantly, the adjudication mechanisms, including the ICJ, ITLOS and arbitration under Annexes VII and VIII, constitute public goods due to the public nature of the dispute resolution function (e.g., through the publication of legal rulings), which the general public can have access to for learning purposes and also for developing international law under the law of the sea regime (e.g., the concept of equitable considerations in the delimitation of maritime boundaries).[735] In addition, the administration of legal proceedings involving the ITLOS, SDC and the ISA also represent public goods as they have a direct impact on the oceans by setting out policies governing the marine environment.

6.2.2.3.2 Implications

Based on the above analysis, all of the functions associated with the LOSC's mechanisms, except for the dispute resolution function of the diplomatic negotiations, exhibit

734. *See* ss 5.3.1.3, 5.3.2.3 and 5.3.3.3 for analysis of physical conditions in action situations 1, 2 and 3 respectively.
735. *See* s. 5.3.3.3.2.1.

intermediate public or public good characteristics. Thus, the LOSC mechanisms, especially the judicial settlement and arbitral tribunals, reflect a wider cooperative strategy (through procedural and substantive rules under international law) to develop the concept of equity and also to address collective action issues under the law of the sea regime.

6.3 IDENTIFYING RELEVANT ASPECTS OF THE LOSC TO ADDRESS ISSUES IN THE ITR

This section compares the patterns of interaction mapped out in the ITR and the LOSC in section 6.2 above to identify relevant aspects of the LOSC's dispute resolution system for addressing the issues of capacity, uncertainty and inequitable solutions at the operational level in tax treaty dispute resolution.

6.3.1 Addressing Capacity Issues

As explained in section 6.2.1.1.1.3, capacity issues within the MAP and build-up of unresolved MAP cases may be explained through bottlenecks at the competent authority level as limited resources are allocated between an increasing number of transfer pricing and non-transfer pricing cases. To address the bottleneck effect within the MAP, it may be useful to consider alternative mechanisms for handling increasing disputes across the ITR, especially with regard to fact-intensive transfer pricing cases that may take up most of the resources across competent authorities. There are various aspects of the LOSC's system that may be useful for addressing such capacity issues in the ITR.

6.3.1.1 Extend MAP System by Adapting the LOSC's Flexible Yet Mandatory Mechanisms

As described in section 6.2.2.1.1, under the LOSC system, any dispute under the Convention must first be submitted to the diplomatic negotiation process. If no agreement is reached, then the dispute is submitted to either compulsory conciliation or adjudication (ITLOS, ICJ or arbitration) depending on the nature of the dispute and whether the concerned parties have chosen a forum of preference under Article 287 or opted to exclude certain disputes from adjudication under Article 298. For example, disputes relating to activities in the Area are resolved solely through the SDC (under ITLOS), and maritime border delimitation disputes are usually addressed through compulsory conciliation unless the parties mutually agree on a different mechanism. If the disputant parties are not able to agree on a specific mechanism, the dispute is submitted to arbitration under Annex VII as the default mechanism.

The LOSC mechanisms may thus be applied in a flexible yet mandatory manner to guarantee some form of resolution of various types of disputes under the law of the sea regime. A similar flexible yet mandatory structure may be adapted in the ITR to ensure that all categories of international tax disputes are guaranteed some form of resolution, including the potential tax disputes under the OECD's proposed Pillar One and Two.[736] More specifically, I recommend using separate mechanisms to address transfer pricing and non-transfer pricing cases for which no MAP agreement is reached within the prescribed timeline of 24 months. This is because the two categories of disputes have very different resource requirements, which may be met more efficiently through different mechanisms.

As explored also in section 6.2.2.1.1, the LOSC emphasises a flexible application of the rules by giving priority to dispute resolution mechanisms under other bilateral or regional treaties which the State party may be bound under. Although such practice of resolving disputes by using mechanisms in other treaties than the applicable tax treaty may help reduce capacity issues in the MAP, it may also contradict efforts towards a more uniform dispute resolution system that would apply to all IF users and, in fact, create more loopholes in the system which may perpetuate inequalities across the ITR. The current tax treaty dispute resolution system already suffers from such fragmentation effects due to the bilateral nature of the MAP that may be applied differently across the DTT network (discussed in section 6.2.1.1.3). As a result, when addressing capacity constraints in the ITR, recommendations proposed in this thesis for expanding the mechanisms under the current tax treaty dispute resolution system will focus on the LOSC mechanisms integrated within the Convention.

6.3.1.2 Focus on Arbitration and Judicial Settlement Mechanisms

As discussed in section 6.2.2.2.2, the *Timor Sea* case is the only publicly known compulsory conciliation case so far, and despite its success under the LOSC, there is not sufficient evidence that compulsory conciliation would have similar results in the ITR. Voluntary conciliation, for its part, may be considered functionally similar to the UN arbitration mechanism in that they both involve an independent third-party decision that is not legally binding on the disputant parties. As discussed in section 6.2.1.3.2, the voluntary and non-binding nature of the UN arbitration procedure may not be very useful as it does not even produce a prophylactic effect, as opposed to the mandatory and binding OECD arbitration. Therefore, conciliation is not recommended in the ITR. Instead, a legally binding and mandatory arbitration mechanism would be more effective in guaranteeing a resolution of the tax dispute, and even if it is not applied, its prophylactic effect may push competent authorities to come to an agreement within the prescribed timelines.

However, as discussed in section 6.2.1.2.2, developing countries are reluctant to adopt mandatory and binding arbitration. Any proposed arbitration mechanisms would need to take into consideration the requirements of developing countries to ensure implementation in all jurisdictions across the IF. In this respect, the LOSC's

736. *See* s. 2.3.1.3.

adjudication mechanisms may provide a useful benchmark for expanding the tax treaty dispute resolution system. The LOSC's arbitration mechanisms could be adapted into the ITR to strengthen the current mechanisms and provide a more uniform arbitration system that all IF users may avail of (as opposed to the dual procedures under the OECD and UN Models). In order to provide more flexibility to the users (taxpayers and competent authorities) and also to address cross-border tax issues which are not covered under MAP (or bilateral tax treaties), an ITT based on the ITLOS may also be useful in the ITR, especially for addressing uncertainty issues as discussed below.

6.3.2 Addressing Uncertainty

As discussed in section 6.2.1.1.1, uncertainty in the ITR is perpetuated through (1) indeterminacy issues through lack of transparency and lack of relevant case law in the ITR; (2) lack of legally binding processes and outcomes, which may result in unresolved MAP cases; and (3) unbalanced allocation of decision-making powers to competent authorities that may encourage mistrust on the part of taxpayers, especially under the UN Model (discussed in section 6.2.1.1.2). Based on the patterns of interaction generated in the LOSC's system, there are several aspects that could be relevant for addressing these issues.

6.3.2.1 Develop International Tax Case Law Through International Tribunal and/or Arbitration

As discussed in section 6.2.2.3, the adjudication mechanisms under the LOSC, including the ICJ, ITLOS and arbitration under Annexes VII and VIII, constitute public goods based on their public dispute resolution function (i.e., publication of rules of procedure and rulings) and their administrative function that contributes to the development of international law (e.g., the concept of equitable considerations under the LOSC) and marine environmental policies under the law of the sea regime. These mechanisms are not only public but also legally binding on the parties.

In contrast, the analysis in section 6.2.1.3 shows that the MAP and arbitration mechanisms under the ITR reflect mostly private good characteristics, with limited impact on the wider international tax governance except for the compliance-monitoring function under the BEPS Action 14 peer review. In order to increase the public good characteristics of the tax treaty dispute resolution mechanisms, it may be useful to introduce more legalistic mechanisms based on the ITLOS and arbitration under Annexes VII and VIII (since they are also public mechanisms). This would also help to address issues of indeterminacy and lack of legally binding outcomes that exacerbate uncertainty in the ITR by expanding the rule of law within tax treaty dispute resolution. Interestingly, the use of a specialised international tribunal in the ITR was also recommended by Altman in 2005 for improving tax treaty dispute resolution.[737]

737. *See* s. 2.3.1.2.

6.3.2.2 *Reallocate Decision-Making Power Across the System*

As discussed in section 6.2.2.1.2, decision-making powers are distributed across the LOSC's dispute resolution system in such a way as to achieve a balance between the principle of sovereign rights and the rule of law. For instance, if disputant parties are not able to reach a diplomatic agreement, then the dispute is generally submitted to judicial settlement or arbitration, where their decision-making powers (to determine rules of procedure or decide on outcomes) are progressively allocated to independent third parties. The increasingly binding processes and outcomes across the LOSC's mechanisms (i.e., from negotiation to conciliation to arbitration and judicial settlement) also contribute to the balance of power between disputant parties and independent third parties within the LOSC's system, although primacy is given to diplomatic negotiations.

Similar arrangements could also be useful in the ITR to ensure a more balanced allocation of decision-making powers across the tax treaty dispute resolution system while still giving priority to the MAP. It is important here, however, to take into account a key difference between the institutional actors of the ITR and the LOSC.[738] In the MAP, competent authorities negotiate on behalf of the private taxpayer to address any tax issues, and any agreement may directly affect the taxpayer's tax returns as well as tax revenues at the national level. This creates a three-way transaction that requires an adequate allocation of rights and decision-making powers among all three parties. On the other hand, under the LOSC, there is no private party involved in the government negotiations. Any agreements between governments are usually drafted into treaties as agreed between the two government parties alone and thus constitute a two-way transaction. Despite such differences, the LOSC mechanisms, especially the functioning of the ITLOS and the SDC, may provide some helpful insight into the balance of rights and responsibilities as they also deal with private parties (e.g., individual contractors involved in mining contracts in the seabed Area).[739]

6.3.3 Addressing Inequitable Solutions

As discussed in section 6.2.1.1.3, despite the implementation of BEPS Action 14 across IF jurisdictions, inequitable solutions across the ITR may be generated through differentiated rules under the MAP (mainly due to restrictions under domestic law) and dual arbitration systems under the UN and OECD Models which lead to unequal treatment across the different jurisdictions of the ITR. These issues of inequitable solutions are usually worse for competent authorities and taxpayers from developing countries when dealing with their counterparts in developed countries that may be technically, economically or politically more advanced (and therefore able to secure more favourable positions during MAP negotiations).

738. *See* s. 2.4.2.2.
739. *See* s. 5.3.3.1.1.1.1.

As mentioned in section 6.2.2.1.3, the participation of States parties and non-States parties (including juridical persons) through specific LOSC forums allows all parties (from developed and developing countries) to be subject to equal rules and, arguably, more equitable solutions across the law of the sea regime. The creation of the ITLOS under the LOSC may be particularly useful for developing countries to achieve equitable solutions based on the analysis of their preferences (*see* section 6.2.2.2.1). The SDC is also relevant as it allows a juridical person (e.g., individual contractor) to take part in court proceedings despite the interstate nature of the LOSC's system. These mechanisms may be relevant in the ITR to achieve an inclusive dispute resolution system for resolving increasingly multilateral disputes under the rule of law.

6.4 ASSESSING INCLUSIVITY

This section applies the second part of Step B of the pIAD analysis to assess and compare inclusivity (participation) at the policymaking and constitutional levels by analysing the relevant actors and the rules that govern the decision-making processes at each level. The aim is to identify relevant consensus-based techniques used in the LOSC's dispute resolution system that may be applied in the ITR to facilitate the implementation of the proposed reforms across the IF while taking into consideration the different institutional contexts of the two regimes.

6.4.1 Inclusivity at the Policymaking Level

6.4.1.1 ITR

6.4.1.1.1 Actors

In the context of the tax treaty dispute resolution system, the policymaking process involves the negotiation of the MAP and arbitration provisions in the bilateral tax treaties between contracting States. The main actors usually include government-level officers from the tax administration as State negotiators with experience and knowledge of tax treaties, international tax issues and domestic tax legislation, although in some cases, an official from the Ministry of Foreign Affairs may also be a member of the negotiating team.[740]

6.4.1.1.2 Policymaking Rules

6.4.1.1.2.1 Standardised Text of MAP Provision Based on OECD and UN Models

The policymaking level rules refer to the rules that guide the design of the MAP and arbitration provisions in the bilateral tax treaties. The MAP provisions negotiated

740. UN Department of Economic and Social Affairs, *Papers on selected topics in negotiation of tax treaties for developing countries* 75 (United Nations 2014).

therein are usually included in Article 25 of the applicable bilateral tax treaty based on Article 25 of the OECD or UN Model. This standardised format has been reinforced even more since the rollout of the BEPS Action Plan in 2015 and the subsequent commitment of all IF jurisdictions to implement mandatory MAP rules under the BEPS Action 14 minimum standard.[741] Thus, despite the bilateral nature of the negotiations regarding the MAP provisions in tax treaties, the MAP provision is largely standardised across the DTT network, irrespective of whether the tax treaty follows the OECD or the UN Model format. This creates limited space for negotiation of the MAP clause by State negotiators in bilateral treaties.

Treaty negotiators may have more decision-making powers when it comes to the supplementary arbitration procedure as it is not part of the BEPS Action 14 minimum standard, although the dual arbitration procedures under the OECD and UN Models lead to non-uniform treatment across the ITR with respect to the resolution of MAP cases.[742] In fact, to date, the OECD arbitration provision has been adopted in tax treaties mostly among developed countries, as developing and emerging nations like China and India remain wary of loss of sovereignty and limited expertise in relation to the arbitration process.[743] There is a slight shift noted, however, in the position of developing countries when it comes to mandatory binding dispute resolution under the Pillar One proposal, as most countries have agreed in principle to such a mechanism.

6.4.1.1.2.2 Modifying MAP Provisions Through Competent Authority Agreements

The tax treaty is generally concluded when the countries exchange instruments of ratification. The treaty enters into force in accordance with the specific rules in the treaty (Article 29 (Entry into force) of the UN Model or Article 31 of the OECD Model). Once a treaty is in force, it may be modified in minor or major ways by the mutual consent of the contracting States. It is commonplace for them to amend a tax treaty by entering into a Protocol to the treaty, although it is usually a lengthy process. To a limited degree, the MAP provisions may allow for tax treaties to be updated without a formal amendment procedure through the interpretative process as it authorises the competent authorities of the two States to resolve issues of interpretation.[744] As such, certain aspects of the MAP provisions may be revised more swiftly through competent authority agreements or exchanges without going through another negotiation and ratification process. Thus, treaty negotiators at the level of the competent authority may have more decision-making power with respect to the modification process, although generally, the structure of the MAP clause would follow the Model treaty provision and BEPS Action 14.

741. *See* Action 14 Peer Review Documents, *supra* n. 31, at paras 12.A1, 14.B3-B5 and 14.B7.
742. *See* Art. 25(5) OECD Model; Art. 25 Alternative B UN Model.
743. *See* s. 4.3.2.2.
744. *See* Art. 25(3) OECD Model; Art. 25(3) UN Model.

6.4.1.2 LOSC

6.4.1.2.1 Actors

The policymaking level in the LOSC involves the negotiation of the dispute resolution provisions under Part XV of the Convention. Since the LOSC is a multilateral treaty, the relevant actors include the group of international negotiators participating in the UNCLOS III negotiations from 1973 to 1982. These included a total of almost 160 delegates grouped under the Western industrialised States, the Socialist States and the Group of 77.[745] Thus, in contrast to the ITR, policymaking in the LOSC is conducted at a multilateral and not bilateral level. The policymaking rules refer specifically to the rules that underpin the international negotiations of the dispute resolution provisions in the LOSC.

6.4.1.2.2 Policymaking Rules

6.4.1.2.2.1 Formalising the Consensus Principle

The UNCLOS III Conference recognised that due to the widely divergent interests on issues of paramount importance to States, a process of simply voting through a majority view would not lead to a lasting legal regime. Therefore, the Rules of Procedure adopted by the Conference in 1974 departed from the pattern normally applicable to UN conferences for the taking of decisions.[746] It incorporated a 'Gentleman's Agreement', approved by the General Assembly in 1973,[747] which provided that the Conference should make every effort to reach agreement on substantive matters by way of consensus and that there should be no voting on such matters until all efforts at consensus had been exhausted. Before any substantive matter could be put to a vote, a determination had to be made by a two-thirds majority of representatives present and voting, including a majority of the states participating in that session of the Conference, that all efforts at reaching agreement had been exhausted. Although UNCLOS III did not invent consensus as a rule of decision-making, it was the first major international conference that decided to rely on this rule and developed a consensus technique that revolutionised global decision-making to ensure an equitable decision-making process.[748]

745. *See* Alan Beesley, *The Negotiating Strategy of UNCLOS III: Developing and Developed Countries as Partners: A Pattern for Future Multilateral International Conferences?* 46(2) L. & *Contemp. Problems* 183 (1983) DOI: 10.2307/1191524.
746. Tommy Koh and Shanmugam Jayakumar, *The Negotiating Process of The Third United Nations Conference on The Law of the Sea* in *United Nations Convention on the Law of the Sea 1982: A Commentary* 29, 99 (Myron H. Nordquist ed., Vol. 1, Martinus Nijhoff Publishers 1985).
747. *UNCLOS III Draft Rules of Procedure: Note by the Secretary-General* UN Doc. A/CONF.62/L.1 (3 Jun. 1974). *See* Appendix for a copy of the Gentleman's Agreement approved by the UN General Assembly at its 2169th meeting on 16 Nov. 1973.
748. Barry Buzan, *Negotiating by Consensus: Developments in Technique at the United Nations Conference on the Law of the Sea* 75(2) Am. J. Int'l L. 324 (1981) DOI: 10.2307/2201255. *See also* Koers, *supra* n. 656, at 28.

6.4.1.2.2.2 Building the Negotiating Text from Scratch

UNCLOS III adopted a revolutionary approach by proceeding without a draft negotiating text (discussed in section 5.3.5.1). Faced with a great number of proposals and variants regarding various aspects of the law of the sea (gathered through the work of the Seabed (preparatory) committee in the years leading up to the opening of the Conference),[749] three Main Committees were formed to draft the negotiating texts of specific topics relating to the law of the sea (that constitute the three parts of the ISNT), each of which included a relevant discussion of the relevant dispute resolution provisions.[750] The dispute resolution provisions were progressively refined in successive versions of the negotiating text when consensus was achieved among the delegates and finally grouped under a separate Part IV of the ISNT by the President of the Conference.[751]

The Conference also vested a lot of authority in the Collegium, namely the President of the Conference, the Chairmen of the three Main Committees, the Chairman of the Drafting Committee and the Rapporteur-General for drafting and revising progressive drafts of the ISNT by giving them the freedom to choose from among the various proposals or draft their own text to reflect the trends in the Conference.[752] The power vested in them was enormous since it was not easy for delegations to subsequently alter the text, and the decision whether to revise it or not was also largely left to the President and Chairmen – a practice that was unprecedented at the UN.[753] It was only after they consolidated the four different parts of the negotiating text into the ICNT in 1977 that the decision-making powers of the Chairmen were diluted among various negotiating groups set up to address certain 'hardcore' issues on which no consensus had been reached yet.[754] This technique allowed for all subsequent revisions to be based on widespread support among all delegates to ensure that the text remained cohesive until its completion in 1982.[755]

Such a delegated approach was not only useful for ensuring that the views of all delegates were reflected in the text and for integrating the fragmented efforts of the various interest groups, but it also resulted in one of the longest and most intricate dispute settlement provisions ever drafted under Part XV of the Convention.[756] Presumably, the wide range of dispute resolution procedures available under Part XV and the freedom to choose any one of the four available adjudicative forums[757] were the result of the compromises made among the delegates to achieve consensus.

749. Constantin A. Stavropoulos, *Procedural Problems of The Third Conference on The Law of the Sea* in Myron Nordquist (ed.) *United Nations Convention on the Law of the Sea 1982: A Commentary* lxiii (Vol. 1, Martinus Nijhoff Publishers 1985).
750. *See* s. 5.3.5.4.2.
751. *See* s. 5.3.5.4.3.
752. Koers, *supra* n. 656, at 29.
753. Koh and Jayakumar, *supra* n. 746, at 56.
754. *See supra* n. 688 for a description of the hardcore issues remaining in the ICNT.
755. Bernardo Zuleta, *'Introduction'* in *United Nations, The Law of the Sea: United Nations Convention on the Law of the Sea with Index and Final Act of the Third United Nations Conference on the Law of the Sea* xxiv (St. Martin's Press in cooperation with the United Nations 1983).
756. *See supra* n. 17.
757. *See* s. 5.3.3.1.5.2.1.

6.4.1.2.2.3 The Package Deal Concept

During UNCLOS III, a small group of States had decried the establishment of a regime for binding third-party dispute settlement, suggesting instead to have dispute settlement provisions annexed to the Convention like an optional protocol.[758] Nonetheless, the majority (including the US) felt that not having the dispute settlement provisions as an integral part of the LOSC could weaken it and jeopardise its ratification and acceptance worldwide.[759] It was also believed that 'the interpretation and application of an instrument containing so many innovations were bound to generate dispute which could only be resolved by the use of a third-party procedure'[760] and thus incorporating the dispute resolution procedures in the LOSC would prevent unilateral interpretations of the treaty provisions by States.[761]

This decision largely owes its making to the failure of the dispute settlement provisions of the 1958 Geneva Conventions on the law of the sea. The 1958 Geneva Conventions provided for dispute settlement provisions in an Optional Protocol rather than as a part of the substantive body of laws.[762] It is noteworthy that to date, no dispute has been referred under the Optional Protocol or the Fishing Convention.[763] Out of a total of 44 states that had originally signed the Optional Protocol, only 37 states actually followed it up with ratifications, definitive signatures or successions.[764] Countries such as the USA, Canada and China, which had initially signed the Optional Protocol, refrained from finally ratifying and accepting it.[765] Moreover, out of an average number of 52 states that became parties to the other four conventions, the Optional Protocol had only 37 parties.[766] Industrialised countries like Japan and Russia, which had actively participated in the other 1958 Geneva Conventions, chose not to get involved with the Optional Protocol at all.[767] Taking all this into account, it would be

758. *United Nations Convention on the Law of the Sea 1982: A Commentary* 43 (Shabtai Rosenne and Louis B. Sohn eds, vol. 5, Martinus Nijhoff Publishers 1989).
759. Sohn, Settlement of Disputes, *supra* n. 665, at 516.
760. Merrills, *supra* n. 572 at 179.
761. Louis B. Sohn, *The Importance of the Peaceful Settlement of Disputes Provisions of the United Nations Convention on the Law of the Sea* in *Entry into Force of the Law of the Sea Convention* 265 (M.H. Nordquist and J.N. Moore eds, Martinus Nijhoff Publishers 1995) (Importance of peaceful settlement of disputes).
762. *Optional Protocol of Signature Concerning the Compulsory Settlement of Disputes* (29 Apr. 1958) 450 UNTS 169 (Optional Protocol).
763. Alan E. Boyle, *UNCLOS, the Marine Environment and the Settlement of Disputes* in *Competing Norms in the Law of Marine Environmental Protection: Focus on Ship Safety and Pollution Prevention* 241, 244 (n. 10) (Hendrik Ringbom ed., Kluwer Law International 1997).
764. *See* Status of Optional Protocol at Chapter XXI (5) of the UN Depository (Status of Optional Protocol) https://treaties.un.org/Pages/ViewDetails.aspx?src=TREATY&mtdsg_no=XXI-5&chapter=21&clang=_en accessed 22 Jul. 2022. The Optional Protocol received 14 Signatures, and seven States that had placed their signatures, failed to ratify, definitively sign or succeed to it.
765. Status of Optional Protocol, *supra* n. 764.
766. *Ibid.* The Convention on the Territorial Sea and the Contiguous Zone had 51 States parties; the Convention on the High Seas had 62 States parties; the Convention on Fishing and Conservation of the Living Resources of the High Seas had 37 States parties and the Convention on the Continental Shelf had 57 States parties.
767. *Ibid.*

fair to say that the dispute settlement provisions as an Optional Protocol to the law of the sea had failed, prompting the delegates at UNCLOS III to keep the dispute settlement provisions integrated within the LOSC itself to ensure its effectiveness.

6.4.2 Inclusivity at the Constitutional Level

6.4.2.1 ITR

Constitutional level rules frame the context in which policymaking rules are applied by determining the participants and the rules governing decisions at the policymaking level. Since one of the defining features at the policymaking level involves the standardised implementation of the MAP provision based on Article 25 of the OECD or the UN Model throughout the 3,000 or so bilateral tax treaties, constitutional rules in the context of the ITR will examine the rules that frame the design of the OECD and UN Models (especially Article 25) including the design of the BEPS Action 14 minimum standard that determines the MAP provisions applied across the IF countries. There are two distinct sets of actors and rules at the OECD and the UN.

6.4.2.1.1 MAP under the OECD Model

The Committee on Fiscal Affairs (CFA), which consists of senior government tax officials from the member countries, is responsible for developing the OECD Model as well as other aspects of international tax cooperation. The CFA operates through several working parties at the CTPA, which contains the permanent secretariat for the CFA.[768] The working parties consist of delegates from the member countries. Working Party No. 1 on Tax Conventions and Related Questions is responsible for the provisions of the OECD Model, and it examines issues related to it on an ongoing basis. Prior to the creation of the BEPS IF in June 2016, the CFA consisted mainly of tax officials from the OECD countries, although some non-OECD countries participated as 'BEPS invitees' or 'BEPS Associates' through the CFA.[769] It follows that most developing and emerging countries were not included in any meaningful way in the treaty negotiating structures prior to 2016, including the development of the BEPS Action Plan, which took place from 2012-2015. This may explain the criticisms from developing countries and the international tax community generally that the BEPS Action Points launched in 2015 do not adequately reflect the concerns of developing and emerging nations.[770]

In relation to MAP specifically, the FTA MAP Forum[771] (created as a subgroup of the FTA) meets regularly to deliberate on general matters affecting all participants'

768. *See* OECD, *CFA Organisation Chart* www.oecd.org/tax/beps/committee-on-fiscal-affairs-and-subsidiary-bodies-organigramme.pdf accessed 2 Apr. 2021.
769. Allison Christians, *BEPS and the New International Tax Order* 6 B.Y.U. L. Rev. 1603, 1605 (2016).
770. *See* generally Christians, *supra* n. 769; Burgers and Mosquera, *supra* n. 93; Martin Hearson, *The Challenges for Developing Countries in International Tax Justice* 54(10) J. Dev. Stud. (2017).
771. *See* FTA Forum, *supra* n. 246.

programs for conducting MAP, including collaborations with other multilateral bodies to further its goals on an ongoing basis. The FTA MAP Forum was also the main party leading the development of the peer review process of the BEPS Action 14 minimum standard (including the Terms of Reference and the assessment methodology) in October 2016. The FTA MAP Forum constitutes only 53 OECD and non-OECD countries, including all G20 members, representing less than half of the IF population (comprising 141 countries as of June 2022). It is interesting to note, therefore, that the majority of the developing countries that make up the IF were left out of the BEPS Action 14 negotiations that determined the requirements of the peer review process that they are subjected to.

6.4.2.1.2 MAP under the UN Model

The work of the United Nations on a model treaty commenced in 1968 with the establishment by the United Nations Economic and Social Council (ECOSOC) of the United Nations Ad Hoc Group of Experts on Tax Treaties between Developed and Developing Countries pursuant to its resolution 1273 (XLIII).[772] The Group of Experts, known as the Committee of Experts on International Cooperation in Tax Matters (Tax Committee) since 2004,[773] produced a Manual for the Negotiation of Bilateral Tax Treaties between Developed and Developing Countries, which led to the publication of the original UN Model 1980. The Model Convention was revised in 2001, in 2011 and more recently in 2017 to reflect the BEPS provisions.

The members of the Tax Committee are tax officials nominated by their governments and appointed by the Secretary-General of the United Nations. They serve in their individual capacity for a period of four years.[774] As of 2013, the Tax Committee comprised 25 members, with a small majority of the members coming from developing countries and countries with economies in transition.[775] The Tax Committee maintains detailed commentaries on the UN Model, and it is also responsible for the publication of several useful manuals on tax issues important for developing countries, such as transfer pricing and the administration of tax treaties. Although the UN Model traditionally tends to follow the patterns set by the OECD Model, especially to reflect the BEPS provisions, there are key provisions with respect to dispute resolution that diverge from its OECD counterpart, reflecting the different tax needs and concerns that developing non-OECD countries may have compared to the more developed OECD countries.[776] Such differences are evident in relation to the reluctance of developing and emerging countries (e.g., China and India) to adopt mandatory arbitration as prescribed in the OECD Model.

772. United Nations Economic and Social Council (ECOSOC) Resolution 1273 XLIII (4 Aug. 1967).
773. ECOSOC Resolution 2004/69 (11 Nov. 2004).
774. Paragraph 10 UN Model.
775. Paragraph 11 UN Model.
776. *See* s. 4.3.2.2.

6.4.2.2 LOSC

The constitutional level rules determine who can take part in the policymaking level rules. In the context of the LOSC, constitutional rules are those that govern the organisation and composition of the negotiation groups at the UNCLOS III. The Conference comprised two parallel negotiating groups: a formal structure of delegates and an informal group comprising private interest groups that emerged alongside the formal group to facilitate the consensus-building efforts and ensure momentum across nine years of negotiations.

6.4.2.2.1 *Formal Structure of UNCLOS III*

The formal group comprised a General Committee, three Main Committees, a Drafting Committee and a Credentials Committee.[777] UNCLOS III was held at a time when a dominant concern of the UN was to close the gap between developing and developed countries, which had rightly been a major theme in the discussions in the preparatory stage and was a major concern of the Conference.[778] The negotiators were also mindful of the inability of UNCLOS I and II in 1958 and 1960, respectively, to agree on prior issues (e.g., the maximum breadth of the territorial sea and fishery limits). Given the overarching objective of achieving universal acceptance among parties holding widely varying interests (as discussed in section 5.3.5), the Conference put maximum efforts to ensure that all states, including developed and especially developing countries, were represented through an equitable geographical distribution of the seats across the committees.[779]

To this end, the delegates of the General Committee, the three Main Committees and the Drafting Committee were divided into five major geographical groups: the African group; Asian group; Latin American group; Western European group; and Eastern European group.[780] Although there were some views issued by the African group that they were under-represented,[781] the Conference finally agreed by consensus on the distribution of seats of the various committees, avoiding recourse to voting on the rule of procedure, which may have catapulted a breakdown of the Conference.[782] In this way, several countries made compromises to move forward in a spirit of cooperation.[783]

6.4.2.2.2 *Emergence of Informal Negotiating Group*

There were 157 countries participating in the formal negotiations of UNCLOS III, which made it extremely difficult to negotiate in such a large body, and it was also difficult to

777. *See supra* n. 654.
778. UNCLOS III UN Doc. A/CONF.62/SR.1 (10 Dec. 1973).
779. *Ibid.*
780. *Ibid.*, at para. 2.
781. *Ibid.*, at paras 12 and 16.
782. Buzan, *supra* n. 748, at 332.
783. UNCLOS III UN Doc. A/CONF.62/SR.3 paras 1 and 5 (10 Dec. 1973).

reduce the size of the negotiating groups because no State was willing to be left out.[784] As a result, several informal private negotiating groups emerged in parallel with the formal structure, alongside the traditional UN regional groups (e.g., the Western industrialised States, the Socialist States and the Group of 77, which included the developing countries) in order to fulfil the need for small but representative negotiating groups.[785] The convenors of these smaller interest groups were individuals who had stature at the Conference. They could choose which delegations to invite to join their respective groups.

The private interest groups cut across geographical regions, ideology and development status and arguably proved to be more influential than the usual UN groups,[786] as the Conference had to acknowledge their existence and allocate facilities for their meetings. For example, the Coastal States group (76 members) and the Landlocked and Geographically Disadvantaged States group (55 members) comprised both developed and developing States, marking the beginning of a partnership process.[787] Examples of other influential interest groups included the 'Margineers Group' or Group of Broad-Shelf States; the Straits States Group; the Group of Archipelagic States; the Group of Maritime States; and the Great Maritime Powers.[788] On the positive side, their central role was to identify and clarify the issues in dispute, as reflected, for example, in the first draft on dispute settlement submitted by a private group co-chaired by Australia, El Salvador, and Kenya.[789] On the negative side, the interest groups consumed a great deal of the Conference's time and resources, and once a group had adopted a common position, it was often rigid in the official negotiations, possibly challenging the consensus-based approaches that underpinned UNCLOS III.[790]

6.4.3 Implications

Although tax treaty dispute resolution – comprising mainly of the MAP – is operated through a bilateral treaty mechanism across the DTT network, the above analysis of the policymaking and constitutional level rules reveals clearly that decision-making regarding the MAP provisions is determined through the constitutional rules that govern the negotiations at the OECD and the UN Tax Committee. In fact, the analysis points to dual decision-making structures across the ITR that separate developed countries that adopt the OECD Model and developing countries that tend to adopt the UN Model. This fragmented approach is emphasised even more through the MAP Forum that decides the MAP requirements under BEPS Action 14, as it constitutes only 53 countries out of the 141 IF countries that are required to adopt the BEPS provisions in their bilateral

784. Tommy Koh, *Negotiating the UN Convention on the Law of the Sea: A Practitioner's Reflection* in *The Oxford Handbook of United Nations Treaties* 540 (Simon Chesterman at al. eds, Oxford Publishing 2019).
785. For a complete list of groups *see* Koh and Jayakumar, *supra* n. 746 at 55.
786. Koh, Negotiating the UN Convention on the Law of the Sea, *supra* n. 784, at 540.
787. Beesley, *supra* n. 745, at 186.
788. *Ibid.*
789. *See* s. 5.3.5.4.1.
790. Beesley, *supra* n. 745, at 186.

treaties. This means that the majority of developing countries do not have access to the decision-making platform that determines the evolution of the MAP.

Moreover, the policymaking level rules show that tax treaty negotiators at the level of the competent authority have very limited decision-making power for influencing the MAP provisions as the text of the MAP article is prescribed by Article 25 of the OECD or UN Model and the applicable rules of BEPS Action 14 minimum standard (for IF jurisdictions) which are decided at the constitutional level. The negotiators of the bilateral treaty may have some more decision-making power when it comes to arbitration, emphasising the institutional differences between developed and developing countries (discussed in section 4.3.2.2). Such dual policy structures arguably affect the distribution of MAP users and the effectiveness of the MAP through a fragmented dispute resolution system across the ITR.[791] It should be noted, however, that more than 135 countries of the IF, including China and India, have agreed in principle to the proposed mandatory dispute resolution mechanism under Pillar One. Although the mechanism under Pillar One may be applied to resolve disputes regarding allocation of profits to market jurisdictions for certain in-scope MNEs only, it has set the first step for a multilateral and binding dispute resolution mechanism for IF users. This development may open new doors for negotiating a greater alignment between the OECD and UN Models regarding dispute resolution across the IF.

In contrast to the ITR, the analysis of the policymaking and constitutional rules applied during the UNCLOS III negotiations for finalising the dispute resolution provisions under Part XV of the LOSC reveals a much more unified decision-making structure (the UN framework) to ensure an equitable dispute resolution system across the regime despite the conflicting objectives and interests of the various parties. To overcome the geopolitical obstacles that threatened the development of a universal treaty, the multilateral conference adopted several innovative techniques at the constitutional level to ensure a balanced geographical representation of states in the decision-making structure, as discussed in section 6.4.2.2. This balanced power structure provided a solid foundation for achieving equitable objectives set out at the policymaking level (i.e., applying a consensus approach, building a negotiating text to ensure that all different views were included and integrating the provisions into the treaty to ensure that they are legally binding).

The ITR is moving towards a more multilateral structure, just as the law of the sea regime, and both regimes also share various similarities in their geopolitical context (discussed in section 2.4.1). As such, certain consensus-building techniques developed during the UNCLOS III negotiations at the policymaking level could be useful to achieve consensus across the IF, given the similar number of participants under the two systems (157 members in UNCLOS III and 141 members in IF meetings). At the constitutional level, the clustering strategies developed at the UNCLOS III within the formal structure to ensure an equitable geographical representation of states could be useful at the IF meetings to ensure that the views of the developed, developing and emerging countries are equitably represented. The formation of parallel informal

791. *See* s. 6.2.1.1.

groups to clarify issues and build up consensus prior to formal negotiations may also be a useful approach at the level of the IF. Such techniques may be relevant not only for facilitating negotiations on the reforms to tax treaty dispute resolution across the IF but also for achieving consensus with respect to the wider debate on the allocation of taxing rights under Pillar One.

6.5 CONCLUSIONS

This chapter explored Step B of the three-step methodology that underpins this research thesis. Step B addresses the second research question with the aim of identifying aspects of the LOSC's dispute resolution system that may be relevant for improving tax treaty dispute resolution. The analysis in Step B is carried out in two parts. The first part integrates the analysis of the institutional arrangements (rules, norms and strategies) across the three action situations that make up the dispute resolution systems under the ITR and the LOSC and compares the resulting patterns of interaction at the operational level. The second part compares the inclusivity (participation) levels across the two dispute resolution systems at the policymaking and constitutional levels.

The comparative analysis in Step B revealed several aspects of the LOSC's system that may be relevant for improving dispute resolution in the ITR at all three levels of decision-making. At the operational level, the LOSC's dispute resolution system comprises at least six different mechanisms involving consensual means (diplomatic negotiation and conciliation) and adjudication procedures (ICJ, ITLOS, and arbitration under Annexes VII and VIII). This flexible yet mandatory structure aims to achieve an equitable balance between countries' exercise of their sovereign rights and the rule of law while giving priority to diplomatic solutions through State negotiations. Similarly, tax treaty dispute resolution in the ITR also gives priority to diplomatic solutions through the MAP, and it could, therefore, benefit from the LOSC's flexible yet mandatory mechanisms for addressing issues of capacity in the MAP system.

More specifically, mechanisms based on the ITLOS and the arbitral tribunals under Annexes VII and VIII would not only introduce more legalistic measures to expand the MAP system but would also provide useful benchmarks for addressing issues of uncertainty and inequitable solutions perpetuated through the current tax treaty dispute resolution system. The public nature of such mechanisms would promote the development of common legal interpretations to counter issues of indeterminacy under international tax law, reallocate decision-making powers away from competent authorities for a more balanced process among relevant actors and also ensure a more uniform application of dispute resolution rules across the IF to level the playing field between developing and developed countries for more equitable solutions.

The analysis of the inclusivity (participation) levels across the policymaking and constitutional levels of the two systems also reveals useful techniques from the LOSC's system that may be contextualised into the ITR to facilitate consensus-building across the 141 jurisdictions of the IF. These techniques were developed to achieve universal consensus among 157 UN member countries that participated in the UNCLOS III negotiations that produced the LOSC. Relevant techniques applicable in the ITR would include integrating any proposed dispute resolution provisions within a multilateral treaty to ensure that all members are subject to the same rules under law; developing a treaty without a draft model text to ensure that all views are reflected therein; promoting a more unified decision-making structure instead of the dual OECD/UN platforms; and also applying clustering strategies at the formal and informal level during IF negotiations to ensure that the views of developed, developing and emerging countries are equitably represented.

CHAPTER 7

Proposed Restructuring of the Tax Treaty Dispute Resolution System

Chapter 7 applies the final Step C of the methodology and proposes a restructuring of the tax treaty dispute resolution system by adapting the relevant aspects of the LOSC's system identified in Step B. Although the MAP is maintained as the primary dispute resolution mechanism, the suggested new structure adds three new mechanisms to ensure the resolution of issues not addressed through the MAP. These include an IF arbitration mechanism for non-transfer pricing disputes, a special IF arbitration mechanism for transfer pricing disputes and an ITT, all of which are based on LOSC mechanisms. The proposed reform also recommends specific consensus-building techniques that comprise the integration of the new dispute resolution system in a multilateral treaty, created from scratch, to be signed by IF and non-IF members, the creation of an IF Secretariat to handle BEPS-related work, including dispute resolution in the ITR and the application of appropriate clustering strategies during IF meetings at the formal committee level and at the level of informal private negotiating groups.

7.1 INTRODUCTION

The comparative analysis in Chapter 6 revealed several aspects of the LOSC's dispute resolution system that may be relevant for improving tax treaty dispute resolution at the operational, policymaking and constitutional levels. This chapter applies the final Step C of the methodology and focuses on the actual restructuring of the system to address the final research question posed in this thesis.

Section 7.2 will recommend necessary policy reforms at the operational level to address issues of capacity, uncertainty and inequitable solutions under the tax treaty dispute resolution system. The proposed restructuring of the institutional arrangements in the ITR will take into consideration the unique elements of the ITR compared to the law of the sea regime (e.g., the annual number of MAP cases relative to the number of maritime dispute cases under the LOSC). An overview of the proposed new dispute resolution system is offered in Figure 7. The following sections 7.3 and 7.4 will propose reforms at the policymaking and constitutional levels, respectively, to facilitate negotiations on the implementation of the new system across the IF based on the analysis of the inclusivity levels in the ITR and the LOSC. Section 7.5 will then review the proposed changes in light of the OECD's proposed dispute resolution mechanism under Pillar One, expected to come into force in 2024, before concluding in section 7.6.

7.2 RECOMMENDATIONS AT THE OPERATIONAL LEVEL

This section proposes a potential restructuring of the tax treaty dispute resolution system based on the relevant aspects of the LOSC's system identified in section 6.3. The new structure aims to address the issues of capacity, uncertainty and inequitable solutions that impact the current MAP system in the ITR.

7.2.1 Key Elements of the Restructured Tax Treaty Dispute Resolution System

7.2.1.1 Giving Primacy to the MAP

In the ITR, almost 80% of tax treaty disputes are resolved annually through the MAP, while around 20% of MAP cases overall may remain unresolved because competent authorities of the contracting States are unable to reach an agreement or the tax issue is not eligible for MAP under the treaty (*see* Table I.3 in Appendix I). In addition, the analysis of norms in section 6.2.1.2 reveals an increasing preference for MAP among taxpayers, especially given the advantages that the MAP presents compared to domestic remedies (in terms of processing time and financial costs). As such, I recommend that the MAP remain the primary tax treaty dispute resolution mechanism. Just as diplomatic negotiations are given primacy under the LOSC's dispute resolution system, the MAP would also be given priority in the suggested new tax treaty dispute resolution system; adjudication mechanisms would only be used to resolve disputes for which no MAP agreement is obtained within the prescribed 24-month timeline or tax disputes that are not eligible under the MAP system.

The proposed reform would also take into consideration the two institutional differences identified in section 2.4.2. The first difference refers to the fact that there are many more disputes lodged through the MAP compared to the LOSC's system on a yearly basis. The second difference relates to the fact that the private taxpayer constitutes a prominent institutional actor in initiating the tax treaty dispute resolution process, whereas the LOSC's dispute resolution system is generally initiated by government entities (although private parties may have a more critical role for initiating dispute resolution relating to activities in the Area through the SDC). The

LOSC mechanisms, therefore, will be adapted into the ITR (and not directly replicated) to take into consideration these contextual differences, as explained in the sections below.

7.2.1.2 Expanding Legalistic Dispute Resolution Mechanisms

Currently, MAP cases for which no MAP agreement is reached within the 24-month prescribed timeline can be subjected to the mandatory and binding OECD arbitration mechanism or the voluntary UN arbitration mechanism, if applicable, in the bilateral treaty. As discussed in section 6.2.1.1.3, the dual arbitration mechanisms under the UN and OECD Models may lead to a fragmented dispute resolution system across the DTT network that not only reduces the effectiveness and predictability of the mechanisms but also subjects taxpayers and competent authorities to differential rules, resulting in inequitable solutions across the ITR.

To address such issues of uncertainty and inequitable solutions, I propose introducing three new adjudication mechanisms through a multilateral treaty, which would be legally binding on all parties to the treaty (similar to the mandatory and binding dispute resolution mechanism proposed through the MC under Pillar One). These mechanisms would include an IF arbitration mechanism, a special IF arbitration mechanism and an ITT based on the LOSC's arbitral tribunal under Annex VII, special arbitral tribunal under Annex VIII and the ITLOS, respectively, as discussed in section 6.3.1.2. Each mechanism would address specific types of disputes to ensure that all disputes are guaranteed some form of resolution (*see* section 6.3.1.1) as in the LOSC's dispute resolution system. The introduction of such public mechanisms would also contribute to the development of international tax law through legal rulings (*see* section 6.3.2.1) and provide a more balanced allocation of resources and decision-making powers across the tax treaty dispute resolution system (*see* section 6.3.2.2). The aim is to create a comprehensive legal framework that can achieve an effective, predictable and equitable resolution of multilateral tax disputes across the ITR while giving priority to diplomatic solutions through the MAP.

7.2.1.2.1 Separate Arbitration Mechanisms for Addressing Non-transfer Pricing and Transfer Pricing Cases

The MAP statistics in Table I.3 in Appendix I reveal a significant discrepancy between the average resolution timelines for transfer pricing cases (30-35 months) and non-transfer pricing cases (17-22 months). As discussed in section 6.2.1.1.1.3, this may be due to the fact-intensive nature of transfer pricing cases, which takes more time for competent authorities to gather the required information before coming to an agreement. The process is complicated even further if there are several jurisdictions involved in the transfer pricing case. Non-transfer pricing cases are generally more straightforward and require less investigation on the part of competent authorities. Given the different resource requirements for these two types of cases, I propose addressing non-transfer pricing and transfer pricing cases through separate mechanisms to increase the efficiency of the dispute resolution process.

Accordingly, non-transfer pricing cases may be addressed through the new IF arbitration mechanism that is based largely on the LOSC's Annex VII arbitration mechanism. The IF arbitration procedure would effectively replace the existing dual arbitration procedures under the OECD and UN Models. This is discussed further in section 7.2.2 below. Alternatively, transfer pricing cases for which no MAP agreement was reached within the 24-month timeline or which were not eligible under the current MAP system may be submitted to the special IF arbitration mechanism that is based on the LOSC's special arbitration procedure under Annex VIII. The special IF mechanism is explained in section 7.2.3, further below.

7.2.1.2.2 An ITT That Addresses Unresolved MAP Cases and Issues Not Covered under the MAP

As discussed in section 6.2.1.1.3, the MAP covers only tax disputes brought under Articles 25(1) and 25(3) of the applicable treaty, excluding other tax issues (e.g., the case of a third-country resident that has a PE in both of the contracting States) that are not included under the treaty. In addition, cases brought under Article 25(3) are not generally eligible for arbitration in the current system unless the competent authorities mutually agree. Such discretionary exclusions may result in unresolved MAP cases and also encourage opportunistic behaviour between competent authorities during MAP negotiations to the detriment of the taxpayer. Moreover, some jurisdictions may also restrict transfer pricing cases from MAP through domestic legislation, in which case the taxpayer may have no choice but to litigate the tax dispute through domestic court. Such unequal treatment puts the taxpayer at a disadvantage compared to other taxpayers who may access the MAP.

Accordingly, the creation of the ITT based on the ITLOS, as proposed in this thesis, would hear unresolved MAP cases and other international tax disputes that are not eligible under the MAP or the treaty (e.g., disputes relating to DSTs or Pillar Two[792]). The ITT would also include a transfer pricing disputes chamber (TPDC) that will exclusively hear transfer pricing disputes and will allow the direct participation of private taxpayers. This mechanism is based on the SDC that operates under the ITLOS and hears only disputes related to the seabed Area. The workings of the ITT and the TPDC are discussed in section 7.2.4, further below.

Despite the importance of the ICJ's rulings under the LOSC, this thesis does not recommend the ICJ's jurisdiction under the new tax treaty dispute resolution system for three reasons. First, in matters of the law of the sea, the ITLOS was created precisely because of the lack of trust of developing countries in the 1970s with regard to the impartiality of the ICJ. Second, even if the ICJ may have proved its competency as the world's leading international court, the ICJ proceedings usually last between 5 and 10

792. If Pillar Two disputes become eligible under the MAP, they may be submitted to the IF arbitration or special IF arbitration mechanisms according to the characterisation of the dispute.

years, which would be excessively lengthy given the rapid changes in MNE's tax planning models. Third, in the case of the LOSC, the ICJ was already a leader in resolving disputes concerning the law of the sea and, therefore, could contribute immensely in terms of case law and precedence. However, in matters of international tax law, the ICJ has no specific experience with adjudicating international tax matters, and since the ITT is being created to handle such cases, there may be overlapping with the ICJ, mitigating the efficiency of the restructured tax treaty dispute resolution system. Having the ITT as the sole international court litigating international tax matters may thus limit potential criticisms with respect to fragmentation of international law as is the case in the law of the sea regime, although there is no evidence for such criticisms as the ICJ and the ITLOS tend to, in fact, refer to each other's rulings to ensure consistency in their judgments.[793]

The three new mechanisms (IF arbitration, special IF arbitration and ITT) proposed along with the existing MAP will form a comprehensive legal framework that aims to achieve an effective, predictable and equitable resolution of the existing and new generation of multilateral tax disputes in the wake of BEPS 2.0. As will be discussed below, the mechanisms will be interlinked to ensure a flexible yet mandatory application of the rules (just as in the LOSC's system) for all IF users. Figure 7 gives an overview of the proposed new structure of the tax treaty dispute resolution system. The details of each mechanism will follow.

Figure 7 Overview of Restructured Tax Treaty Dispute Resolution System

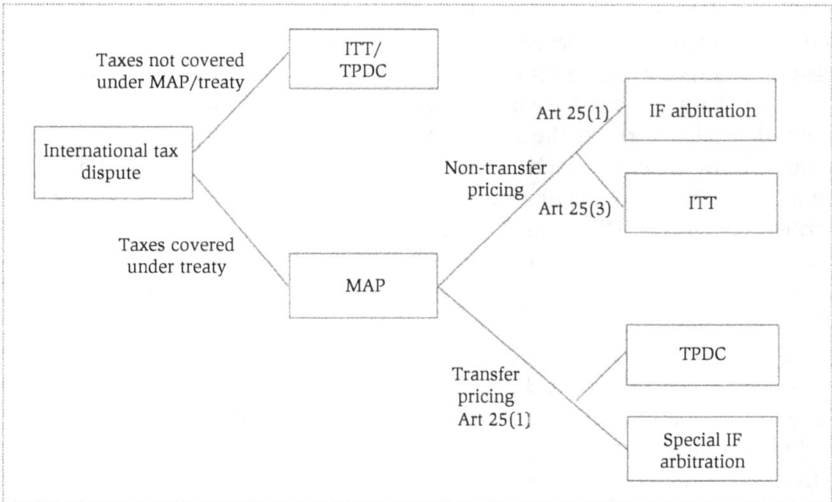

793. *See supra* n. 583.

7.2.2 IF Arbitration Mechanism

As shown in Figure 7, the proposed IF arbitration mechanism addresses non-transfer pricing disputes for which no MAP agreement was reached within the prescribed timeline of 24 months (as specified under the BEPS Action 14 minimum standard). The IF arbitration procedure is based largely on the OECD mandatory arbitration with certain specific modifications, as explained below. The analysis in section 6.2.1.1 has shown that having dual arbitration mechanisms under the OECD and the UN Models creates a fragmented dispute resolution system that leads to an uneven application of the rules and, hence, inequitable processes and outcomes across the ITR. In addition, the voluntary arbitration procedure under the UN Model threatens the taxpayer's rights to a fair resolution of the dispute by allocating excessive control to competent authorities that may decide not to proceed to arbitration even if no MAP agreement is reached (*see* section 6.2.1.1.2). Even if they choose to trigger the arbitration process, the competent authorities are not obligated to implement the arbitration decision if it is not for their mutual benefit, possibly at the expense of the taxpayer. The proposed IF arbitration procedure that replaces the existing dual arbitration procedures is intended to ensure a more standardised and mandatory application of the rules for all IF users, irrespective of whether they come from developed, developing or emerging countries.

7.2.2.1 Mandatory and Legally Binding Procedure

The proposed IF arbitration mechanism would be mandatory and legally binding on competent authorities that are not able to reach a MAP agreement within a prescribed 24-month timeline. This is based on the experience of countries regarding the limited success of voluntary tax arbitration, which has never been applied despite being included in many bilateral treaties.[794] A mandatory mechanism would allow the taxpayer the right to trigger the arbitration procedure and thus put more pressure on competent authorities to reach a workable MAP agreement within the prescribed 24-month timeline. A 24-month timeline is recommended instead of the 3-year period prescribed under the UN Model to reduce the risks of exceeding the statute of limitations set under a country's domestic legal framework should the taxpayer choose to use domestic remedies. The new IF mechanism is also legally binding in order to ensure a guaranteed resolution to the dispute and to ensure a more independent decision-making mechanism once the dispute is submitted to the arbitrators.

To a large degree, the proposed IF arbitration mechanism is based on the current OECD arbitration procedure and avoids those aspects of the voluntary UN arbitration procedure that arguably fail to guarantee an effective and equitable solution to MAP disputes, as discussed in section 6.2.1.1. Just as with the current OECD arbitration procedure, the decision of the arbitrators would be implemented within a 6-month period once the decision is approved by the taxpayer. Even if the arbitration procedure

794. *See e.g.*, Rosenbloom, *supra* n. 29. In 2014, the US had four double tax treaties in force that contained voluntary arbitration provisions but there is no known arbitration case pursuant to these arbitration provisions.

is intended to have mostly a 'prophylactic' effect,[795] it would arguably be more effective as a deterrent if it is mandatory and legally binding on the competent authorities. However, there are certain institutional issues that have been expressed mostly by the developing countries with respect to the OECD Model arbitration, which need to be addressed so that developing countries are also willing to adopt the IF arbitration mechanism.[796] The LOSC's arbitration under Annex VII provides several aspects which may be useful in this respect, such as instituting a five-member arbitration panel instead of three members and applying the independent opinion method instead of the baseball approach, as discussed below.

7.2.2.2 Constitution of Arbitration Panel

As discussed in section 4.3.2.2, developing countries are particularly reluctant to adopt mandatory arbitration because they feel disadvantaged in comparison to their more developed counterparts in terms of expertise and familiarity with arbitration. Also, developing countries have the perception that judges may come mostly from developed countries and would, therefore, be acquainted with mostly developed country issues, resulting in a biased procedure.

In order to address this independence issue in the proposed IF arbitration mechanism, it is first recommended that the arbitration panel comprise a five-member panel instead of the current three-member panel under the OECD and UN Models. This is based on the composition of the arbitral tribunal under Annex VII of the LOSC (*see* position rules in section 5.3.3.1.2.2.2). Each competent authority would still appoint one arbitrator to the panel (who may be its national) and mutually agree on the remaining three arbitrators. The three arbitrators will be third State nationals (i.e., other than those of the disputant competent authorities) unless the parties otherwise agree. The competent authorities would then jointly appoint the Chair of the arbitration panel among those three members. It is expected that such a five-member panel may ensure a more equitable geographical representation of arbitrators from developed, developing and emerging countries.

Second, in order to be appointed to an arbitration case, the arbitrator must be independent of the competent authorities, tax administrations and ministries of finance of either contracting state, including all persons directly affected by the case, as specified under the OECD Model procedure. Additionally, the arbitrators would be required to provide a statement to declare their independence. If the competent authorities are not able to appoint an arbitrator or mutually agree on the three arbitrators within a reasonable time limit (to be determined), the necessary appointment(s) will be made by the President of the ITT (instead of the OECD Secretariat). This is based on the rule for appointing arbitrators under the LOSC's Annex VII, as discussed in section 5.3.3.1.2.2.2.

795. *See* s. 4.3.3.2.1.
796. *See* s. 4.3.2.2.

Additionally, based on the Annex VII arbitration mechanism, all arbitrators would be chosen preferably from a preapproved list of potential judges/arbitrators maintained by the proposed IF Secretariat (*see* discussion in section 7.4.1 below). This process of drawing up a preapproved list of potential judges and arbitrators is based on the LOSC's Annex VII mechanism, where each State party nominates up to four members to their list. However, in the ITR, given the lack of resources and international tax expertise being faced in developing countries especially, it is recommended that each IF member nominate two competent members to the preapproved list. All members being nominated to the list would be persons experienced in international tax law who enjoy the highest reputation for fairness, competence and integrity. This would be particularly useful for developing countries to have swift access to a pool of experts nominated by both developed, developing and emerging countries.

7.2.2.3 Applying the Independent Opinion Method

Although the current arbitration processes under the UN and the OECD Models allow competent authorities to decide mutually on the procedure to be used, i.e., the baseball approach or the independent opinion method, both Models recommend using the baseball approach as the default process. The baseball approach allows for a slightly more rapid resolution of the case compared to the independent opinion method (10 and 13 months under the OECD and UN Models, respectively, for the baseball approach compared to 16 months under both Models for the independent opinion method). More importantly, however, it disallows the publication of the arbitration decision even in redacted format, as it constitutes more of a compromise transaction between two competent authorities regarding a tax issue rather than an independent interpretation of the legal provisions in the treaty. This constitutes a major block in achieving a common interpretation of international tax rules in order to increase certainty across the ITR, as discussed in section 6.2.1.1.1.

Accordingly, in order to increase the predictability related to the IF arbitration mechanism and also allow for the proceedings to be held in a neutral space that would bolster the appearance of independence, it is recommended that the arbitration proceedings be administered by the PCA, just as most of the Annex VII arbitration proceedings.[797] In fact, the publication of arbitral decisions under Annex VII of the LOSC on the website of the PCA, subject to the rules of procedures devised by the arbitral tribunal with the approval of the disputing parties (as discussed in section 5.3.3.1.3.2), is one of the factors that contributes to the LOSC's reliable legal framework.

To make the arbitration process more impartial and transparent, the proposed IF arbitration mechanism would apply the independent opinion method as the default procedure unless the competent authorities agree otherwise, in spite of the slightly longer resolution period compared to the baseball approach. The same timeline of 16

797. The PCA at The Hague administered all but one of the UNCLOS Annex VII arbitrations to date. *See supra* n. 529 for the list of Annex VII cases administered by the PCA.

months may be retained for the independent opinion procedure as specified under the current UN and OECD Models. This would give the opportunity to both competent authorities to present their claims and objections that will be reviewed by the arbitration panel before issuing an arbitration award. Based on Annex VII arbitration, the disputant parties (i.e., the competent authorities) will facilitate the work of the panel by providing relevant information and enabling the participation of taxpayers (if deemed necessary by the panel). This is currently the process in the OECD arbitration procedure as well if the independent opinion method is used. The proceedings and the decision could then be published with the consent of the parties in redacted format, which may help to develop relevant case law in the ITR to increase the transparency and reliability of the arbitration process. This is similar to the arbitration process under the LOSC, where the consent of the disputing parties is also needed (*see* section 5.3.3.1.3.2).

7.2.3 Special IF Arbitration Mechanism

As explained in section 6.2.1.1.1.3, transfer pricing cases are generally fact-sensitive and may involve difficult evaluations of comparability, markets, and financial or other industry information. The gathering and procurement of such information from the taxpayer explains the longer resolution timelines under the MAP. In order to remove the pressure off competent authorities, it is proposed that all transfer pricing cases brought under Article 25(1) for which no MAP agreement was reached within the prescribed 24-month timeline be submitted to either the TPDC (discussed in section 7.2.4.4 below) or the special IF arbitration mechanism as shown in Figure 7. The taxpayer may decide to submit the unresolved MAP case to either mechanism.

7.2.3.1 Mandatory and Legally Binding 'Findings of Fact' and Non-binding Recommendations

The special IF arbitration mechanism will take the form of a fact-finding mechanism based on the special arbitral tribunal under Annex VIII of the LOSC. The jurisdiction of Annex VIII arbitration is limited to four different categories of disputes relating to (l) fisheries, (2) protection and preservation of the marine environment, (3) marine scientific research, or (4) navigation, including pollution from vessels and by dumping.[798] In the context of the ITR, the scope of the special IF mechanism will be limited to transfer pricing disputes only. This includes any transfer pricing cases brought to MAP under Article 25(1) for which no MAP agreement was reached within 24 months; it may include allocation cases in relation to amounts A and B under Pillar One (i.e., profit allocations to market jurisdictions as specified in the MC under Pillar One) if it is eligible under Article 25(1) in the treaty. Just like the IF arbitration mechanism, this special mechanism would also be a mandatory procedure, and it can be triggered by the taxpayer if no MAP agreement is reached in the prescribed 24-month timeline.

798. *See* s. 5.3.3.1.6.1.2.

Alternatively, the special arbitration procedure may also be triggered voluntarily through mutual agreement of the competent authorities within a period of 6 months of receiving the MAP request from the taxpayer if they consider that the 24-month deadline may not be met. The approval of the taxpayer would be required for the competent authorities to submit the MAP case to the special IF arbitration mechanism within 6 months of receiving the request. This alternate mechanism allows some flexibility on the part of competent authorities to ensure that the transfer pricing case can meet the 24-month resolution deadline (since the special arbitration procedure is expected to last 16 months, just like the IF arbitration). It would also help to free up resources at the level of the competent authorities, for example, in cases involving complex transfer pricing transactions across multilateral jurisdictions. This alternate procedure is a contextualised application of the flexible application of rules in the LOSC that considers the three-way transactions in the MAP system (as discussed in section 2.4.2.2).

Unless the competent authorities otherwise agree, the findings of fact will be considered conclusive (i.e., binding and final) to be used by the competent authorities for resolving the MAP case in the same way that Annex VIII arbitration decisions are used (*see* section 5.3.3.1.6.2.2). The decision may be published in redacted format with the consent of the parties. In addition, if all parties to the dispute so request, the special arbitral tribunal may also formulate recommendations which, without having the force of a decision, will only constitute the basis for a review by the competent authorities of the questions giving rise to the dispute. This procedure is also based on the Annex VIII mechanism.

7.2.3.2 Constitution of Fact-Finding Panel

The fact-finding panel would include five arbitrators, just as in the special arbitration under Annex VIII of the LOSC. Each competent authority would appoint two arbitrators from the preapproved list of judges/experts maintained by the proposed IF Secretariat (as discussed in section 7.4.1 below), one of whom may be its national. The competent authorities would then jointly appoint a fifth member from a third State, preferably from the same list, to be the Chair of the five-member panel. If the competent authorities are not able to appoint an arbitrator or jointly agree on the Chair within a specified timeline, then the President of the proposed ITT may make the necessary appointment(s), just as in the IF arbitration mechanism.

It is expected that the fact-finding panel may be better equipped than competent authorities to gather information from taxpayers located across different jurisdictions. Just as in Annex VIII arbitration, the disputant parties in the ITR (i.e., the competent authorities) will assist the panel in gathering necessary information and evidence from taxpayers or experts, and the panel may also request information from the taxpayers directly if need be. Based on the Annex VIII mechanism, where there are more than two competent authorities involved as disputant parties, as is often the case in transfer pricing cases, any additional parties having the same interests may jointly agree on the appointment of the two arbitrators. Where there are several parties having separate interests or whether there is a disagreement as to whether they are of the same interest, each of the parties will appoint one arbitrator to the panel. This process will be repeated to the maximum extent possible, as recommended under the Annex VIII rules, discussed in section 5.3.3.1.2.2.2.

7.2.3.3 Applying the Independent Opinion Method

As discussed in section 7.2.2.3 in relation to the proposed IF arbitration mechanism, the independent opinion method is also prescribed as the default mechanism for arbitrators to reach a legally binding decision in the special IF arbitration mechanism (in the form of a finding of facts). In addition, to increase the independence of the process, it is recommended that the special IF arbitration mechanism be administered by the PCA (just as the IF arbitration) following the approach of the Annex VII proceedings, given that no public Annex VIII arbitration proceeding has yet been instituted.

7.2.4 ITT

7.2.4.1 Competence

As shown in Figure 7, the proposed ITT would address non-transfer pricing disputes lodged under Article 25(3) where no MAP agreement was reached within the 24-month timeline since these MAP cases are generally not eligible for arbitration under tax treaties. The ITT may also be used to adjudicate international tax disputes that may not be covered under MAP or the tax treaty, e.g., tax disputes arising from schemes like DSTs or carbon taxes under the Paris Agreement (similar to the extended jurisdiction of the ITLOS that may hear disputes brought under other agreements than the LOSC – *see* section 5.3.3.1.6.1.1). In this way, the ITT may provide access to not only IF members but also non-IF members to contribute to the wider field of international tax governance.

7.2.4.2 Organisation of the ITT

Just like the ITLOS, to ensure continuity, the ITT would also be composed of a certain number of rotating judges elected to fixed-year terms by the members of the IF, although a more restricted panel may be proposed (instead of the 21 judges of the ITLOS) due to the restrictive budget of developing countries as discussed in section 4.3.2.2. The judges would be elected based on their independence, character, and expertise. Each IF member may nominate two persons with such credentials to a list from which the judges of the ITT would be elected by the IF members by secret ballot for a renewable fixed term (to be determined). The elections would be held at the meeting of the IF and would be convened by the proposed IF Secretariat (discussed in section 7.4.1 below) as agreed by the IF members. The expenses of the ITT, including the annual allowances of the elected judges, will be funded by the IF members. When an entity other than an IF member is a party to a case submitted by it to the ITT, the Tribunal will fix the amount that that party has to contribute towards the expenses of the ITT. These proposed procedures are based on the workings of the ITLOS (as discussed in section 5.3.3.1.2.2.1).

To ensure an equitable geographical representation, no two judges may be of the same nationality. Moreover, just as at the ITLOS, the ITT as a whole must represent the principal legal systems of the world. In the case of the ITR, this requires the judges to display a balanced knowledge of general provisions under the OECD and the UN Models and domestic tax laws under the common law and civil law systems. These may be relevant in relation to interpretation provisions that refer to applicable domestic laws as prescribed under the VCLT rules of interpretation (e.g., for establishing residency under Article 4 of the OECD Model). The ITT would develop its own rules of procedure, and it may form special chambers composed of three or more of its elected members for dealing with a particular category of dispute if the parties so request as with the ITLOS (discussed in section 5.3.3.1.4.2.1).

7.2.4.3 Rules of Procedure and Finality of Outcomes

As with the ITLOS, disputes would be submitted directly by the disputant party to the ITT, and the Tribunal would then notify all parties concerned (*see* section 5.3.3.1.4.1.1). The questions will be decided through a majority of the judges of the ITT who are present. Any decision rendered by the ITT (same as the ITLOS and the ICJ) will be final and will have to be complied with by the competent authorities, although any such decision will be binding on the contracting States only (based on the scope rules of the ITLOS as discussed in section 5.3.3.1.6.1.1).

The ITT proceedings would generally be public unless the Tribunal decides otherwise, and the decision would be published (in redacted form in specific situations). Such practice would encourage the development of international tax case law in the ITR, which all taxpayers and competent authorities may have access to. Just as the ITLOS and the ICJ have contributed to interpreting the limits of 'equitable considerations' as used in the LOSC, it is expected that the ITT will have a similar role in developing the concept of equitable solutions in the ITR. One example would be the interpretation of the 'principle of value creation' to address issues of indeterminacy in the ITR.

7.2.4.4 TPDC

The ITT would also include a transfer pricing dispute chamber, the TPDC, that exclusively hears disputes related to transfer pricing, especially if these are not covered under the applicable tax treaty and, therefore, not eligible for MAP. As shown in Figure 7, the TPDC may also be used to litigate transfer pricing prices brought under Article 25(1), for which no MAP agreement was reached within 24 months. The TPDC thus provides an alternative forum for resolving transfer pricing disputes along with the special IF mechanism. The flexibility of the system is enhanced as the taxpayer may decide which forum to use after the 24-month is passed. The TPDC is based on the SDC operating under the ITLOS that deals exclusively with disputes concerning activities in the seabed Area and thus provides a forum for non-State entities, including juridical persons (e.g., private contractors) to lodge a case (*see* section 5.3.3.1.1.1.1). Similarly, the TPDC would provide a forum for private taxpayers to present their transfer pricing case and take part in the proceedings alongside competent authorities.

In addition to unburdening the tasks of competent authorities, this procedure may help to balance the allocation of rights across the ITR by giving taxpayers more control over the dispute resolution process. Just as the SDC, the TPDC would also be composed of members selected by a majority of the members of the ITT for a specific term that may be renewed for a second term. As part of the ITT, the decisions issued by the TPDC are legally binding on the competent authorities, and the procedure will be public unless the parties otherwise agree (as discussed in section 5.3.3.1.3.1).

7.3 RECOMMENDATIONS AT THE POLICYMAKING LEVEL

Based on the inclusivity analysis in section 6.4.1, this section formulates recommendations at the policymaking level to facilitate the implementation by consensus of the proposed new dispute resolution structure across the IF. The recommendations are based on the analysis of consensus-building techniques applied during the UNCLOS III negotiations that produced the universally agreed LOSC. It is noted that decision-making during IF meetings is based on consensus, and in this respect, the LOSC's consensus approach, although novel at the time, has already been adopted across the IF.

7.3.1 Incorporate Dispute Resolution Provisions in a Multilateral Treaty

Currently, the MAP and arbitration provisions are adopted at a bilateral level in tax treaties based on the OECD and UN Models. Although the BEPS Action 14 minimum standard and the peer review process may standardise the MAP provisions across the DTT network, mandatory and binding arbitration provisions are adopted on an optional basis in DTTs and are not subject to any minimum standard. As a result, arbitration under the OECD or UN Model is not applied effectively in the tax treaty dispute resolution process, evidenced through the build-up of unresolved MAP cases in Table I.1 in Appendix I. Even the MC being developed at the OECD under Pillar One proposes a mandatory and binding dispute resolution mechanism that applies to certain disputes under Pillar One (in relation to the new proposed nexus for allocating global income) without addressing Pillar Two disputes.[799] This may suggest a more optional or discretionary approach for resolving disputes under Pillar Two.

Based on the failure of the dispute settlement system proposed under the Optional Protocol of the 1958 Geneva Convention (discussed in section 6.4.1.2.2.3), I recommend that the three dispute resolution mechanisms proposed in section 7.2 (that

799. *See* s. 2.3.1.3.

would apply to both Pillar One and Pillar Two disputes) be included in a multilateral treaty so that all IF members become legally subject to the same set of rules at a multilateral level. This technique would not only increase certainty among the IF members regarding the applicability of the mechanisms but also create a legal obligation that may push countries to make the compromises necessary to establish universal consensus on Pillar One in the ITR, as experienced during the UNCLOS III negotiations that produced the universally agreed LOSC.[800]

7.3.2 Develop a Multilateral Treaty Without a Draft Model Text

The delegates across the IF come from developed, developing and emerging countries, often having different interests and objectives. To ensure that all views are given due consideration during the IF meetings before they can even be discussed, I recommend adopting the technique used during UNCLOS III, which includes proceeding without a draft model text, as discussed in section 6.4.1.2.2.2. This technique may be useful to avoid the situation where developing countries' interests and needs are overlooked, as with the BEPS Action Plan developed in 2015 (developing countries were involved only as BEPS Invitees or Associates with no substantial decision-making powers[801]). It is noted, however, that with technological advances, in order to prepare for the IF meetings currently, the OECD Secretariat usually sends draft texts to delegates well in advance so that they can work on the text and send back revisions that will then be discussed at the meetings. While this practice may be useful for all members to insert their views, it is important for the OECD Secretariat (or the proposed IF Secretariat discussed in section 7.4.1) to ensure that all views are reflected accurately in the final treaty to be discussed.

7.4 RECOMMENDATIONS AT THE CONSTITUTIONAL LEVEL

Based on the inclusivity analysis in section 6.4.2, this section proposes two techniques adapted from the UNCLOS III for achieving a more equitable decision-making structure across the IF.

7.4.1 Build a Unified Decision-Making Structure: Creation of an IF Secretariat

As discussed in section 6.4.2.1, in spite of the standardisation of the MAP across the IF through BEPS Action 14, there is a clear dual decision-making structure in the ITR that impacts the development of MAP, especially arbitration between developed and developing countries. Traditionally, the OECD policy space provided a platform for mostly Western, developed countries (OECD countries) to develop the OECD Model. The UN Tax Committee then emerged in the 1980s, giving a voice to the developing

800. Stevenson, *supra* n. 691.
801. *See* s. 6.4.2.1.1.

countries, specifically (non-OECD countries), with the development of the UN Model. Although such a dual structure may have been necessary to emphasise the tax realities of the developing countries vis-à-vis their more developed counterparts in the past, most of these countries are now part of the IF and, as such, may negotiate on equal footing on BEPS-related matters. Arguably, the proposed implementation of a mandatory and binding mechanism under Pillar One for all IF members also suggests increased alignment between the OECD and UN rules.

There are, however, important ideological and practical divides that remain between the OECD and the UN policy spaces that may impair collaboration across the IF. For example, negotiations regarding MAP are currently conducted at the level of the FTA MAP Forum, comprising 53 OECD and non-OECD members,[802] which leaves out most developing countries. This study argues that to encourage universal consensus across the developed, developing and emerging countries of the IF through compromises, as under the UNCLOS III, it is important that all countries can participate on equal footing in the negotiations, preferably on neutral negotiation grounds. As such, instead of the dual decision structures that affect dispute resolution in the ITR, I recommend instituting an independent IF Secretariat to spearhead international negotiations among the IF members regarding reforms to the tax treaty dispute resolution system (which could also be extended to other aspects of international tax). Although no such Secretariat exists under the LOSC, it aims to provide a neutral platform to ensure more levelled negotiations among the IF members, similar to the UNCLOS III negotiations. This is especially important given the perceived shift in the centre of gravity of the political economy and the rise of China as a significant player in both the ITR and the law of the sea regime (as discussed in sections 4.3.4 and 5.3.4, respectively).

One of the main tasks of the proposed IF Secretariat would be to administer the preapproved list of judges/experts drawn up by the IF members (each member would nominate two potential judges) that may be appointed as arbitrators of the five-member panel of the IF arbitration or special IF arbitration mechanisms (as recommended in sections 7.2.2.2 and 7.2.3.2 respectively). The development of such a preapproved list of potential judges and arbitrators is based on the LOSC's mechanisms to ensure that a pool of qualified judges is readily available when needed. More importantly, it also ensures an equitable geographical distribution of the potential judges and arbitrators across all jurisdictions of the IF.

7.4.2 Apply Clustering Strategies Across IF Meetings

As discussed in section 6.4.2.2, there was significant emphasis on the need for an equitable geographical distribution of the delegates at the UNCLOS III negotiations in order to achieve a fair consensus-based decision-making structure. While most of the countries under the UN were represented by almost 160 delegates, the composition of the formal committees of the Conference was decided through consensus to ensure a

802. *See* FTA MAP Forum, *supra* n. 246.

well-balanced geographical representation of all delegates present. Similarly, in the present-day ITR, for achieving a fair and inclusive decision-making process across the 141-member IF, I recommend adopting an equitable geographical distribution of seats (covering developed, developing and emerging countries) across the various committees set up across IF meetings, as agreed through consensus of all the parties.

Additionally, during the UNCLOS III conference, several informal negotiating groups were also formed in parallel to the formal negotiations to reach an agreement within smaller groups before being submitted for universal consensus across the conference. These informal groups clustered delegates based on their common interests and objectives in relation to the law of the sea rather than their geographical memberships. Similar clustering strategies may be applied during IF meetings at the informal level through smaller private groups to clarify issues and develop consensus among groups having conflicting interests. Such groups may include traditional groups like the African Tax Administration Forum (ATAF), the Centre de Rencontre et d'Etudes des Dirigeants des Administrations Fiscales (CREDAF) or the Southern African Development Community (SADC). Such practice of breaking up the conference into smaller informal groups may also remove the political pressure associated with more formal meetings, thus encouraging developing countries to express their views and be better represented in the negotiation process. It is noteworthy that such multilateral participation among working group members from different parts of the globe may be largely facilitated through the use of virtual meetings, thus reducing the costs associated with such international conferences for all parties.

7.5 REVIEW OF PROPOSED RESTRUCTURING IN LIGHT OF PILLAR ONE DISPUTE RESOLUTION MECHANISM

As discussed in section 2.3.1.3, although the OECD's proposed mandatory and binding dispute resolution mechanism under Pillar One brings the promise of the first multilateral system of binding dispute resolution in the ITR (on an elective basis), there are a number of potential issues identified with the mechanism that may mitigate its effectiveness for resolving disputes relating to the allocation of residual profits (amount A) to market jurisdictions. These include (1) a mix of mandatory, binding and advisory approaches[803] that may encourage opportunistic behaviour among competent authorities and exacerbate power disparities that compromise the independence of the parties; (2) the default application of baseball arbitration approach in a multilateral dispute may arguably leave competent authorities unsatisfied as any single offer cannot settle the positions for the remaining parties while also restricting the development of case law in the ITR; and (3) the approach under Pillar One covers specific categories of disputes relating to amount A and potentially excludes disputes brought under Pillar Two which may lead to an increase in the number of unresolved disputes across the ITR especially if it is not correlated with the MAP system. It is also unsure at this point how the competent authorities will be handling the increased workload related to

803. Report on Pillar One Blueprint, *supra* n. 74, at paras 800-803.

Amount A disputes under Pillar One, given that competent authorities are already burdened by the ever-increasing number of MAP cases (as shown in Table I.1 in Appendix I).

The proposed reform in this research thesis reflects similar key considerations included in Pillar One, most notably, the need for a flexible yet mandatory and binding process that leads to an effective resolution of disputes and increased tax certainty across the ITR. The suggested new structure based on the LOSC's system meets these requirements to achieve an effective and predictable resolution of multilateral tax disputes. In addition, however, the proposed reform goes beyond the Pillar One proposal not only by expanding the existing mechanisms to a multilateral framework but also by suggesting new mechanisms, including the ITT, the IF arbitration mechanism and the special IF arbitration mechanism (*see* section 7.2) for addressing the increasing complexities and capacity issues linked with the MAP. Such an expanded and legalistic dispute resolution system not only relieves some of the capacity issues in the MAP but also increases tax certainty for both taxpayers and governments and aims for a more balanced allocation of power across the system through the rule of law to achieve equitable solutions across the ITR.

More specifically, the mechanisms proposed in this thesis also address the issues linked with the application of the baseball approach (opacity of procedures, lack of case law and dissatisfaction) by recommending the independent opinion approach to be used in the proposed IF and special IF arbitration mechanisms to strengthen the independent review process under arbitration. Finally, the suggested new structure also recommends addressing disputes under Pillar Two through the ITT or the IF arbitration mechanism in accordance with the characterisation of the dispute.[804] Pillar One disputes, however, which constitute allocation cases, would be addressed through the TPDC if they are not eligible under MAP, otherwise, they may also be addressed through the special IF arbitration mechanism. As such, the comprehensive legal framework being proposed in this thesis addresses not only the technical shortcomings identified with the Pillar One mechanism in section 2.3.1.3 but also attempts to achieve a balance between governments' exercise of their sovereign rights and the rule of law under public international law.

7.6 CONCLUSIONS

Several aspects of the LOSC's dispute resolution system were adapted into the ITR for reforming the tax treaty dispute resolution system. The new system suggested in this thesis addresses not only the existing MAP issues but also the potential issues identified with the dispute resolution mechanism proposed under Pillar One. At the operational level, although the MAP remains the primary means of dispute resolution, three new adjudication mechanisms were proposed, including the IF arbitration and special IF arbitration mechanisms and the ITT (based on arbitration under Annex VII and Annex VIII of the LOSC and the ITLOS respectively). The IF arbitration mechanism addresses

804. *See* s. 7.2.1.2.2.

specifically non-transfer pricing MAP cases brought under Article 25(1), and the special IF arbitration mechanism deals with transfer pricing cases brought under Article 25(1) for which no MAP agreement was reached within the prescribed timeline of 24 months. The arbitration process is usually triggered by the taxpayer. However, competent authorities may, subject to the approval of the taxpayer, submit a transfer pricing dispute to the special IF arbitration within 6 months of receiving the MAP request if they consider that the 24-month deadline may not be met.

To address tax disputes that are not covered under MAP or the treaty, this thesis recommends the creation of an ITT, which includes a special transfer pricing dispute chamber, the TPDC, that may specifically hear transfer pricing cases. This is based on the SDC that operates under the ITLOS and hears only disputes relating to activities in the seabed Area. If the transfer pricing dispute is brought under Article 25(1), it may be submitted to either the TPDC or to special IF arbitration. The taxpayer may decide which of the two forums to use. The ITT will also hear cases relating to the interpretation and application of the treaty brought under Article 25(3), which are not usually eligible for arbitration. The jurisdiction of the ITT may also be extended to other international tax agreements or treaties if they explicitly confer jurisdiction on the ITT (e.g., disputes regarding carbon taxes under the Paris Agreement). The proposed structure addresses disputes arising under both Pillar One and Pillar Two.

In order to facilitate the implementation of the proposed new mechanisms across the IF, the reform proposal also includes recommendations at the policymaking and constitutional levels of decision-making to enhance consensus-building across the ITR. At the policymaking level, recommendations include: (1) incorporating the provisions implementing the new dispute resolution system in a multilateral treaty (similar to the MC under Pillar One) to ensure that all users are subject to equal rules under law; and (2) developing the multilateral treaty without a draft model text to ensure that the views of all users are reflected therein. Recommendations at the constitutional level include (1) the creation of an IF Secretariat to implement BEPS-related work, especially in relation to dispute resolution instead of the dual OECD/UN policy spaces; and (2) applying appropriate clustering strategies at the formal and informal levels of the IF meetings to ensure a balanced geographical representation of delegates in the various committees and also promote the creation of private negotiating groups during the IF meetings to build consensus at a smaller scale before joining the official negotiations. Such measures aim to promote more equitable decision-making processes across the ITR.

CHAPTER 8
Conclusion

The aim of this book is to contribute to the development of an improved tax treaty dispute resolution system that is more appropriate in an increasingly interconnected and multilateral ITR. Based on the LOSC's dispute resolution system, the new tax treaty dispute resolution system proposed constitutes a comprehensive legal framework that aims to achieve a more effective, predictable and equitable resolution of multilateral tax disputes in the ITR. The structure strives to achieve a balance between states' right to tax sovereignty and the rule of law across the ITR. The proposed reform also offers consensus-building techniques that may facilitate negotiations on the new dispute resolution system to reach a universal agreement across the developed and developing countries of the IF. Just as agreement on the LOSC's dispute resolution system led to the finalisation of the LOSC itself, it is expected that the innovative reforms proposed in this book may not only improve the tax treaty dispute resolution process but also facilitate international cooperation for developing a multilateral convention on tax in the ITR.

The aim of this research thesis is to contribute to the development of an improved tax treaty dispute resolution system that may address more appropriately the tsunami of cross-border tax disputes expected in the ITR within the next few decades. In fact, the OECD MAP Statistics already shows a steadily growing inventory of outstanding MAP cases from 2016-2020 (*see* Table I.1 in Appendix I)[805] despite the positive impact of the BEPS Action 14 on the effectiveness of the MAP. To this end, this thesis applies a comparative institutional analysis method to examine and compare the dispute resolution systems under the ITR and the LOSC to identify aspects of the LOSC's system that may be used to improve tax treaty dispute resolution in the ITR. This endeavour is crystallised in three research questions: (1) What are the institutional arrangements

805. There is slight decrease in the number of outstanding MAP cases in 2020 which may be attributed to the COVID-19 pandemic.

that underpin the current tax treaty dispute resolution system and the LOSC's dispute resolution system? (2) Which aspects of the LOSC's dispute resolution system may be relevant for improving tax treaty dispute resolution? and (3) How can the tax treaty dispute resolution system be restructured by adapting the relevant aspects identified in the LOSC's system?

As I argue in Chapter 2, the LOSC's system is an appropriate benchmark for this purpose based on the common geopolitical context that underpins both the ITR and the law of the sea regime, despite the substantive legal differences between international tax rules and laws that govern the oceans. There are five geopolitical similarities discussed in section 2.4.1. First, the governance structure under both regimes is based on consensus-based decision-making across approximately a similar number of Member States. Second, both regimes deal with scarce resources (i.e., the global tax base and the oceans), which need to be distributed in an equitable manner across jurisdictions to prevent global conflict.[806] Third, since jurisdictions have public access to both the global tax base and the oceans, there are collective action issues being faced in both regimes, which need to be managed through cooperative mechanisms. Fourth, customary international law plays an important role in both regimes, which may impact the political relations among the Member States. Finally, both the ITR and the law of the sea regime place significant emphasis on maintaining diplomatic relations among Member States as reflected through the dispute resolution mechanisms that operate within the regimes. There are, however, important institutional differences in relation to dispute resolution across the two regimes, as discussed in section 2.4.2. These include the frequency of disputes and the actors involved in the dispute resolution processes, and they are taken into account when comparing the two systems.

Given the different institutional contexts of the dispute resolution systems under the ITR and the LOSC, I apply a comparative institutional analysis method based on the pIAD framework to analyse and compare the institutional arrangements that underpin the two systems. The pIAD framework is a politicised version of Elinor Ostrom's IAD framework developed in the 1980s to study institutions, the different components of which are discussed in Chapter 3, along with the research approach based on a three-step analytical process (Steps A, B and C). The pIAD framework is applied in Steps A and B to ensure an accurate analysis of the two dispute resolution systems at the operational, policymaking and constitutional levels, which constitute the three levels of institutionalised decision-making. As discussed in section 3.4, the pIAD framework constitutes an ideal tool for the purposes of this comparative exercise as it breaks up each dispute resolution system into smaller components that may be compared more accurately, given the different institutional contexts within which they operate. Moreover, the pIAD framework avoids the pitfalls associated with single institutional analysis (e.g., cycling issues) and provides a complete analysis of the two systems.

806. Even if the size of the global tax base can be increased by increasing effective tax rates, it is still considered a scarce resource for jurisdictions as the tax base being allocated to each jurisdiction is limited through distributive rules.

Each Step A, B and C of the methodology corresponds to one of the three research questions posed respectively. Step A of the pIAD analysis maps out the relevant institutional arrangements (rules, norms and strategies) underpinning the dispute resolution systems under the ITR and the LOSC within their respective political, economic and discursive context. The results of Step A in the ITR and the LOSC are mapped out in Chapters 4 and 5, respectively. Step B then integrates the analysis of the mapped-out institutional arrangements and compares the resulting patterns of interaction in the two systems to identify aspects of the LOSC's system that could be relevant for improving tax treaty dispute resolution. Step B of the pIAD analysis also compares the inclusivity (participation) levels in both systems to identify relevant consensus-building techniques developed through the LOSC that could be applied to facilitate the implementation of the proposed reform in the ITR. Step B is explored in Chapter 6 of the thesis. Finally, Step C offers a potential restructuring of the tax treaty dispute resolution system based on relevant aspects adapted from the LOSC's system (as a benchmark). The suggested new structure is set out in Chapter 7.

The proposed reform includes recommendations at the operational, policymaking and constitutional levels. At the operational level, I propose three new mechanisms, in addition to the MAP, to address the issues of capacity, uncertainty and inequitable solutions that the current MAP and arbitration mechanisms generate in the ITR (as discussed in section 2.2). These mechanisms include the IF arbitration, the special IF arbitration and the ITT based on the LOSC's Annex VII arbitration, Annex VIII arbitration and the ITLOS, respectively. The IF arbitration process addresses non-transfer pricing cases, while the special IF arbitration process deals with transfer pricing cases, both of which are brought to the MAP under Article 25(1). The ITT tackles cases which are not eligible under the MAP or the bilateral tax treaty, and it also addresses MAP cases brought under Article 25(3) that relate to the interpretation or application of the treaty but which may not be eligible under the current arbitration procedures. The ITT also includes a transfer pricing dispute chamber (TPDC) that hears only transfer pricing cases. This is based on the LOSC's SDC that hears only disputes relating to activities in the seabed Area. The jurisdiction of the ITT could also be extended to hear disputes brought under agreements other than bilateral tax treaties (e.g., carbon tax disputes under the Paris Agreement). These three mechanisms form a mandatory yet flexible dispute resolution system in the ITR, just as the LOSC mechanisms on which they are based, while prioritising the MAP as the primary tax treaty dispute resolution mechanism.

At the policymaking level, I recommend incorporating the proposed mechanisms (IF arbitration, special IF arbitration and the ITT) in a multilateral treaty that all interested parties may ratify, just as the MC proposed under Pillar One. This will ensure that all parties to the treaty are subject to a uniform and legally binding dispute resolution system if the dispute is not resolved on a diplomatic basis through the bilateral MAP. In addition, to ensure that the final treaty text reflects the views of all parties, it is recommended that the negotiation text be developed from scratch instead of relying on a draft model, as was done in the case of the LOSC (as discussed in the discourse analysis in section 5.3.5).

At the constitutional level, I recommend applying certain specific consensus-building techniques that were developed during the UNCLOS III negotiations that produced the LOSC to facilitate the universal adoption of the proposed multilateral treaty (including the new dispute resolution structure) across the IF. These techniques include first the creation of an IF Secretariat to promote a more unified and neutral decision-making structure across the ITR, as opposed to the competing OECD and UN policy spaces. The IF Secretariat may take over any BEPS-related initiatives with the aim of achieving a more equitable balance of powers among the developed G20 countries and the developing countries under the G77. Second, I propose applying clustering strategies at the formal level in IF meetings to achieve an equitable geographical representation of jurisdictions across IF committees and at the informal level to promote the creation of private negotiating groups in parallel to build consensus within smaller groups prior to the formal negotiations. These measures aim to increase inclusivity across the IF to enable developed, developing and emerging countries to negotiate on a more level playing field.

To sum up, the comparative exercise in this research thesis has revealed many insightful lessons from the law of the sea regime and the LOSC's dispute resolution system for improving tax treaty dispute resolution. The LOSC's system is especially useful as a comparative benchmark as the ITR today seems to be mirroring similarly disruptive geopolitical dynamics between developed and developing countries as experienced under the law of sea regime in the mid-20th century. Since the LOSC's dispute resolution system was purposely designed to avoid political and economic pressures and ensure the principle of equality before the law, especially for developing countries, it contains much of the foundational work needed to build a similar system in the ITR. This includes achieving a large measure of uniformity in the application and interpretation of the applicable treaty; ensuring that all members have recourse to legal mechanisms to avoid political and even military confrontation; and recognising that a generally accepted, effective and flexible dispute resolution system provides the necessary stability in the face of current and future disputes of a rapidly evolving regime.[807] Motivated through similar principles, the new tax treaty dispute resolution system proposed in this thesis constitutes a comprehensive legal framework that aims to achieve an effective, predictable and equitable resolution of multilateral tax disputes in the 21st century by striking a balance between states' right to tax sovereignty and the rule of law across the ITR.

On a final note, the proposed reform to tax treaty dispute resolution, as presented in this study, could not be more timely. There is no doubt that the OECD's proposed mandatory and binding dispute resolution mechanism under Pillar One, that is expected to be implemented in 2024, has opened new doors for restructuring dispute resolution in the ITR, especially by rallying developing countries to accept mandatory and binding arbitration. However, as discussed in section 2.3.1.3 above, the OECD's proposal, in its current form, is also expected to have limited scope and even exacerbate the power imbalances at the competent authority level between developed

807. These principles are outlined in the provisional working paper presented by the Working Group on dispute settlement during the first session of UNCLOS III. *See supra* n. 658.

and developing countries. The comprehensive tax treaty dispute resolution system proposed in this thesis aims to address not only the issues of the current MAP system but also the potential technical issues identified under the OECD's dispute resolution mechanism proposed under Pillar One.

APPENDIX I OECD MAP Statistics

Table I.1 MAP Caseloads

	Opening Inventory 1 January			*Cases Started in the Year*			*Cases Closed in the Year*			*Ending inventory 31 December*		
Year	*Transfer Pricing*	*Other*	*Total*	*Transfer Pricing*	*Other*	*Total*	*Transfer Pricing*	*Other*	*Total*	*Transfer Pricing*	*Other*	*Total*
2016	*	*	0	*	*	1496	*	*	353	*	*	1143
2017	576	611	1187	779	1297	2076	251	730	981	1104	1178	2282
2018	1132	1206	2338	930	1455	2385	394	1079	1473	1668	1582	3250
2019	1918	1803	3721	1156	1534	2690	691	1196	1887	2383	2141	4524
2020	2058	1841	3899	1178	1330	2508	667	1058	1725	2569	2113	4682

Source: OECD MAP Statistics.

* No data provided.

Table I.2 Resolution Timeline

	Average Time to Close MAP Cases (Months)	
Year	*Transfer Pricing Cases*	*Other Cases*
2016	30	17
2017	30	17
2018	33	14
2019	30.5	22
2020	35	18.5

Source: OECD MAP Statistics.

Table I.3 MAP Outcomes

Year	*Some Form of Agreement Reached**	*Unilateral Relief Granted*	*Resolved via Domestic Remedy*	*Denied MAP Access*	*Not Resolved for Various Reasons*
2016	61%	19%	4%	4%	11%
2017	57%	20%	3%	6%	14%
2018	60%	17%	4%	6%	13%
2019	58%	15%	5%	6%	16%
2020	52%	16%	7%	3%	22%

Source: OECD MAP Statistics.

* Includes agreement fully and partially eliminating double taxation and taxation not in accordance with tax treaty.

Appendix II LOSC Article 287 Declarations

Table II.1 DOALOS, Settlement of Disputes Mechanism: Recapitulative Tables (30 August 2019)

		Choice of Procedure: Declarations under Article 287 (Numbers Indicate the Order of Preference)			
		ITLOS	*ICJ*	*Annex VII Arbitral Tribunal*	*Annex VIII Special Arbitral Tribunal*
1	Algeria	**1**	–	–	–
2	Angola	**1**	–	–	–
3	Argentina	**1**	–	–	**2**
4	Australia	**1**	**1**	–	–
5	Austria	**1**	**3**	–	**2**
6	Bangladesh	**1**	–	–	–
7	Belarus	In respect of the prompt release of detained vessels or their crews	–	**1**	**1**
8	Belgium	**1**	**1**	–	–
9	Bulgaria	**1**	–	–	–
10	Cabo Verde	**1**	**2**	–	–
11	Canada	**1**	–	**1**	–
12	Chile	**1**	–	–	**2**
13	China			No choice under Article 287 made	
14	Croatia	**1**	**2**	–	–

Choice of Procedure: Declarations under Article 287
(Numbers Indicate the Order of Preference)

		ITLOS	*ICJ*	*Annex VII Arbitral Tribunal*	*Annex VIII Special Arbitral Tribunal*
15	Cuba	–	Cuba rejects the ICJ jurisdiction for any type of disputes	–	–
16	Democratic Republic of the Congo	**1**	–	–	–
17	Denmark	–	**1**	Not accepted for any of the categories of disputes mentioned in Article 298	–
18	Ecuador	**1**	**1**	–	**1**
19	Egypt	–	–	**1**	–
20	Equatorial Guinea			No choice under Article 287 made	
21	Estonia	**1**	**1**	–	–
22	Fiji	**1**	–	–	–
23	Finland	**1**	**1**	–	–
24	France			No choice under Article 287 made	
25	Gabon			No choice under Article 287 made	
26	Germany	**1**	**3**	**2**	–
27	Greece	**1**	–	–	–
28	Guinea-Bissau	-	Guinea-Bissau rejects the ICJ jurisdiction for any type of disputes	–	–

		Choice of Procedure: Declarations under Article 287 (Numbers Indicate the Order of Preference)			
		ITLOS	*ICJ*	*Annex VII Arbitral Tribunal*	*Annex VIII Special Arbitral Tribunal*
29	Honduras	–	**1**	–	–
30	Hungary	**1**	**2**	–	**3**
31	Iceland			No choice under Article 287 made	
32	Italy	**1**	**1**	–	–
33	Kenya			No choice under Article 287 made	
34	Latvia	**1**	**1**	–	–
35	Lithuania	**1**	**1**	–	–
36	Madagascar	**1**	–	–	–
37	Mexico	**1**	**1**	–	**1**
38	Montenegro	**1**	**2**	–	–
39	The Netherlands	**1**	**1** In the event another State Party has chosen ICJ and ITLOS without indicating precedence, The Netherlands should be considered as having chosen the ICJ only.	–	–

Choice of Procedure: Declarations under Article 287
(Numbers Indicate the Order of Preference)

		ITLOS	*ICJ*	*Annex VII Arbitral Tribunal*	*Annex VIII Special Arbitral Tribunal*
40	Nicaragua	–	1	–	–
41	Norway	–	1	–	–
42	Oman	1	1	–	–
43	Palau			No choice under Article 287 made	
44	Panama	1	–	–	–
45	Portugal	1	1	1	1
46	Republic of Korea			No choice under Article 287 made	
47	Russian Federation	In matters relating to the prompt release of detained vessels and crews		1	1
48	Saint Vincent and the Grenadines	1	–	–	–
49	Saudi Arabia	–	–	–	–
50	Singapore			No choice under Article 287 made	
51	Slovenia	–	–	1	–
52	Spain	1	1	–	–
53	Sweden	–	1	–	–
54	Switzerland	1	–	–	–
55	Thailand			No choice under Article 287 made	
56	Timor-Leste	1	1	1	1
57	Togo	1	1	–	–

		Choice of Procedure: Declarations under Article 287 (Numbers Indicate the Order of Preference)			
		ITLOS	*ICJ*	*Annex VII Arbitral Tribunal*	*Annex VIII Special Arbitral Tribunal*
58	Trinidad and Tobago	**1**	**2**	–	–
59	Tunisia	**1**	–	**2**	–
60	Ukraine	In respect of the prompt release of detained vessels or their crews	–	**1**	**1**
61	United Kingdom of Great Britain and Northern Ireland	–	**1**	–	–
62	United Republic of Tanzania	**1**	–	–	–
63	Uruguay	**1**	–		
	Number of countries that indicate preferred procedure (i.e., 1)	**39**	**21**	**8**	**7**

Source: UN, Division for Ocean Affairs and the law of the sea (DOALOS) – Recapitulative Tables www.un.org/Depts/los/settlement_of_disputes/choice_procedure.htm, accessed 20 March 2021.

* If number 1 appears for more than one procedure, no order of preference has been specified.

Table II.2 List of Developed Countries under World Economic and Prospects (WESP) Report

Europe			*Other Countries*	*Major Developed Economies (G7)*
European Union	*New EU Member States*	*Other Europe*		
EU-15	Bulgaria	Iceland	Australia	Canada
Austria	Croatia	Norway	Canada	Japan
Belgium	Cyprus	Switzerland	Japan	France
Denmark	Czech Republic		New Zealand	Germany
Finland	Estonia		United States	Italy
France	Hungary			United Kingdom
Germany	Latvia			United States
Greece	Lithuania			
Ireland	Malta			
Italy	Poland			
Luxembourg	Romania			
The Netherlands	Slovakia			
Portugal	Slovenia			
Spain				
Sweden				
United Kingdom				

Source: Country Classification WESP www.un.org/en/development/desa/policy/wesp/wesp_current/2014wesp_country_classification.pdf accessed 20 March 2021.

Bibliography

Books, Articles and Research Papers

Alan Beesley, *The Negotiating Strategy of UNCLOS III: Developing and Developed Countries as Partners: A Pattern for Future Multilateral International Conferences?* (46(2) Law & Contemporary Problems 183, 1983).

Alan E. Boyle, *Dispute Settlement and the Law of the Sea Convention: Problems of Fragmentation and Jurisdiction* (46 International & Comparative Law Quarterly 37, 1997).

Alan E. Boyle, *UNCLOS, the Marine Environment and the Settlement of Disputes* in Hendrik Ringbom (ed.) Competing Norms in the Law of Marine Environmental Protection: Focus on Ship Safety and Pollution Prevention (Kluwer Law International, 1997).

Albert W. Koers, *The Third United Nations Conference on the Law of the Sea: Some Remarks on Its Contribution Towards the Making of International Law*, in Wybo P. Heere (ed.) International Law and Its Sources: Liber Amicorum Maarten Bos (T.M.C. Asser Institute, 1989).

Alex Cobham, Tax Justice Network Blog (25 November 2021) https://taxjustice.net/2021/11/25/power-concedes-nothing-without-a-demand-the-oecd-the-g77-and-a-un-framework-convention-on-tax-proposal/ (accessed 20 May 2022).

Alf H. Hoel and Ingrid Kvalvik, *The Allocation of Scarce Natural Resources: The Case of Fisheries* (30(4) Marine Policy 347, 2006).

Allison Christians, *BEPS and the New International Tax Order* (6 BYU Law Review 1603, 2016).

Allison Christians, *How Nations Share* (87 Indiana Law Journal 1407, 2012).

Andre Nollkaemper, *International Adjudication of Global Public Goods: The Intersection of Substance and Procedure* (23 European Journal of International Law 769, 2012).

Andreas Osthagen, *Maritime Boundary Disputes: What Are They and Why Do They Matter?* (120 Marine Policy 6, 2020).

Andronico O. Adede, *Settlement of Disputes Arising under the Law of the Sea Convention* (69 American Journal of International Law, 1975).

Anshuman Chakraborty, *Dispute Settlement under the United Nations Convention on the Law of the Sea and Its Role in Oceans Governance* (LLM thesis, Victoria University of Wellington 2006).

Anthony Mason, *International Law as a Source of Domestic Law* in Brian R. Opeskin and Donald R. Rothwell (eds) International Law and Australian Federalism (Melbourne University Press, 1997).

ASEAN Secretariat, *Declaration in the Conduct of Parties in the South China Sea* (14 May 2012), https://asean.org/declaration-on-the-conduct-of-parties-in-the-south-china-sea-2 (accessed 10 May 2022).

Asgeir Johannesson, *The Politics of Historical Discourse Analysis: A Qualitative Research Method?* (31(2) Discourse: Studies in the Cultural Politics of Education 251, 2010).

Ashley J. Roach, *Today's Customary International Law of the Sea* (45(3) Ocean Development & International Law 239, 2014).

Aslaug Asgeirsdottir and Martin Steinwand, *Dispute Settlement Mechanisms and Maritime Boundary Settlements* (Review of International Organizations, 2015).

Barry Buzan, *Negotiating by Consensus: Developments in Technique at the United Nations Conference on the Law of the Sea* (75(2) The American Journal of International Law 324, 1981).

Benjami A. Juanpere, *The Resolution of Tax Disputes and International Tax Arbitration* (5(1) European Journal of Business and Management Research 1, 2020).

Bernard H. Oxman, *The Rule of Law and the United Nations Convention on the Law of the Sea* (7 European Journal of International Taxation 353, 1996).

Bernardo S. Amor, *The International Court of Justice and the Law of the Sea* (Anuario Mexicano de Derecho Internacional 3, 2012).

Boleslaw A. Boczek, *International Law: A Dictionary xxii* (Scarecrow Press, 2005).

Bret Wells and Cym H. Lowell, *Income Tax Treaty Policy in the 21st Century: Residence vs. Source* (5(1) Columbia Journal of Tax Law 1, 2013).

Canada Revenue Agency, *Mutual Agreement Procedure: Program Report – 2018 (Annex A)* www.canada.ca/en/revenue-agency/services/tax/international-non-residents/competent-authority-services/2018map.html#toc17 (accessed 20 March 2021).

Cesare P.R. Romano, *The Settlement of Disputes under the 1982 Law of the Sea Convention: How Entangled Can We Get?* (103(1) Journal of International Law and Diplomacy 84, 2004).

Chloe Burnett, *International Tax Arbitration* (36(3) Australian Tax Review 173, 2007).

Chris Xing et al., *China after BEPS, for Now ...* (International Tax Review, 28 November 2017) www.internationaltaxreview.com/article/b1f7nb1h471zlm/china-after-beps-for-now (accessed 10 March 2021).

Clive Schofield and I. Arsana, *The Delimitation of Maritime Boundaries: A Matter of Life or Death for East Timor?* in Damien Kingsbury and Michael Leach (eds) East Timor: Beyond Independence (Melbourne University Press, 2007).

Colin Hay, *Constructivist Institutionalism* (Oxford University Press, 2008).

Constantin A. Stavropoulos, *Statement by C.A. Stavropoulos. Procedural Problems of the Third Conference on the Law of the Sea*, in Myron Nordquist (ed.) United

Nations Convention on the Law of the Sea 1982: A Commentary (vol. 1, Martinus Nijhoff Publishers, 1985).

Dai Tamada, *The Timor Sea Conciliation: The Unique Mechanism of Dispute Settlement* (31(1) European Journal of International Law 321, 2020).

Dani Rodrik and Tanguy Van Ypersele, *Capital Mobility, Distributive Conflict and International Tax Coordination* (54(1) Journal of International Economics 57, 2001).

Daniel Augenstein, *To Whom It May Concern: International Human Rights Law and Global Public Goods* (23(1) Indiana Journal of Global Legal Studies 225, 2016).

Daniel H. Cole, *The Varieties of Comparative Institutional Analysis* (Articles by Maurer Faculty, 2012) www.repository.law.indiana.edu/facpub/834 (accessed 19 December 2018).

David Rosenbloom, *Mandatory Arbitration of Disputes Pursuant to Tax Treaties: The Experience of the United States*, in Michael Lang and Jeffrey Owens (eds) International Arbitration in Tax Matters (IBFD, 2016).

Deloitte, Global Transfer Pricing Alert 2017-012 (6 April 2017) www2.deloitte.com/content/dam/Deloitte/global/Documents/Tax/dttl-tax-global-transfer-pricing-alert-17-012-6-april-2017.pdf (accessed 20 February 2023).

Dharshini Amaratunga, *Maritime Boundary Delimitation: Building and Preparing a Negotiating Team* (24(1-2) Commonwealth Law Bulletin 516, 1998).

Diheng Xu, *Regional Tax Coordination Between China and ASEAN under the Belt and Road Initiative* (2019), https://papers.ssrn.com/sol3/papers.cfm?abstract_id=3349398 (accessed 10 March 2021).

Dirk Broekhuijsen and Irma Mosquera Valderrama, *Revisiting the Case of Customary International Tax Law* (23 International Community Law Review 79, 2021).

Donald C. Watt, *The Future Governance of the Seas: An Inaugural Lecture for the Inauguration of the M Sc Course in Sea Use: Law, Economics and Policy – Making* (The London School of Economics and Political Science, London, 10 October 1979).

Douglas H. Yarn, *Conflict* in Douglas H. Yarn (ed.) Dictionary of Conflict Resolution (Jossey-Bass, 1999).

Douglass C. North, *Institutions, Institutional Change and Economic Performance* (Cambridge University Press, 1991).

Eduardo Baistrocchi, *Patterns of Tax Treaty Disputes: A Global Taxonomy* in Eduardo Baistrocchi (ed.) A Global Analysis of Tax Treaty Disputes (Cambridge University Press, 2017).

Eduardo Baistrocchi, *The International Tax Regime and Global Power Shifts* (20(2) Virginia Tax Review, 2021).

Eduardo Baistrocchi, *The Transfer Pricing Problem: A Global Proposal for Simplification* (59(4) Tax Law, 2006).

Edward L. Miles, *Global Ocean Politics: The Decision Process at the Third United Nations Conference on the Law of the Sea 1973-1982* (Brill Nijhoff, 1998).

Elinor Ostrom, *An Agenda for the Study of Institutions* (48(1) Public Choice 3, 1986).

Elinor Ostrom, *Institutional Rational Choice: An Assessment of the Institutional Analysis and Development Framework* in Paul A. Sabatier (ed.) Theories of the Policy Process (Westview Press, 2007).

Elinor Ostrom, *Understanding Institutional Diversity* (Princeton University Press, 2005).

Elliot L. Richardson, *Dispute Settlement under the Convention on the Law of the Sea: A Flexible and Comprehensive Extension of the Rule of the Law to Ocean Space* in Thomas Buergenthal (ed.) Contemporary Issues in International Law: Essays in Honor of Louis B. Sohn (N P Engel, 1984).

Elmer Pergament et al., *The 'Competent Authority' Rules for Section 482 Relief: An Analysis of Rev. Proc. 70-18* (35 Journal of Taxation, 1971).

Eric A. Posner and John C. Yoo, *A Theory of International Adjudication* (John M. Olin Program in Law and Economics Working Paper No. 206, 2004).

Eric A. Posner and John C. Yoo, *Judicial Independence in International Tribunals* (93 California Law Review 1, 2005).

Erik Voeten, *The Politics of International Judicial Appointments* (9(2) Chicago Journal of International Law 387, 2009).

Ernst and Young, *2016-2017 Transfer Pricing Survey Series: Controversy, Avoidance and Resolution* (EY Publications, 2017).

Ernst and Young, *OECD Releases People's Republic of China Stage 2 Peer Review Report on Implementation of Action 14 Minimum Standard* (27 October 2021) https://taxnews.ey.com/news/2021-1960-oecd-releases-peoples-republic-of-china-stage-2-peer-review-report-on-implementation-of-action-14-minimum-standard (accessed 20 May 2022).

Ernst-Ulrich Petersmann, *Mini-Symposium on Multilevel Governance of Interdependent Public Goods* (15 Journal of International Economic Law 709, 2012).

Fabrizio Cafaggi, *Global Public Goods Amidst a Plurality of Legal Orders: A Symposium* (23 European Journal of International Law 643, 2012).

Floriane Clement, *Analysing Decentralised Natural Resource Governance: Proposition for a 'Politicised' Institutional Analysis and Development Framework* (43 Policy Sciences 129, 2010).

Gerhard Erasmus, *Dispute Settlement in the Law of the Sea* (Acta Juridica, University of Cape Town 15, 1986).

Gilbert Guillaume, *The Use of Precedence by International Judges and Arbitrators* (2(1) Journal of International Dispute Settlement 5, 2011).

Gustaf Lindecrona and Nils Mattsson, *Arbitration in Taxation* (Kluwer Law and Taxation Publishers, 1981).

Hans Mooij, *Tax Treaty Arbitration* (35(2) Arbitration International 195, 2018).

Harm Mark Pit, *Arbitration under the OECD Model Convention: Follow-Up under Double Tax Conventions: An Evaluation* (42(6-7) Intertax 445, 2014).

HMRC, *Policy Paper: Mutual Agreement Procedure Decisions Relating to the Diverted Profits Tax* (HMRC, 27 October 2021), www.gov.uk/government/publications/mutual-agreement-procedure-map-decisions-relating-to-the-diverted-profits-tax/mutual-agreement-procedure-map-decisions-relating-to-the-diverted-profits-tax (accessed 20 March 2022).

Howard Mann, *The Expanding Universe of International Tax Disputes: A Principled Analysis of the OECD International Tax Dispute Settlement Proposals* (31(1) Asia-Pacific Law Review 268, 2023).

Howard S. Schiffman, *The Protection of Whales in International Law: A Perspective for the Next Century* (22 Brook Journal of International Law 303, 1996).

Huaigao Qi, *Joint Development in the South China Sea: China's Incentives and Policy Choices* (8(2) Journal of Contemporary East Asia Studies 220, 2019).

Hugh Ault and Jacques Sasseville, *2008 OECD Model: The New Arbitration Provision* (63(5) Bulletin for International Taxation 210, 2009).

Igor V. Karaman, *Dispute Resolution in the Law of the Sea* (Brill Publications, 2012).

Inge Kaul and Ronald U. Mendoza, *Advancing the Concept of Public Goods* in Inge Kaul (ed.), Providing Global Public Goods: Managing Globalization (Oxford University Press, 2003).

Inge Kaul, Isabelle Grunberg and Marc A. Stern, *Defining Global Public Goods* in Inge Kaul, Isabelle Grunberg and Marc A. Stern (eds), Global Public Goods: International Cooperation in the 21st Century (Oxford University Press, 1999).

Irene Burgers and Irma Mosquera, *Corporation Taxation and BEPS: A Fair Slice for Developing Countries* (10(1) Erasmus Law Review 29, 2017).

Ivan A. Shearer, *The Relationship Between International Law and Domestic Law* in Brian R. Opeskin and Donald R. Rothwell (eds) International Law and Australian Federalism (Melbourne University Press, 1997).

James N. Rosenau, *Governance in the Twenty-First Century* (1 Global Governance 13, 1995).

Jean-Pierre Cot, *Expectations Attached to Conciliation Reconsidered* in Christian Tomuschat et al. (eds) Conciliation in International Law: The OSCE Court of Conciliation and Arbitration (Brill, 2016).

Jeff Owens, *Mandatory Tax Arbitration: The Next Frontier Issue* (46(8/9) Intertax 610, 2018).

Jerome Monsenego, *Does the Achmea Case Prevent the Resolution of Tax Treaty Disputes Through Arbitration?* (47(8) Intertax 728, 2019).

Jinyan Li, *The Great Fiscal Wall of China: Tax Treaties and Their Role in Defining and Defending China's Tax Base* (66(9) Bulletin for International Taxation 452, 2012).

Joe Duffy and Tomas Bailey, *Tax Disputes Post-BEPS: A Perfect Storm* (International Tax Review, 17 March 2017) www.internationaltaxreview.com/article/b1f7n6czfxf1jf/tax-disputes-post-beps-a-perfect-storm (accessed 15 Nov. 2021).

John W. Burton, *Conflict: Resolution and Prevention* (vol. 1 of Conflict Series, St Martin's Press, 1990).

John C. Klotsche, *United States: Jousting with the Tax Man: An Extreme Makeover, IRS Edition* (3 July 2009) quoted in M. Markham, Advance Pricing Agreements: Past, Present and Future 19 (Kluwer Law International, 2012).

John Collier and Vaughan Lowe, *The Settlement of Disputes in International Law: Institutions and Procedures* (Oxford University Press, 1999).

John E. Noyes, *The Third-Party Dispute Settlement Provisions of the 1982 United Nations Convention on the Law of the Sea: Implications for States Parties and for*

Non-parties, in M. H. Nordquist and J. N. Moore (eds) Entry into Force of the Law of the Sea Convention (Martinus Nijhoff Publishers, 1995).

John F. Avery Jones, *Types of Arbitration Procedure* (49(8/7) Intertax, 2019).

John G. Merrills, *International Dispute Settlement* (Cambridge University Press, 2017).

John R. Stevenson, Address to the Plenary Session of the Law of the Sea Conference (11 July 1974) US Department of State Press Release 301.

Jon M. Van Dyke, *Louis B Sohn and the Settlement of Ocean Disputes* (33 George Washington International Law Review 31, 2000).

Jonathan Charney, *The Impact of the International Legal System of the Growth of International Courts and Tribunals* (31 N.Y.U. Journal of International Law & Policy 697, 1999).

Jonathan Schwarz, *Mutual Agreement Procedure: Taxpayer Access to Information* (Kluwer International Tax Blog, 12 June 2019) http://kluwertaxblog.com/2019/06/12/mutual-agreement-procedure-taxpayer-access-to-information/ (accessed 4 March 2022).

Joost Pauwelyn, *The WTO 20 Years On: 'Global Governance by Judiciary' or, Rather, Member-Driven Settlement of (Some) Trade Disputes Between (Some) WTO Members?* (27(4) European Journal of International Law (2016).

Joshua Paine, *International Adjudication as a Global Public Good?* (29(4) European Journal of International Law 1223, 2019).

Julien Chaisse, *The Treatment of (National) Taxes in Tax and Non-Tax (International) Agreements* (6th meeting of the Asia – Pacific FDI network) www.unescap.org/sites/default/files/5.%20Julien%20Chaisse_Tax.pdf (accessed 21 March 2021).

Keyuan Zou, *China's Marine Legal System and the Law of the Sea* (Martinus Nijhoff, 2005).

Keyuan Zou, *Implementation of the United Nations Law of the Sea Convention in China* in Seokwoo Lee and Warwick Gullet (eds) Asia-Pacific and the Implementation of the Law of the Sea (Maritime Cooperation in East Asia Series: vol. 1, Brill Nijhoff, 2016).

Keyuan Zou, *Implementing the United Nations Convention on the Law of the Sea in East Asia: Issues and Trends* (9 Singapore Y.B. International Law & Contributors 37, 2005).

Keyuan Zou, *International Law in the Chinese Domestic Context* (44(3) Valparaiso University Law Review 935, 2010).

Keyuan Zou, *The Sino-Vietnamese Agreement on Maritime Boundary Delimitation in the Gulf of Tonkin* (36 Ocean Development and International Law 13, 2005).

Keyuan Zou, *The South China Sea* in Donald R. Rothwell, Alex G. Oude Elferink, Karen N. Scott, Tim Stephens (eds) The Oxford Handbook of the Law of the Sea (Oxford University Press, 2015).

Library of Congress, *International Tribunal for the Law of the Sea Confirms Sovereignty of Mauritius over Chagos Archipelago* (23 February 2021) www.loc.gov/item/global-legal-monitor/2021-02-23/international-international-tribunal-for-the-law-of-the-sea-confirms-sovereignty-of-mauritius-over-chagos-archipelago/ (accessed 30 March 2022).

Lingliang Zeng, *Conceptual Analysis of China's Belt and Road Initiative: A Road Towards a Regional Community of Common Destiny* (15 Chinese Journal of International Law 517, 2016).

Lofti Maktouf, *Resolving International Tax Disputes Through Arbitration* (4 Arbitration International 32, 1988).

Louis B. Sohn, *Settlement of Disputes Arising Out of the Law of the Sea Convention* (12 San Diego Law Review 495, 1975).

Louis B. Sohn, *The Importance of the Peaceful Settlement of Disputes Provisions of the United Nations Convention on the Law of the Sea* in M.H. Nordquist and J.N. Moore (eds) Entry into Force of the Law of the Sea Convention (Martinus Nijhoff Publishers, 1995).

Louis B. Sohn, *UN Conference on the Law of the Sea* (12(1) International Law, 1978).

Louis Kriesberg, *The Development of the Conflict Resolution Field* in William Zartman and Lewis Rasmussen (eds) Peacemaking in International Conflict (United States Institute of Peace Press, 1997).

Mahdi El-Baghdadi, *The Binding Nature of the Disputes Settlement Procedure in the Third U.N. Convention on the Law of the Sea: The International Seabed Authority* (6(2) Journal of Mineral Law & Policy 173, 1991).

Mancur Olson, *The Logic of Collective Action: Public Goods and the Theory of Groups* (Harvard University Press, 1965).

Margaret M. Polski and Elinor Ostrom, *An Institutional Framework for Policy Analysis and Design* in Daniel H. Cole and Michael D. McGinnis (eds), Elinor Ostrom and the Bloomington School of Political Economy: Volume 3, A Framework for Policy Analysis (Rowman and Littlefield Publishers Inc, 2010).

Marianne Schneider-Petsinger, *Reforming the World Trade Organisation* (Chatham House, 11 September 2020) www.chathamhouse.org/2020/09/reforming-world-trade-organization (accessed 20 February 2021).

Martin Hearson and Wilson Prichard, *China's Challenge to International Tax Rules and the Implications for Global Economic Governance* (94(6) International Affairs 1287, 2018).

Martin Hearson, *The Challenges for Developing Countries in International Tax Justice* (54(10) The Journal of Development Studies, 2017).

Martin Lishexian Lee, *The Interrelation Between the Law of the Sea Convention and Customary International Law* (7 San Diego International Law Journal 405, 2006).

Martti Koskenniemi and Paivi Leino, *Fragmentation in International Law? Postmodern Anxieties* (15 Leiden Journal of International Law 553, 2002).

Masahiko Aoki, *Towards a Comparative Institutional Analysis: Motivations and Some Tentative Theorization* (47(1) Japanese Economic Review, 1996).

Maya Ganguly, *Tribunal and Taxation: An Investigation of Arbitration in Recent US Tax Conventions* (29 Wisconsin International Law Journal 735, 2012).

Michael Devereux and John Vella, *Are We Heading Towards a Corporate Tax System Fit for the 21st Century?* (35 Fiscal Studies 449, 2014).

Michael Lang et al., *The Impact of Bilateral Investment Treaties on Taxation* (IBFD, 2017).

Michael Lang, *BEPS Action 6: Introducing an Anti-abuse Rule in Tax Treaties* (74 Tax Notes International 655, 2014).

Michael Lang, *Introduction to the Law of Double Taxation Conventions* (IBFD, 2013).

Michael Lennard, *Act of Creation: The OECD/G20 Test of 'Value Creation' as a Basis for Taxing Rights and Its Relevance to Developing Countries* (25(3) Transnational Corporations 55, 2018).

Michael Sutherland and Susan Nichols, *Maritime Boundary Delimitation for Ocean Governance* in FIG Technical Program Proceedings, XXII FIG International Congress (Washington DC, 2002).

Michelle Markham, *Litigation, Arbitration and Mediation in International Tax Disputes: An Assessment of Whether This Results in Competitive or Collaborative Relationships* (11(2) Contemporary Asia Arbitration Journal 283, 2018).

Michelle Markham, *Seeking New Directions in Dispute Resolution Mechanisms: Do We Need a Revised Mutual Agreement Procedure?* (70 (1-2) Bulletin for International Taxation 82, 2016).

Mindy Herzfeld, *The Case Against BEPS: Lessons for Tax Coordination* (21 Florida Tax Review 52, 2017).

Mitchell B. Carroll, *International Tax Law: Benefits for American Enterprises and Enterprises Abroad* (2(4) International Lawyer 692, 1968).

Mosquera Valderrama, *BEPS Principal Purpose Test and Customary International Law* (33(3) Leiden Journal of International Law 745, 2020).

Natalie Klein, *Dispute Settlement in the UN Convention on the Law of the Sea* (Cambridge University Press, 2009).

Neil K. Komesar, *Imperfect Alternatives: Choosing Institutions in Law Economics, and Public Policy* (University of Chicago Press, 1994).

Nico Krisch, *International Law in Times of Hegemony: Unequal Power and the Shaping of the International Legal Order* (16(3) European Journal of International Law, 2005).

Nico Krisch, *The Decay of Consent: International Law in an Age of Global Public Goods* (108 American Journal of International Law 1, 2014).

Nirmala Sitharaman, Speech at the G-20 Finance Ministers' Meeting on International Tax in Cairns, Australia (21 September 2014) www.indiainfoline.com/article/news-top-story/nirmala-sitharaman-speech-at-g-20-finance-ministers%E2%80%99-meeting-114092300001_1.html (accessed 10 March 2021).

Oliver E. Williamson, *The Economic Institutions of Capitalism: Firms, Markets, Relational Contracting* (The Free Press, 1985).

Olivier Marquais, *Lalive Lecture by Professor Sean Murphy: A Rising Tide: Dispute Settlement under the Law of the Sea* (Geneva, 15 July 2015) www.international-arbitration-attorney.com/law-of-the-sea-dispute-settlement-mechanism (accessed 11 July 2021).

Øystein Jensen and Nigel Bankes, *Compulsory and Binding Dispute Resolution under the United Nations Convention on the Law of the Sea: Introduction* (48(3-4) Ocean Development & International Law 209, 2017).

Peggy B. Musgrave, *Taxation of Foreign Investment Income: An Economic Analysis* (John Hopkins Press, 1963).

Pierre Marie Dupuy, *The Danger of Fragmentation or Unification of the International Legal System and the International Court of Justice* (31 N.Y.U. Journal of International Law and Policy 791, 1999).

Qiang Cai, *A Package Deal Is Not a Bad Deal: Reassessing the Method of Package Negotiation Under the Mutual Agreement Procedure* (46(10) Intertax 746, 2018).

Ramazan Bicer, *The Effectiveness of Mutual Agreement Procedures as a Means for Settling International Transfer Pricing Disputes* (21 International Transfer Pricing Journal 76, 2014).

Reuven Avi-Yonah and Haiyan Xu, *China and BEPS* (7(1) Laws 4, 2018).

Reuven Avi-Yonah, *Does Customary International Tax Law Exist?* (University of Michigan Law & Economic Research Paper No. 19-005, 2019).

Reuven Avi-Yonah, *International Tax as International Law* (57 Tax Law Review, 2004).

Reuven Avi-Yonah, *International Tax as International Law: An Analysis of the International Tax Regime* (Cambridge Tax Law Series, 2007).

Richard A. Musgrave and Peggy B. Musgrave, *Inter-Nation Equity* in Richard Bird and John G. Heads (eds) Modern Fiscal Issues: Essays in Honor of Carl S Shoup (University of Toronto Press, 1972).

Richard J Payne and Jamal R Nassar, *The New International Economic Order at Sea* (17(1) The Journal of Developing Areas 31, 1982).

Richard M. Bird, *Reforming International Taxation: Is the Process the Real Product?* (International Center for Public Policy, Working Paper Series paper 1503, 2016).

Rishi Gulati, *Judicial Independence at International Courts and Tribunals: Lessons Drawn from the Experiences of the International Court of Justice and the Appellate Body of the World Trade Organisation* (KFG Working Paper No. 41, 2020). https://papers.ssrn.com/sol3/papers.cfm?abstract_id=3519891 (accessed 23 March 2021).

Robert A. Green, *Antilegalistic Approaches to Resolving Disputes Between Governments: A Comparison of the International Tax and Trade Regimes* (23 Yale Journal of International Law 79, 1998).

Robert Howse, *The World Trade Organization 20 Years On: Global Governance by Judiciary* (27(1) European Journal of International Law 9, 2016).

Robert O. Keohane, *After Hegemony: Cooperation and Discord in the World Political Economy* (Princeton University Press, 1984).

Robert T. Cole, *Competent Authority Procedure: International Tax Counsel Gives His Views* (35(8) The Journal of Taxation 10, 1971).

Roberto Lavalle, *Conciliation under the United Nations Convention on the Law of the Sea: A Critical Overview* (2(1) Austrian Review of International and European Law 25, 1997).

Robin R. Churchill and Alan V. Lowe, *The Law of the Sea* (Manchester University Press, 1999).

Robin R. Churchill, *Compulsory Dispute Settlement under the United Nations Convention on the Law of the Sea: How Has It Operated? Pt. 1* (9 June 2016) www.jus.uio.no/pluricourts/english/blog/guests/2016-06-09-churchill-unclos-pt-1.html (accessed 20 Jul. 2021).

Rosalyn Higgins, *The International Court and Southwest Africa* (42(4) International Affairs 573, 1966).

Rudolf Dolzer and Christoph Schreuer, *Principles of International Investment Law* (Oxford University Press, 2012).

Ruth Lapidoth, *Equity in International Law* (81 American Society of International Law 138, 1987).

Samuel Cogolati, Linda Hamid and Nils Vanstappen, *Global Public Goods and Democracy in International Legal Scholarship* (5(1) Cambridge Journal of International and Comparative Law 4, 2016).

Sean D. Murphy, *International Judicial Bodies for Resolving Disputes Between States* in Cesare P.R. Romano, Karen J. Alter, and Yuval Shany (eds) The Oxford Handbook of International Adjudication (Oxford University Press, 2013).

Shabtai Rosenne and Louis B. Sohn (eds) *United Nations Convention on the Law of the Sea 1982: A Commentary* (vol. 5, Martinus Nijhoff Publishers, 1989).

Shabtai Rosenne, *The Law and Practice of the International Court* (vol. 2, A W Sijthoff, 1965).

Shriram Govind and Shreya Rao, *Designing* an Inclusive and Equitable Framework for Tax Treaty Dispute Resolution: An Indian Perspective (46(4) Intertax 313, 2018).

Shruti Srivastava, *At G20 Talks, India to Come out Strongly Against 'Mandatory' Arbitration for Tax* (The Indian Express, 13 November 2014) http://indianexpress.com/article/business/economy/at-g20-talks-india-to-come-out-strongly-against-mandatory-arbitration-for-tax/ (accessed 10 March 2021).

Sienho Yee, *Intervention in an Arbitral Proceeding under Annex VII to the UNCLOS* (14 Chinese Journal of International Law 79, 2015).

Sol Picciotto, *Constructing Compliance: Game Playing, Tax Law, and the Regulatory State* (29(1) Law & Policy 11, 2007).

Sol Picciotto, *Indeterminacy, Complexity, Technocracy and the Reform of International Corporate Taxation* (24 Social & Legal Studies 165, 2015).

Sol Picciotto, *International Law: The Legitimation of Power in World Affairs* in P. Ireland and Per Laleng (eds) The Critical Lawyer's Handbook (Pluto Press, 1997).

Sophia Kopela, *Historic Titles and Historic Rights in the Law of the Sea in the Light of the South China Sea Arbitration* (Lancaster University Law School) https://eprints.lancs.ac.uk/id/eprint/84981/1/Historic_titles_and_historic_rights_ODIL.pdf (accessed 6 July 2022).

Spyridon E. Malamis and Qiang Cai, *International Tax Dispute Resolution in Light of Pillar One: New Challenges and Opportunities* (75(2) Bulletin for International Taxation 94, 2021).

Spyridon E. Malamis, *The future of OECD Tax Arbitration: The Relevance of Investment Treaty and WTO Dispute Settlement Practice in Promoting a Gradual Evolution of the International Tax Dispute Resolution System* (48(11) Intertax 966, 2020).

Stefan Talmon, *The Chagos Marine Protected Area Arbitration: A Case Study of the Creeping Expansion of the Jurisdiction of UNCLOS Part XV Courts and Tribunals* (65 International & Comparative Law Quarterly 927, 2016).

Stefano Castagna, *ICSID Arbitration: BITs, Buts and Taxation – An Introductory Guide* (70(7) Bulletin for International Taxation, 2016).

Stephen B. Golberg et al., *Dispute Resolution: Negotiation, Mediation and Other Processes* (Wolters Kluwer Law & Business/Aspen Publishers, 2003).

Steve Charnovitz, *Judicial Independence in the World Trade Organization* in Steve Charnovitz (ed.) The Path of World Trade Law in the 21st Century (World Scientific Publishing, 2015).

Stjepan Gadžo, *The Principle of 'Nexus' or 'Genuine Link' as a Keystone of International Income Tax Law: A Reappraisal* (46(3) Intertax, 2008).

Ted L. McDorman and Aldo Chircop, *The Resolution of Maritime Disputes* in Edgar Gold (ed.) Maritime Affairs: A World Handbook (Longman Group UK, 1991).

Ted L. McDorman, *Ocean Dispute Settlement in the Baltic Sea* in Renate Platzöder and Philomene Verlaan (eds) The Baltic Sea: New Developments in National Policies and International Co-operation (Martinus Nijhoff Publishers, 1996).

Tommy Koh and Shanmugam Jayakumar, *The Negotiating Process of The Third United Nations Conference on The Law of the Sea* in Myron H. Nordquist (ed.) United Nations Convention on the Law of the Sea 1982: A Commentary (vol. 1, Martinus Nijhoff Publishers, 1985).

Tommy Koh, *A Constitution for the Oceans*, Remarks of the President of the Third United Nations Conference on the Law of the Sea at the Conference at Montego Bay (10 December 1982) www.un.org/depts/los/convention_agreements/texts/koh_english.pdf (accessed 2 February 2022).

Tommy Koh, *Negotiating the UN Convention on the Law of the Sea: A Practitioner's Reflection* in Simon Chesterman, David M. Malone and Santiago Villalpando (eds) The Oxford Handbook of United Nations Treaties (Oxford University Press, 2019).

USTR, Termination of Action in the Digital Services Tax Investigation of India and Further Monitoring (Federal Register, 2 December 2021) www.federalregister.gov/documents/2021/12/02/2021-26198/termination-of-action-in-the-digital-services-tax-investigation-of-india-and-further-monitoring (accessed 5 March 2022).

Willem Riphagen, *Dispute Settlement in the 1982 United Nations Convention on the Law of the Sea*, in Christos L. Rozakis and Constantine A. Stephanou (eds) The New Law of the Sea (North-Holland Publishing Company, 1983).

WTO, *A Handbook on the WTO Dispute Settlement System* (2nd ed., Cambridge University Press, 2017).

Xinmin Ma, *China and the UNCLOS: Practices and Policies* (5 The Chinese Journal of Global Governance 1, 2019).

Yann-Huei Song and Stein Tønnesson, *The Impact of the Law of the Sea Convention on Conflict and Conflict Management in the South China Sea* (44 Ocean Development and International Law 235, 2013).

Yogesh K. Tyagi, *The System of Settlement of Disputes under the Law of the Sea Convention: An Overview* (25(2) Indian Journal of International Law 191, 1985).

B. Zuleta, *Introduction* in United Nations, The Law of the Sea. United Nations Convention on the Law of the Sea with Index and Final Act of the Third United Nations Conference on the Law of the Sea (St. Martin's Press, Published in cooperation with the United Nations, 1983).

Zvi Daniel Altman, *Dispute Resolution under Tax Treaties* (Doctoral Series vol. 11, 1-5, IBFD Publications, 2005).

Reports

European Commission, Resolution of Double Taxation Disputes in the European Union (Taxation and Customs Union) (19 October 2016) https://ec.europa.eu/taxation_customs/business/company-tax/resolution-double-taxation-disputes_en_en (accessed 20 November 2021).

ICJ, *The International Court of Justice: Handbook*, www.icj-cij.org/public/files/publications/handbook-of-the-court-en.pdf (accessed 29 March 2022).

ILC, Report of the International Law Commission on the Work of its 70th Session from 30 April-1 June and 2 July-10 August 2018, UN Doc. A/73/10.

Independent World Commission on the Oceans, *The Ocean Our Future: The Report of the Independent World Commission on the Oceans* (Cambridge University Press, 1998).

IMF and OECD, 'Tax Certainty: IMF/OECD Report for the G20 Finance Ministers' (March 2017) www.oecd.org/tax/tax-policy/tax-certainty-report-oecd-imf-report-g20-finance-ministers-march-2017.pdf (accessed 21 March 2021).

ITLOS, *A Guide to Proceedings Before the International Tribunal for the Law of the Sea* (2016) www.itlos.org/fileadmin/itlos/documents/guide/1605-22024_Itlos_Guide_En.pdf (accessed 20 March 2022).

League of Nations, Double Taxation and Tax Evasion Document F.212 (Geneva, February 1925).

League of Nations, Report Presented by the Committee of Technical Experts on Double Taxation and Tax Evasion, Doc C.216.M.85.1927 II (Geneva, April 1927).

League of Nations, Report presented by the General Meeting of Government Experts on Double Taxation and Tax Evasion, Doc C.562.M.178.1928.II (Geneva, October 1928).

League of Nations, Fiscal Committee, London and Mexico Model Tax Conventions: Commentaries and Text, Doc C 88.M.88. 1946.II.A (Geneva, November 1946).

OECD, Committee on Fiscal Affairs Organisation Chart www.oecd.org/tax/beps/committee-on-fiscal-affairs-and-subsidiary-bodies-organigramme.pdf (accessed 2 April 2021).

OECD, Forum on Tax Administration www.oecd.org/tax/forum-on-tax-administration/about/ (accessed 1 November 2020).

OECD, MAP Statistics Reporting Framework www.oecd.org/tax/dispute/mutual-agreement-procedure-statistics-reporting-framework.pdf (accessed 20 July 2020).

OECD, MLI Matching Database www.oecd.org/tax/treaties/mli-matching-database.htm (accessed on 8 March 2021).

OECD, *Transfer Pricing and Multinational Enterprises: Three Taxation Issues* (OECD Publishing, 1984).

OECD, Improving the Process for Resolving International Tax Disputes (2004) www.oecd.org/ctp/treaties/33629447.pdf (accessed 10 March 2021).

OECD, *Proposals for Improving Mechanisms for the Resolution of Tax Treaty Disputes: Public Discussion Draft 2006* (OECD Publishing, 2006).

OECD, *Manual on Effective Mutual Agreement Procedures* (OECD Publishing, 2007).

OECD, *Addressing the Tax Challenges of the Digital Economy, Action 1 – 2015 Final Report* (OECD Publishing, 2015).

OECD, *Explanatory Statement, OECD/G20 Base Erosion and Profit Shifting Project* (OECD Publishing, 2015).

OECD, G20 finance ministers endorse reforms to the international tax system for curbing avoidance by multinational enterprises' (9 October 2015) www.oecd.org/tax/beps/g20-finance-ministers-endorse-reforms-to-the-international-tax-system-for-curbing-avoidance-by-multinational-enterprises.htm (accessed 9 March 2021).

OECD, *Making Dispute Resolution Mechanisms More Effective, Action 14-2015 Final Report* (OECD Publishing, 2015).

OECD, MAP Program Statistics for the 2015 reporting period, Country: Luxembourg (2015) www.oecd.org/ctp/dispute/MAP%20PROGRAM%20STATISTICS%20FOR%202015%20LUX.pdf (accessed 10 November 2021).

OECD, *Preventing the Granting of Treaty Benefits in Inappropriate Circumstances, Action 6 – 2015 Final Report* (OECD Publishing, 2015).

OECD, *BEPS Action 14 on More Effective Dispute Resolution Mechanisms: Peer Review Documents* (OECD Publishing, 2016).

OECD, Multilateral Convention to Implement Tax Treaty Related Measures to Prevent Base Erosion and Profit Shifting (2016) www.oecd.org/tax/beps/multilateral-convention-to-implement-tax-treaty-related-measures-to-prevent-BEPS.pdf (accessed 20 March 2022).

OECD, *Resumption of Application of Substantial Activities for No or Nominal Tax Jurisdictions – BEPS Action 5* (OECD Publishing, 2018).

OECD, MAP Statistics (2019) www.oecd.org/tax/dispute/mutual-agreement-procedure-statistics-2019.htm (accessed 3 January 2022).

OECD, MAP Statistics (2020) www.oecd.org/tax/dispute/mutual-agreement-procedure-statistics-2020-per-jurisdiction-inventory.htm (accessed 26 January 2022).

OECD, OECD/G20 BEPS IF (5th meeting of the Inclusive Framework in Lima, Peru on 27-28 June 2020) www.oecd.org/tax/beps/flyer-inclusive-framework-on-beps.pdf (accessed 2 October 2020).

OECD, *Tax Challenges Arising from Digitalisation: Report on Pillar One Blueprint – Inclusive Framework on BEPS* (OECD Publishing, 2020).

OECD, *Statement on a Two-Pillar Solution to Address the Tax Challenges Arising from the Digitalisation of the Economy* (OECD/G20 Base Erosion and Profit Shifting Project, 8 October 2021) www.oecd.org/tax/beps/statement-on-a-two-pillar-solution-to-address-the-tax-challenges-arising-from-the-digitalisation-of-the-economy-july-2021.pdf (accessed 4 March 2022).

OECD, *Transfer Pricing Guidelines for Multinational Enterprises and Tax Administrations 2022* (OECD Publishing, 2022).

UN, Division for Ocean Affairs and the Law of the Sea (DOALOS) www.un.org/Depts/los/index.htm (accessed 31 July 2021).

UN, *Handbook on the Delimitation of Maritime Boundaries* (Division for Ocean Affairs and the Law of the Sea Office for Legal Affairs, United Nations 2000).

UN, LA41TR/221/Full Powers Guidelines/2010 https://treaties.un.org/doc/source/publications/NV/2010/Full_Powers-2010.pdf (accessed 10 October 2021).

UN, Department of Economic and Social Affairs, *Papers on Selected Topics in Negotiation of Tax Treaties for Developing Countries* (United Nations, 2014).

UN, *Secretariat Paper on Alternative Dispute Resolution in Taxation*, E/C.18/2015/CRP.8 (2015).

UN, *Chapter 5 on MAP Arbitration of the Handbook on Avoidance and Resolution of Tax Disputes*, E/C18/2020/CRP.28 (2020).

UN, Third United Nations Conference on the Law of the Sea (1973-1982) (UNCLOS III) https://legal.un.org/diplomaticconferences/1973_los/ (accessed 10 January 2022).

UN, *United Nations Model Rules for the Conciliation of Dispute Between States Res 50/50*, UN Doc. A/RES/50/50 (29 January 1996) https://documents-dds-ny.un.org/doc/UNDOC/GEN/N96/762/31/PDF/N9676231.pdf?OpenElement (accessed 21 July 2022).

UNCLOS III, UN Doc. A/CONF.62/SR.1 (New York, 10 December 1973).

UNCLOS III, UN Doc A/CONF.62/SR.2 (New York, 7 December 1973).

UNCLOS III, UN Doc. A/CONF.62/SR.3 (New York, 10 December 1973).

UNCLOS III, *Draft Rules of Procedure: Note by the Secretary-General*, UN Doc. A/CONF.62/L.1 (3 June 1974).

UNCLOS III, UN Doc. A/CONF.62/L.7 (Caracas, 20 June to 29 August 1974).

UNCLOS III, UN Doc. A/CONF.62/SR.51 (Caracas, 20 June to 29 August 1974).

UNCLOS III, UN Doc. A/CONF.62/WP.8/Part I (Geneva, 17 March to 9 May 1975).

UNCLOS III, UN Doc. A/CONF.62/WP.8/Part II (Geneva, 17 March to 9 May 1975).

UNCLOS III, UN Doc. A/CONF.62/WP.8/Part III (Geneva, 17 March to 9 May 1975).

UNCLOS III, UN Doc. A/CONF.62/WP.8/Rev.1/Part I (New York, 15 March to 7 May 1976).

UNCLOS III, UN Doc. A/CONF.62/WP.8/Rev.1/Part II (New York, 15 March to 7 May 1976).

UNCLOS III, UN Doc. A/CONF.62/WP.8/Rev.1/Part III (New York, 15 March to 7 May 1976).

UNCLOS III, UN Doc. A/CONF.62/WP.9/Add.1 (New York, 31 March 1976).

UNCLOS III, UN Doc. A/CONF.62/WP.9, UN Doc. A/CONF.62/WP.9/Rev.1 (New York, 15 March to 7 May 1976).

UNCLOS III, UN Doc. A/CONF.62/WP.9/L.20 (New York, 23 May to 15 July 1977).

UNCLOS III, UN Doc. A/CONF.62/WP.10/Add.1 (New York, 22 July 1977).

UNCLOS III, UN Doc. A/CONF.62/SR.78 (New York, 28 June 1977).

UNCLOS III, UN Doc. A/CONF.62/62 (Geneva, 13 April 1978).

UNCLOS III, UN Doc. A/CONF.62/WP.9/L.52 (New York, 29 March and 1 April 1980).

UNCTAD, Investment Policy Hub https://investmentpolicy.unctad.org/international-investment-agreements (accessed 4 March 2022).

Table of Cases

Arbitration between Barbados and the Republic of Trinidad and Tobago, relating to the delimitation of the exclusive economic zone and the continental shelf between them (Decision of 11 Apr. 2006) UN Reports of International Arbitral Awards, Vol XXVII paras 138, 140, 136

Case Concerning the Continental Shelf (*Tunisia/Libyan Arab Jamahiriya*) [1982] ICJ Rep para 100, 136

Conservation and Sustainable Exploitation of Swordfish Stocks in the South-Eastern Pacific Ocean (*Chile/European Union*) ITLOS Case No. 7 http://www.itlos.org/index.php?id = 99 (accessed 25 July 2021), 116

Kevin McCabe v. The Commissioners for HM Revenue and Customs [2020] UKUT 0266 (TCC), 12

Maritime Delimitation and Territorial Questions between Qatar and Bahrain (Qatar v. Bahrain) (Merits) [2001] ICJ Rep 40, 111, 133

Maritime Delimitation in the Area between Greenland and Jan Mayen (Denmark v. Norway) [1993] ICJ Rep 38, 62, 133

Maritime Delimitation in the Black Sea (Romania v. Ukraine) [2009] ICJ Rep 101, 104

Nestle Company Inc v. Commissioner (1963) 22 TCM 46, 62, 23

North Sea Continental Shelf (Germany v. Netherlands) (Judgment of 20 January 1969) [1969] ICJ Rep 3, 123

Request for an Advisory Opinion submitted by the Sub-Regional Fisheries Commission (SRFC), ITLOS Case No. 21 www.itlos.org/en/main/cases/list-of-cases/case-no-21/ (accessed 20 March 2022), 127

Second Stage of the Proceedings between Eritrea and Yemen (Maritime Delimitation) (Award of 17 December 1999) UN Reports of International Arbitration Awards, Vol. XXII paragraph 109, 136

Territorial and Maritime Dispute between Nicaragua and Honduras in the Caribbean Sea (Nicaragua v. Honduras) [2007] ICJ Rep 443, 133

Territorial Sovereignty and Scope of the Dispute (Eritrea/Yemen) (Award of 9 Oct. 1998) UN Reports of International Arbitration Awards, Vol. XXII paragraph 126, 137

Table of Treaties and Conventions

Index

SERIES ON INTERNATIONAL TAXATION

1. Alberto Xavier, *The Taxation of Foreign Investment in Brazil,* 1980 (ISBN 90-200-0582-0).
2. Hugh J. Ault & Albert J. Rädler, *The German Corporation Tax Law with 1980 Amendments,* 1981 (ISBN 90-200-0642-8).
3. Paul R. McDaniel & Hugh J. Ault, *Introduction to United States International Taxation,* 1981 (ISBN 90-6544-004-6).
4. Albert J. Rädler, *German Transfer Pricing/Prix de Transfer en Allemagne,* 1984 (ISBN 90-6544-143-3).
5. Paul R. McDaniel & Stanley S. Surrey, *International Aspects of Tax Expenditures: A Comparative Study,* 1985 (ISBN 90-654-4163-8).
6. Kees van Raad, *Nondiscrimination in International Tax Law,* 1986 (ISBN 90-6544-266-9).
7. Sijbren Cnossen (ed.), *Tax Coordination in the European Community,* 1987 (ISBN 90-6544-272-3).
8. Ben Terra, *Sales Taxation. The Case of Value Added Tax in the European Community,* 1989 (ISBN 90-6544-381-9).
9. Rutsel S.J. Martha, *The Jurisdiction to Tax in International Law: Theory and Practice of Legislative Fiscal Jurisdiction,* 1989 (ISBN 90-654-4416-5).
10. Paul R. McDaniel & Hugh J. Ault, *Introduction to United States International Taxation* (3rd revised edition), 1989 (ISBN 90-6544-423-8).
11. Manuel Pires, *International Juridicial Double Taxation of Income,* 1989 (ISBN 90-6544-426-2).
12. A.H.M. Daniels, *Issues in International Partnership Taxation,* 1991 (ISBN 90-654-4577-3).
13. Arvid A. Skaar, *Permanent Establishment: Erosion of a Tax Treaty Principle,* 1992 (ISBN 90-6544-594-3).
14. Cyrille David & Geerten M.M. Michielse (eds), *Tax Treatment of Financial Instruments,* 1996 (ISBN 90-654-4666-4).
15. Herbert H. Alpert & Kees van Raad (eds), *Essays on International Taxation,* 1993 (ISBN 90-654-4781-4).
16. Wolfgang Gassner, Michael Lang & Eduard Lechner (eds), *Tax Treaties and EC Law,* 1997 (ISBN 90-411-0680-4).
17. Glória Teixeira, *Taxing Corporate Profits in the EU,* 1997 (ISBN 90-411-0703-7).
18. Michael Lang et al. (eds), *Multilateral Tax Treaties,* 1998 (ISBN 90-411-0704-5).
19. Stef van Weeghel, *The Improper Use of Tax Treaties,* 1998 (ISBN 90-411-0737-1).

20. Klaus Vogel (ed.), *Interpretation of Tax Law and Treaties and Transfer Pricing in Japan and Germany*, 1998 (ISBN 90-411-9655-2).
21. Bertil Wiman (ed.), *International Studies in Taxation: Law and Economics; Liber Amicorum Leif Mutén*, 1999 (ISBN 90-411-9692-7).
22. Alfonso J. Martín Jiménez, *Towards Corporate Tax Harmonization in the European Community*, 1999 (ISBN 90-411-9690-0).
23. Ramon J. Jeffery, *The Impact of State Sovereignty on Global Trade and International Taxation*, 1999 (ISBN 90-411-9703-6).
24. A.J. Easson, *Taxation of Foreign Direct Investment*, 1999 (ISBN 90-411-9741-9).
25. Marjaana Helminen, *The Dividend Concept in International Tax Law: Dividend Payments Between Corporate Entities*, 1999 (ISBN 90-411-9765-6).
26. Paul Kirchhof, Moris Lehner, Kees van Raad, Arndt Raupach & Michael-Rodi (eds), *International and Comparative Taxation: Essays in Honour of Klaus Vogel*, 2002 (ISBN 90-411-9841-5).
27. Krister Andersson, Peter Melz & Christer Silfverberg (eds), *Liber Amicorum Sven-Olof Lodin*, 2001 (ISBN 90-411-9850-4).
28. Juan Martín Jovanovich, *Customs Valuation and Transfer Pricing: Is It Possible to Harmonize Customs and Tax Rules?*, Second Edition, 2018 (ISBN 978-90-411-6134-5).
29. Stefano Simontacchi, *Taxation of Capital Gains under the OECD Model Convention: With Special Regard to Immovable Property*, 2007 (ISBN 978-90-411-2549-1).
30. Michael Lang, Josef Schuch, & Claus Staringer (eds), *Tax Treaty Law and EC Law*, 2007 (ISBN 978-90-411-2629-0).
31. Duncan Bentley, *Taxpayers' Rights: Theory Origin and Implementation*, 2007 (ISBN 978-90-411-2650-4).
32. Sergio André Rocha, *Interpretation of Double Taxation Conventions: General Theory and Brazilian Perspective*, 2008 (ISBN 978-90-411-2822-5).
33. Robert F. van Brederode, *Systems of General Sales Taxation: Theory, Policy and Practice*, 2009 (ISBN 978-90-411-2832-4).
34. John G. Head & Richard Krever (eds), *Tax Reform in the 21st Century: A Volume in Memory of Richard Musgrave*, 2009 (ISBN 978-90-411-2829-4).
35. Jens Wittendorff, *Transfer Pricing and the Arm's Length Principle in International Tax Law*, 2010 (ISBN 978-90-411-3270-3).
36. Marjaana Helminen, *The International Tax Law Concept of Dividend*, Second Edition, 2017 (ISBN 978-90-411-8394-1).
37. Robert F. van Brederode (ed.), *Immovable Property under VAT: A Comparative Global Analysis*, 2011 (ISBN 978-90-411-3126-3).
38. Dennis Weber & Stef van Weeghel, *The 2010 OECD Updates: Model Tax Convention & Transfer Pricing Guidelines - A Critical Review*, 2011 (ISBN 978-90-411-3812-5).
39. Yariv Brauner & Martin James McMahon, Jr. (eds), *The Proper Tax Base: Structural Fairness from an International and Comparative Perspective— Essays in Honour of Paul McDaniel*, 2012 (ISBN 978-90-411-3286-4).
40. Robert F. van Brederode (ed.), *Science, Technology and Taxation*, 2012 (ISBN 978-90-411-3125-6).

41. Oskar Henkow, *The VAT/GST Treatment of Public Bodies*, 2013 (ISBN 978-90-411-4663-2).
42. Jean Schaffner, *How Fixed Is a Permanent Establishment?*, 2013 (ISBN 978-90-411-4662-5).
43. Miguel Correia, *Taxation of Corporate Groups*, 2013 (ISBN 978-90-411-4841-4).
44. Veronika Daurer, *Tax Treaties and Developing Countries*, 2014 (ISBN 978-90-411-4982-4).
45. Claire Micheau, *State Aid, Subsidy and Tax Incentives under EU and WTO Law*, 2014 (ISBN 978-90-411-4555-0).
46. Robert F. van Brederode & Richard Krever (eds), *Legal Interpretation of Tax Law*, 2014 (ISBN 978-90-411-4945-9).
47. Radhakishan Rawal, *Taxation of Cross-border Services*, 2014 (ISBN 978-90-411-4947-3).
48. João Dácio Rolim, *Proportionality and Fair Taxation*, 2014 (ISBN 978-90-411-5838-3).
49. Paulo Rosenblatt, *General Anti-avoidance Rules for Major Developing Countries*, 2015 (ISBN 978-90-411-5839-0).
50. Gaspar Lopes Dias V.S., *Tax Arbitrage through Cross-Border Financial Engineering*, 2015 (ISBN 978-90-411-5875-8).
51. Geerten M.M. Michielse & Victor Thuronyi (eds), *Tax Design Issues Worldwide*, 2015 (ISBN 978-90-411-5610-5).
52. Oktavia Weidmann, *Taxation of Derivatives*, 2015 (ISBN 978-90-411-5977-9).
53. Chris Evans, Richard Krever & Peter Mellor (eds), *Tax Simplification*, 2015 (ISBN 978-90-411-5976-2).
54. Reuven Avi-Yonah & Joel Slemrod (eds), *Taxation and Migration*, 2015 (ISBN 978-90-411-6136-9).
55. Alexander Bosman, *Other Income under Tax Treaties: An Analysis of Article 21 of the OECD Model Convention*, 2015 (ISBN 978-90-411-6610-4).
56. John Abrahamson, *International Taxation of Manufacturing and Distribution*, 2016 (ISBN 978-90-411-6664-7).
57. Frederik Boulogne, *Shortcomings in the EU Merger Directive*, 2016 (ISBN 978-90-411-6713-2).
58. Angelika Meindl-Ringler, *Beneficial Ownership in International Tax Law*, 2016 (ISBN 978-90-411-6833-7).
59. Andreas Waltrich, *Cross-Border Taxation of Permanent Establishments: An International Comparison*, 2016 (ISBN 978-90-411-6832-0).
60. Sergio André Rocha & Allison Christians (eds), *Tax Sovereignty in the BEPS Era*, 2017 (ISBN 978-90-411-6707-1).
61. Peter Antony Wilson, *BRICS and International Tax Law*, 2018 (ISBN 978-90-411-9435-0).
62. Louise Otis, Brigitte Alepin & Blanca Moreno-Dodson (eds), *Winning the Tax Wars: Tax Competition and Cooperation*, 2018 (ISBN 978-90-411-9460-2).
63. Marta Castelon, *International Taxation of Income from Services under Double Taxation Conventions: Development, Practice and Policy*, 2018 (ISBN 978-90-411-9594-4).

64. D.M. Broekhuijsen, *A Multilateral Tax Treaty: Designing an Instrument to Modernise International Tax Law*, 2018 (ISBN 978-90-411-9872-3).
65. John Abrahamson, *International Taxation of Energy Production and Distribution*, 2018 (ISBN 978-90-411-9101-4).
66. Leopoldo Parada, *Double Non-taxation and the Use of Hybrid Entities: An Alternative Approach in the New Era of BEPS*, 2018 (ISBN 978-90-411-9991-1).
67. Richard Snoeij, *International Tax Aspects of Sovereign Wealth Investors: A Source State Perspective*, 2018 (ISBN 978-90-411-9431-2).
68. Aleksandra Bal, *Taxation, Virtual Currency and Blockchain*, 2019 (ISBN 978-94-035-0103-1).
69. Werner Haslehner, Georg Kofler, Katerina Pantazatou & Alexander Rust (eds), *Tax and the Digital Economy: Challenges and Proposals for Reform*, 2019 (ISBN 978-94-035-0361-5).
70. Eva Escribano, *Jurisdiction to Tax Corporate Income Pursuant to the Presumptive Benefit Principle: A Critical Analysis of Structural Paradigms Underlying Corporate Income Taxation and Proposals for Reform*, 2019 (ISBN 978-94-035-0640-1).
71. Jérôme Monsenego & Jan Bjuvberg (eds), *International Taxation in a Changing Landscape: Liber Amicorum in Honour of Bertil Wiman*, 2019 (ISBN 978-90-411-9234-9).
72. Kasper Dziurdź, *Non-discrimination in Tax Treaty Law and World Trade Law: The Impact of Formal, Substantive and Subjective Approaches*, 2019 (ISBN 978-94-035-0904-4).
73. Félix Daniel Martínez Laguna, *Hybrid Financial Instruments, Double Nontaxation and Linking Rules*, 2019 (ISBN 978-94-035-1074-3).
74. Jan Gooijer, *Tax Treaty Residence of Entities*, 2019 (ISBN 978-94-035-1301-0).
75. John Abrahamson, *International Taxation of Banking*, 2020 (ISBN 978-94-035-1094-1).
76. Richard Krever & François Vaillancourt (eds), *The Allocation of Multinational Business Income: Reassessing the Formulary Apportionment Option*, 2020 (ISBN 978-94-035-0614-2).
77. Ajit Kumar Singh, *Exploring the Nexus Doctrine in International Tax Law*, 2021 (ISBN 978-94-035-3363-6).
78. Galya Savir, *Regulation and Tax in Space*, 2021 (ISBN 978-94-035-3393-3).
79. Rita Julien, *Credit Method Compatibility and Constraints under EU Law: An Analysis of the Case Law of the CJEU*, 2022 (ISBN 978-94-035-2363-7).
80. Sergio André Rocha & Allison Christians (eds), *A Multilateral Convention for Tax: From Theory to Implementation*, 2022 (ISBN 978-90-411-9428-2).
81. Brigitte Alepin, Lyne Latulippe & Louise Otis (eds), *Coordination and Cooperation: Tax Policy in the 21st Century*, 2022 (ISBN 978-94-035-3740-5).
82. Chunyang Zhang, *The Role of Tax Law in Mergers and Acquisitions: A Chinese Perspective*, 2022 (ISBN 978-94-035-3741-2).
83. Florian Navisotschnigg, *Substance in International Tax Law: DEMPE Approach, Substantial Activity Requirement and Beneficial Ownership*, 2022 (ISBN 978-94-035-4895-1).

84. Mees Vergouwen, *The Effect of Directives Within the Area of Direct Taxation on the Interpretation and Application of Tax Treaties*, 2023 (ISBN 978-94-035-0907-5).
85. Rachna Matabudul, *Tax Treaty Dispute Resolution: Lessons from the Law of the Sea*, 2023 (ISNB 978-94-035-3407-7).

www.ingramcontent.com/pod-product-compliance
Lightning Source LLC
Chambersburg PA
CBHW071242230926
51849CB00001B/201
* 9 7 8 9 4 0 3 5 3 4 0 7 7 *